Advance Praise for Local Flavor

"*Local Flavor* is an exciting collection of original recipes by Philadelphia's hottest chefs. Though conceived in restaurant kitchens, this food is suited for anyone who loves to cook."
Alonna F. Smith, Author, *The Philadelphia Food Companion*

"What a delicious cookbook! I didn't know whether to start cooking or to make a reservation. Connie Correia Fisher has compiled innovative 'I must try these' recipes from Philadelphia area chefs. This cookbook is a welcome addition to my bookshelf."
Rosalie Saferstein, Food Writer, *Food Bytes*, **NJ Online**

"The recipe directions are written in an easy to follow, straightforward manner, and would allow people to believe that they could actually prepare the same meal as a chef. The real test of the cookbook has therefore been met; the ability to motivate action."
William G. Walker, Agricultural Marketing Specialist, N.J. Department of Agriculture

"*Local Flavor* gives area chefs the opportunity to come out from the kitchen and feeds the general public's interest in regional cuisine. What a great idea!"
Lynne Byck, Marketing Director, The Restaurant School

Local Flavor

Local Flavor

Favorite Recipes of Philadelphia Area Chefs

Connie Correia Fisher
with Joanne Correia

Small Potatoes Press
1106 Stokes Avenue, Collingswood, NJ 08108
609-869-5207

dedicated to
the chefs who feed our imaginations and tummies
and our husbands who feed our hearts.

Published by Small Potatoes Press
1106 Stokes Avenue, Collingswood, NJ 08108.

Front and back cover photos by George Feder
Photo page 161 by Connie Correia Fisher
Photo page 319 by George Feder

ISBN 0-9661200-0-0

ATTENTION ORGANIZATIONS, SCHOOLS, AND EDUCATIONAL FACILITIES:
Quantity discounts are available on bulk purchases of this book for educational purposes or fund-raising. Special books or book excerpts can also be created to fit specific needs. For information, please contact Small Potatoes Press, 1106 Stokes Avenue, Collingswood, NJ 08108. Call (609) 869-5207 or fax (609) 869-5247.

Table of Contents

Preface . . . 8

Introduction . . . 11

Starters . . . 13

Soups & Salads . . . 43

Risottos & Pastas . . . 73

Shellfish and Seafood . . . 97

Meats, Game and Poultry . . . 163

Sides . . . 193

Salsas, Sauces & Such . . . 215

Desserts . . . 237

Brunch . . . 281

Index . . . 308

Preface

As a kid, I always thought there was something mysterious about other peoples' kitchens. They had tools and gadgets that my mom's kitchen didn't. Their cabinets and drawers held strange ingredients and spices. Some people snoop through other peoples' medicine cabinets. For me — it was kitchens.

My own kitchen was rather dull. My parents were hard working people who put considerably more effort into raising us four kids with love and laughter than into what we ate. They weren't bad cooks, just limited in imagination and time. Mom's favorite recipe was "left-over hash." There was no drama, no farm fresh herbs, no lavish buffets. Experimenting (i.e., playing with our food) was discouraged. The biggest mystery in our kitchen: What was in all the Tupperware®?

When we ate out as a family, we always went to the same one or two places and usually only for birthdays or the occasional Sunday breakfast. But no matter where we ate, I always thought it was a special thing. There was a big kitchen back there with "neat-o" ingredients and "cool" equipment. Despite the fact that I never was successful in sneaking into those mysterious kitchens, gradually my scope of food knowledge grew. I often ate out with my best friend and her mom, who both have great taste. We'd travel to bistros and cafes in Buck's County and Philadelphia, throughout South Jersey, and down the shore in search of good food from assorted ethnic backgrounds.

I loved being in those restaurants. It wasn't just the food either. It was the intriguing smells that wafted into the dining room; the random clatter of plates and pots. I was sure that something mystical was going on behind those swinging doors. What magical things went on in there? How could they create this good food, this excitement, this funky puff pastry thing? What were the secrets of the kitchen? I wanted to know.

To find, out I went to college at Johnson & Wales University in Rhode Island. I'd like to say that I became a great chef, but that would be a big ol' lie. I failed eggs. I was responsible for a small fire in the flambé demonstration classroom. I ruined a 6-year-old's birthday with a tray loaded with glasses of orange juice. (Use your imagination.) I did learn some things — steam burns hurt, trays are heavy, and walk-in freezers are not good places for claustrophobics. When I misplaced my *mise en place*, I had to face facts — kitchen life was not for me.

And yet, the mysteries of the food world <u>were</u> revealed to me in each ruined sauce, each culinary disaster. I learned to understand, if not unlock, the secrets of the kitchen. I realized that a chef needed to be able to follow directions as well as lead a staff; to be calm under pressure but exuberant in his or her pursuit of knowledge; to have a firm grasp of technical skills and full love of food; to respect rules of safety and expand the rules of artistry.

This understanding imparted in me a profound respect for anyone who works with a spatula. It also led me to publish a magazine called *Cuizine* which celebrates and promotes our regional restaurants. Culinary skills not withstanding, publishing *Cuizine* allows me to keep expanding my knowledge of the kitchen. My business meetings are commonly held over fry-o-lators and most of my meals out are "working" dinners. I interact daily with chefs and restaurant owners who literally burst with enthusiasm for their work. This book grew out of a desire to share some of their knowledge and passion with you.

The Philadelphia region boasts everything from world-class cheesesteaks to nationally recognized restaurants; from diners to dim sum. And the chefs in this area are as diverse as the food choices. These professionals receive their training on the job, from their moms, and at the well-known institutions. Their areas of expertise range from Asian fusion to Nuevo Latino; from classic French to classic Kosher. All work long, hard hours; deserve much recognition; and have something to share.

When I first conceived of this cookbook, I had modest goals. I hoped that maybe 30 or 40 chefs would have time to contribute their kitchen secrets. As hundreds of recipes came rushing into my mailbox and through my fax machine, I was overwhelmed by the chefs' willingness to share knowledge and the creative community in which they work.

I learned that the true secret of the kitchen is generosity. No one was paid for his or her work. *Local Flavor* is a gift from the chefs of the Delaware Valley to you. They contributed because it is in their nature to create and to give.

Connie Correia Fisher

"Coming to Philadelphia to cook and to eat
is for me a recurring pleasure. The cooking in its
restaurants always entices and I believe that only a
very few cities in this country can boast as many competent,
and better, chefs and restaurants."

Eileen Yin-Fei Lo, Author,
The Chinese Way:
Healthy Low-Fat Cooking from China's Regions

What's inside . . .

I have been preparing food for my family for 30 years. In the course of editing this book, I have finally begun to learn how to cook. It all started with the easy but yummy Grilled Salmon with Tomato, Olive Oil, and Fresh Herbs donated by Chef Jean Francois Taquet. It worked! (My family was stunned.) I saw how the ingredients and flavors played off each other. I was hooked and cooking became fun.

One of the great things about this book is its levels of complexity. We were hoping that not all the chefs would send in sophisticated knock-your-socks-off-35-ingredients recipes. (Those are great for special occasions and weekends but not so practical on hectic Tuesday nights.) Although some chefs did, many chefs sent in uncomplicated dishes that anyone can pull off. There truly is something here for everyone. Novices will enjoy simple salsas that can perk up any main course, the easy desserts, and the useful advice. Experienced home cooks will relish the more challenging dishes with their intriguing spices and flavors.

We made every effort to include all recipes received; therefore, some dishes have two or three variations. (Can you ever have too many recipes for crème brûlée?) There are also a whole bunch o' fish recipes and not many for red meat, reflecting the growing trend in restaurants today.

We have also endeavored to keep each recipe in the chef's own voice. You'll notice that procedures vary from recipe to recipe and are not boiler plated as in other cookbooks.

We hope this collection will inspire you to expand your cooking horizons or, at the very least, entice you into making reservations at one of the participating restaurants!

Joanne Correia

Starters

Wild Boar and Scottish Hare Terrine 15

Eggplant Pate 16

Easy Gravlox and Smoked Salmon Mousse Appetizers 17

Smoked Trout with Horseradish Honey Mustard Sauce 18

Navajo Fry Bread 19

Grilled Oriental Shrimp Kabobs 20

Key West Conch Fritters with Vodka Dip 22

Grilled Stuffed Portobellos 24

Crab Dumplings 25

Har Gow 26

Little Juicy Steamed Buns 28

Empanadas de Cangrejo Moro 30

Smoked Chicken and Cheddar Roll Ups 31

Marinated Steak Wrap 32

Calamari Sarento 33

Oyster Gratin with Caviar 34

Escargot Napoleon with Shiitake and Cream 35

Shiitake Seared Atlantic Salmon with Corn Ragout 36

Grilled Vegetable Napoleons with Baby Lettuces 38

Portobello Pizza 40

Wild Boar and Scottish Hare Terrine

Executive Chef Tom Hannum
Hotel Dupont, Wilmington, DE

1 cup sun-dried cherries
1/2 cup brandy
3 lbs. boneless wild boar meat
3 lbs. boneless Scottish hare
1 T. fresh chopped sage
1 T. fresh chopped thyme
salt and pepper to taste
olive oil
1 cup red wine
flour
2 eggs, beaten
1/2 cup pistachio nuts
1/4 cup fresh chopped parsley
1/2 lb. sliced bacon

Toss cherries with brandy and let marinate for 1 hour. Strain and reserve liquid. Pass 2 pounds each of boar and hare meat through a meat grinder; place in large bowl and set aside.

Dice remaining meats. Toss sage, thyme, and salt and pepper and add to diced meats. Sauté in olive oil until lightly browned. Remove meats and deglaze with red wine. Reduce liquid by half and reserve. Combine liquid from cherries and red wine reduction. Stir in enough flour to make a thick paste. Stir in eggs. Add this mixture to the ground meats along with the cherries, diced meats, pistachios, parsley, and salt and pepper. Mix well. Chill for 1 hour.

Preheat oven to 350°. Line a terrine mold with bacon. Pack meat mixture in the mold; cover and place in a water bath in oven. Bake for 90 minutes or until internal temperature reaches 160°. Let terrine cool for about 1 hour; then uncover. Weigh down by placing another terrine mold on topl of mixture and refrigerate for 4 hours.

Serves 6

Eggplant Pate

Director of School of Culinary Arts Michael Baskette
The Art Institute of Philadelphia, Philadelphia, PA

1 large eggplant, peeled and diced
2 oz. virgin olive oil
1 medium onion, finely chopped
1 medium green or red bell pepper, finely chopped
1 tsp. chopped fresh garlic
1 cup minced fresh tomatoes
1 T. dried basil leaf
1/4 cup chopped ripe olives
1 tsp. ground black pepper
2 tsp. salt
juice of 1 lemon

Sauté eggplant in the olive oil until very tender and begins to brown. Remove the eggplant, but reserve the remaining oil in the pan. Sauté the onions, bell peppers, and garlic in the same oil for 2 minutes. The vegetables should be tender but not brown. Combine vegetables and ingredients from tomatoes through salt in a large mixing bowl and stir well. Add the lemon juice and adjust seasonings if necessary. Serve chilled with toasted garlic bread or crackers.

Serves 9

Easy Gravlox and Smoked Salmon Mousse Appetizers

Owners Howard Landsman and Melissa Killeen
Laurel Springs Smoke House, Laurel Springs, NJ

๏

10 oz. smoked salmon, sliced
6 oz. cream cheese, softened
10 oz. crème fraîche
1 lemon
50 small baked pastry shells
1 lb. gravlox, presliced
2 oz. beluga caviar
dill sprigs (optional)

Place the smoked salmon in a food processor. Puree for about 1 minute. Force the salmon through a sieve. (This step is not absolutely necessary, except for a perfectly smooth mousse.) Place the smoked salmon in an electric mixer bowl and add the softened cream cheese. Add 2 tablespoons of the crème fraîche and a squeeze of lemon juice. At medium speed, whip until the mixture is light and smooth, about 2 to 3 minutes.

In a separate bowl with a clean, dry, balloon whisk, add 6 tablespoons of crème fraîche and whip until it holds a peak. Fold the whipped crème fraîche into the smoked salmon/creme fraiche mixture and then taste. Adjust with more whipped crème fraîche if there is too strong a smoked salmon taste. Refrigerate 2 to 3 hours.

Prepare a tray with the baked pastry shells. The tray must be able to fit into your refrigerator. Cut the sliced gravlox into pieces to fit in the bottom of each shell. Fill a pastry tube/bag with the mousse mixture. Squeeze a decorative amount over the gravlox in the shells. Refrigerate 1 hour or more.

In a mesh sieve, drain the caviar. Decorate each tart with 3 to 4 eggs. Garnish with dill sprigs if desired. Can be prepared and refrigerated up to 1 day prior to serving.

Makes 40 to 50 appetizers

Smoked Trout with Horseradish Honey Mustard Sauce

Owners Howard Landsman and Melissa Killeen
Laurel Springs Smoke House, Laurel Springs, NJ

1/4 cup prepared white horseradish, drained
1/2 cup honey mustard, preferably coarse grained with seeds
1/4 cup crème fraîche
6 smoked trout fillets
1 loaf pumpernickel broad, thinly sliced (small appetizer loaves can also be used)
4 Granny Smith apples, thinly sliced
parsley sprigs

In a medium bowl, place the horseradish, honey mustard, and crème fraîche. Whip to blend. Lay out trout fillets and cut into pieces that are the width of 2 fingers. Spread some of the horseradish sauce on each of the pumpernickel slices used. Add smoked trout, top with an apple slice, and garnish with a parsley sprig.

Makes 50 to 60 canapes

About the Chefs

Names: Howard Landsman and Melissa Killeen

Education/Training: self-taught

Inspirations/Influences: Jack McDavid, Giavanni Massiglia, Phillipe Chin, and Howard's mother

Hobbies: cooking, skiing, sailing, gardening

Family: husband and wife team with a desire to revolutionize the smoked fish industry by using and selling fresh fish!

Hometown: Laurel Springs, NJ

Favorite Food to Eat: American-Fusion at Jack's Firehouse, Chanterelles, and La Grolla

Favorite Food to Prepare: fish!

Favorite Cookbook: *Union Street Cafe* and books by Julee Rosso and Shelia Lukins

Navajo Fry Bread

Executive Chef Bill McConnell
Martini's Lounge & Restaurant, Philadelphia, PA

2 cups all-purpose flour
1 tsp. salt
1 T. cumin
2 tsp. baking powder
1 to 1¼ cups milk (approximately)
oil for frying
2 8-oz. boneless chicken breasts, grilled
4 tomatillos, sliced thin
1 cup shredded cheddar cheese
lime juice
paprika for garnish

Combine flour, salt, cumin, and baking powder in a bowl and mix well. Add milk and mix with a fork, adding a little flour to prevent sticking. Set aside for 10 minutes. Heat oil. Pinch off egg-sized pieces of dough and squash down pieces on table until each is 1/4-inch thick and 4 x 4-inches wide.

Preheat oven to 350°. Fry dough squares in oil until golden brown, about 3 minutes. Place bread slices on sheet pan and top each with thin slices of chicken breasts, 4 slices of tomatillo, and a sprinkling of cheese. Bake for 5 minutes. Squeeze lime juice on plate and place bread on top. Sprinkle paprika over all.

Serves 8 to 10

Grilled Oriental Shrimp Kabobs

Chef/Owner Mark Smith
Sensational Cook Caterers, Westmont, NJ

20 16-20-sized shrimp
Marinade (see recipe)
1 red pepper, cut into 1/2-inch squares
1 green pepper, cut into 1/2-inch squares
10 button mushrooms
1 onion, cut into 1-inch squares

Marinate shrimp for 1½ hours. Skewer shrimp, alternating with peppers, mushrooms, and onion (4 shrimp per skewer). Grill 4 minutes each side, brushing with leftover marinade sauce.

Serves 5

Marinade

2 T. brown sugar
1 tsp. five-spice powder
1 T. chopped fresh garlic
1 T. chopped fresh ginger
1/4 cup soy sauce
3 T. frozen orange concentrate
1/4 cup sesame oil
1/4 cup vegetable oil

Combine marinade ingredients in a bowl. Mix well.

About the Chef

Name: Mark E. Smith

Education/Training: 15 years hotel and restaurant experience

Inspirations/Influences: regional differences in flavors, preparation, and spices

Hobbies: gardening, the Flyers,

Family: married, living in Cherry Hill, NJ

Hometown: Norwalk, OH

Favorite Food to Eat: sushi

Favorite Food to Prepare: English trifle with raspberry sauce

Favorite Cookbook: *Classical Cooking - The Modern Way* by Eugene Pauli

Key West Conch Fritters with Vodka Dip

Executive Chef/Owner Bill Beck
Pompano Grille, Philadelphia, PA

2 eggs, beaten
1½ cups all-purpose flour
I T. sugar
1½ tsp. baking powder
pinch of cayenne
1/3 tsp. dry thyme leaves
1/3 tsp. dry mustard
1 lb. conch meat, ground
1 cup buttermilk
1 tsp. minced jalapeño pepper
1/2 cup medium diced red onion
1/2 cup medium diced red bell pepper
1/2 cup chopped celery
2 cloves garlic, minced
1/2 cup chopped scallions
1 tsp. Worcestershire sauce
salt and pepper to taste
oil
Vodka Dip (see recipe)

Add dry ingredients one by one to beaten eggs. Mix well with a whisk. Add remaining ingredients. Mix with a rubber spatula, using a folding motion. Adjust to taste with salt and pepper.

In sauce pot, heat 3 inches of oil to 350º. Drop batter into oil, using 2 tablespoons in a "scoop and release" motion. Fry fritters until they are golden brown. Serve with Vodka Dip.

Serves 8 to 12

Vodka Dip

1 cup mayonnaise
1 tsp. tomato paste
1/4 cup vodka
1/4 cup chopped scallions
1/4 cup chopped fresh parsley
2 tsp. lemon juice
1 tsp. ground cumin
1 tsp. Tabasco sauce

In a small bowl, whisk mayonnaise with tomato paste; then whisk in rest of ingredients. Refrigerate at least 3 hours, if possible, so that flavors can properly marry.

NOTE: Fish store can grind conch meat.

Grilled Stuffed Portobellos

Executive Chef Anthony DiBernardo
Owner Frank Muratore
Café Portobello, Washington Township, NJ

3 T. butter
1/2 cup diced Spanish onion
1/4 cup diced red bell pepper
1/4 cup diced green bell pepper
1/4 cup diced yellow bell pepper
5 T. flour
1/4 tsp. cayenne pepper
1 T. Worcestershire sauce
1/2 tsp. Old Bay seasoning
salt and pepper to taste
6 portobello mushroom caps
2 T. olive oil
1 lb. lump crab meat, picked through for shells
1/4 cup chopped green onion

Heat butter in saucepan. Add Spanish onion and peppers; cook until tender. Add flour; stir to incorporate. Stir in cayenne pepper, Worcestershire sauce, Old Bay, and salt and pepper. Set aside to cool completely.

Rub mushrooms with olive oil and season with salt and pepper. Grill for 3 minutes on each side or until tender. Set aside to cool.

Once vegetable mixture is cooled, combine it with crabmeat and green onion. Mix gently but thoroughly. Divide crab mixture between portobello caps. Arrange stuffed mushrooms on baking sheet and place under broiler for 8 to 10 minutes or until mixture is lightly browned and warmed through.

Serves 6

Crab Dumplings

Executive Chef Jason Ruch
New World Cafe, Cinnaminson, NJ

2 lbs. jumbo crabmeat, cleaned
1 red pepper, diced
1 yellow pepper, diced
3 ribs celery, diced
1 small white onion, diced
3 T. fresh ground ginger
2 T. fresh ground garlic
3 T. soy sauce
peanut oil
1 package wonton skins

Sauté all ingredients, except skins, in peanut oil until soft. Cool. Place a portion of dumpling mix in the center of each skin. Wet top and one edge of skin with water (using your finger) and fold into a triangle. Crimp edges with fork and deep fry at 350° for 3 minutes or bake at 350° for 10 minutes or until crisp.

Yields approximately 25 dumplings.

About the Chef

Name: Jason Ruch

Education/Training: various chefs

Inspirations/Influences:
co-workers, paycheck

Hobbies: playing guitar

Family: single

Hometown: Mt. Holly, NJ

Favorite Food to Eat:
Oriental

Favorite Food to Prepare:
Southwestern

Favorite Cookbook: *Gourmet Box Lunch*

Har Gow
Shrimp Dumplings

Chef/Owner Joseph Poon
Joseph Poon, Philadelphia, PA

1 lb. white shrimp
4 tsp. potato starch
4 oz. fresh water chestnuts, peeled and finely diced (available in Asian specialty
   grocers and some supermarkets)
1 tsp. salt
1/2 tsp. ground white pepper
1 tsp. sugar
Wrappers (see recipe)

Devein and clean shrimp. Rinse under cold water for 10 minutes, then pat dry.
Chill shrimp in refrigerator for 30 minutes before dicing. Put shrimp and potato
starch in a large bowl and mash until sticky. Add water chestnuts, salt, pepper,
and sugar. Mix well.

Place about 1 teaspoon of filling in the center of each wrapper. Fold it in half
and pinch about ¼ of the opening closed. Using fingers, make about 6 small
pleats along the center the opening and then press it closed.

To steam, place a stoneware bowl or other heat-tempered bowl in the center
of a wok or deep skillet. Fill the wok or skillet with 4 to 6 cups of water, just
enough to surround the **outside** of the bowl with 1 to 2 inches of water. Put a
large plate on the bowl. Place dumplings on the plate. Cover wok or skillet with a
lid. Using high range-top heat, bring water to a boil and steam for 4 minutes.

Makes approximately 48 dumplings

Wrappers

16 oz. wheat starch
2 oz. potato starch
2 cups boiling water

In a bowl, combine the wheat starch and potato starch and pour in the boiling water. Knead into a dough and divide into 4 equal parts. Roll each part into a long rod and cut each rod into 12 small pieces. Using the flat side of a cleaver, a steel presser, or rolling pin, form each piece of dough into a thin, transparent, round wrapper about 3 inches in diameter.

About the Chef

Name: Joseph K. K. Poon

Education/Training: nutrition and food, educted in Hong Kong under British Colony

Inspirations/Influences: I love it! When I was 18 years old, I worked in Hong Kong for airport catering. I was really amazed to see all the chefs making all kinds of food.

Hobbies: teaching vegetable carving, creating new recipes

Family: I take care of my 89-year-old mom and 90-year-old dad who live with me.

Hometown: Hong Kong

Favorite Food to Eat: any kind of food that is simple to make and tasty

Favorite Food to Prepare: Peking duck

Favorite Cookbook: *Art Culinary*

Little Juicy Steamed Buns

Executive Chef Michael Wei
Yangming, Bryn Mawr, PA

1 lb. ground pork
1¼ tsp. kosher salt
2 tsp. sugar
2 egg whites, beaten
2 T. rice wine
1/4 tsp. white pepper
1/2 cup chicken stock
1/2 cup chopped scallions
1/2 cup minced mushrooms
1/4 cup minced Chinese chives
1/2 cup crab meat
Skins (see recipe)
Dipping Sauce (see recipe)

In a bowl, combine the ground pork, salt, sugar, egg whites, rice wine, and pepper and mix well. Slowly add the chicken stock while continuing to mix the contents of the bowl. Add the scallions, mushrooms, and chives and mix. Add the crab meat and mix vigorously. Cover the bowl and refrigerate.

Place 1 tablespoon of the filling on a skin. Grab the edge of the skin with thumb and index finger, and hold the bottom of the skin in the palm of other hand. Pinch the edge of the skin against thumb and start to move it in a counter-clockwise direction while holding the filling and skin in your hand. Use your thumb as a pivot while pinching.

Cover the bottom of the steamer with a thin cloth or leafy vegetable (i.e., lettuce, napa). Place the buns over the cloth and steam for 8 minutes. The buns should look puffy when done. Once done, take steamer off heat and serve the buns with dipping sauce.

Makes 60 to 65 buns

Skins

1 lb. flour plus 1/2 cup flour for rolling
1 1/3 cup warm water

Slowly mix the water with the 1 pound of flour. Knead the flour and slowly add more water. Continue kneading the dough until it becomes smooth. Place the dough into a container; cover it for 10 minutes.

Knead dough again until it is soft and has a bright white appearance. Roll the dough into a long cylinder with a diameter of 1-inch. Cut the dough into 60 to 65 pieces. Spread some flour onto work surface and roll each piece of dough into a thin circle with a diameter of 3 inches. While rolling, remember to roll the edges of the dough so the center of the skin is a little bit thicker.

Dipping Sauce

1/2 cup peeled and minced ginger
2 cup Chinese red vinegar
2 T. sugar

Mix ingredients together in a bowl and refrigerate.

Empanadas de Cangrejo Moro

Stone Crab Claw Empanadas

Executive Chef Guillermo Pernot
Vega Grill, Manayunk, PA

2 lbs. stone crab claw meat, cleaned
2 scallions, minced
1/2 cup chopped cilantro
1/2 habañero pepper, minced
2 shallots, minced
salt and pepper to taste
3 T. lime juice
2 T. mayonnaise
36 Empanadas Disks (see recipe)

Mix together well all the ingredients except empanada disks. Place disks on floured surface and fill each one with 1 tablespoon of the filling. Fold each empanada and seal all sides with a fork. Refrigerate for 20 minutes.

When ready to serve, fry for 4 minutes in enough oil to cover. Serve immediately.

Yields 36 empanadas

Empanadas Disks

4½ cups flour
1½ tsp. salt
3 T. sugar
12 T. butter
3 eggs, beaten
9 T. white wine
flour for dusting

Mix flour, salt, and sugar in a bowl. Cut in butter using a fork. Make a well in the center of the flour mixture and add eggs and wine. Stir mixture until blended. Divide mixture into 36 portions and roll into circles 1/8-inch thick.

Yields 36 disks

Smoked Chicken
and Cheddar Roll Ups

Executive Chef Chris Todd
Arroyo Grille, Manayunk, PA

12 12-inch flour tortillas
2 lb. shredded smoked chicken breast
1 lb. cheddar cheese, shredded
2 red onions, sliced and grilled
2 cups spicy tomatillo salsa
4 roasted red peppers, cut into strips

Lay all ingredients out on tortillas. Roll up like egg rolls. Serve immediately.

Serves 12

Marinated Steak Wrap

Chef/Owner Toby Weitzman
Creative Catering Company, Cherry Hill, NJ

1/4 cup olive oil
2 cloves garlic
3 T. honey
1 tsp. ginger
4 T. balsamic vinegar
1/4 cup water
1/4 cup soy sauce
2 lb. flank steak
2 T. horseradish
3 T. Dijon mustard
4 T. mayonnaise
3 red peppers, quartered
2 yellow peppers, quartered
2 large green zuchini, quartered
1 large yellow zuchini, quartered
1 package tortilla wraps

Combine olive oil, garlic, honey, ginger, vinegar, water, and soy sauce to make a marinade. Marinate steak in marinade in refrigerator over night.

Mix horseradish, Dijon, and mayonnaise. Set aside. Grill vegetables and julienne. Grill flank steak to desired temperature; then slice thin. Open tortillas and spread with horseradish sauce. Arrange a thin layer of grilled julienne veggies and sliced steak. Fold over, repeat, and fold. Secure with attractive toothpick. Continue to fill tortillas. Serve cut on a diagonal at room temperature.

Serves 4 to 6

Calamari Sarento

Executive Chef Dany Chevalier
Nicholas Nickolas, The Rittenhouse Hotel, Philadelphia, PA

4 T. olive oil
1½ cups freshly cleaned calamari
2 T. oregano
1 cup diced tomatoes, seeds removed
2 oz. snake sauce (equal parts Tabasco and Worcestershire sauces)
1 cup beef broth
2 large spoonfuls Garlic Butter (Recipe appears on page 235.)
6 oz. Pecorino Romano cheese
salt and pepper to taste

Heat a sauté pan to high but not smoking. Add olive oil. Place calamari in pan and sauté. Add oregano, tomatoes, snake sauce, beef broth, garlic butter, and salt and pepper to taste. Simmer for approximately 2 minutes. Add cheese and stir. Serve in a soup bowl or on a plate.

Serves 2

About the Chef

Name: Dany Chevalier

Education/Training: self-taught

Inspirations/Influences: the love of food

Hobbies: photography, music

Family: single; from a family of five children

Hometown: Boca Raton, FL

Favorite Food to Eat: pasta

Favorite Food to Prepare: Italian

Favorite Cookbook: *Charlie Trotter's Seafood*

Oyster Gratin with Caviar

Chef/Owner Jean Francois Taquet
Restaurant Taquet, Wayne, PA

24 oysters
1 shallot, chopped
2 oz. Chardonnay wine
1 pint heavy cream
1 oz. caviar
1 bunch chives, chopped

Open the oysters and pour their juice into a sauté pan with the shallot and wine. Cook to reduce to half. Pour in 1 cup of the cream and reduce to half again. Cool the sauce and set aside.

Whip the remaining heavy cream and incorporate the caviar. Place the oysters on the half shell, incorporate the cooled sauce with the whipped caviar cream, and pour over the oysters. Place oysters under the broiler until golden in color. Garnish with chives.

Serves 4

Escargot Napoleon with Shiitake and Cream

Executive Chef Peter McAndrews
Rembrandt's Restaurant, Philadelphia, PA

1 sheet puff pastry
2 tsp. butter
1 tsp. garlic
6 oz. escargot
1½ cups heavy cream
1/2 cup shiitake mushrooms
1 T. soy sauce
1 T. lemon juice
fried leeks (optional)

Preheat oven to 350°. Brush puff pastry with 1 teaspoon butter and bake about 15 minutes or until golden. Cut into 4 desired shapes.

Sauté garlic in remaining butter until brown. Add escargot and cream. Let reduce until thick. Add mushrooms, soy, and lemon juice. Cook for 3 minutes. Arrange pastry on 4 plates. Separate tops from bottoms. Pour 2/3 of cream and escargot mixture evenly into the pastry bottoms. Replace tops and pour remaining cream mixture on top. Garnish with fried leeks if desired.

Serves 4

About the Chef

Name: Peter McAndrews

Education/Training: Penn State University; have worked in restaurants from age 13

Inspirations/Influences: fresh ingredients

Hobbies: cooking, drinking wine

Family: married, two cats

Hometown: Philadelphia, PA

Favorite Food to Eat: good bread and cheese, Italian

Favorite Food to Prepare: fresh pastas

Favorite Cookbook: *Life & Times of James Beard*

Shiitake Seared Atlantic Salmon with Corn Ragout

Chef Adam Sturm
Azalea Restaurant, Omni Hotel, Philadelphia, PA

1 cup shiitake mushrooms, stems removed and julienned 1/4-inch thick
4 4-oz. salmon fillets (appetizer portion)*
2 oz. butter
Corn Ragout and Sauce (see recipe)
1 bunch chives, minced

Place the mushrooms on top of the salmon fillets. Heat a large sauté pan and add the butter. Place the fillets in pan, mushroom-side down, and sauté for 5 minutes on each side. While the salmon is sautéing, finish cooking the ragout and warm the sauce. Place the ragout in the center of the plate with the salmon on top and the sauce around. Garnish with the chives.

Serves 4

*For an entree, substitute 4 6-oz. salmon fillets.

About the Chef

Name: Adam Sturm

Education/Training: French Culinary Institute, Restaurant Bouley, "21" Club, and Restaurant Arpege in Paris

Inspirations/Influences: fresh ingredients, eating out, traveling, and buying a new piece of equipment

Hobbies: mountain biking, cross country skiing

Family: single; parents and sister live in New York City

Hometown: New York City, NY

Favorite Food to Eat: mushrooms, truffles, foie gras, and potatoes (oh, and sushi!)

Favorite Food to Prepare: really fresh seafood and shellfish; anything seasonal

Favorite Cookbook: *Simple Cuisine* by Jean-Georges Vongerichten

Corn Ragout and Sauce

3 ears corn, kernels removed
1 stalk lemon grass, finey minced (remove outer leaves first)
1 oz. ginger, peeled and grated on a box grater
2 leeks, split lengthwise and cut into "half moons" about 1/4-inch thick (wash
     well under cold water)
2 oz. butter
1/4 cups white wine
2 cups clam broth
1/2 bunch asparagus, sliced into 1/8-inch rounds
1/2 bunch cilantro, chiffonaded
1 bunch chives

Combine corn, lemon grass, ginger, leeks, and butter in a large saucepan. Sauté
for 15 minutes over low heat, making sure not to brown the corn ragout. Remove
half of the ingredients and reserve. Deglaze the pan with the wine and reduce
until most of the liquid is evaporated. Add the clam broth and return to a simmer.
Puree smooth and reserve. Season to taste.

   Add asparagus and cilantro to the reserved ragout.

Grilled Vegetable Napoleons with Baby Lettuces

Executive Chef/Owner Lynn Buono
Feast Your Eyes Catering, Philadelphia, PA

4 sheets butter puff pastry
2.2 lbs. Montrachet cheese
1 lb. cream cheese
3/4 cup heavy cream
1½ tsp. chopped fresh rosemary
2 tsp. chopped fresh thyme
1/4 tsp. dried marjoram
1½ tsp. kosher salt
1/4 tsp. ground black pepper
1½ lb. plum tomatoes (about 6)
1¼ lb. Japanese eggplant
1½ lb. beets (about 6), boiled and peeled
1½ lb. yams (about 3)
1¼ lb. zucchini (about 3)
1½ lb. yellow squash (about 3)
1½ lb. shiitake mushroom caps
1/2 cup olive oil
1 tsp. kosher salt
1 tsp. minced peeled garlic
36 sprigs thyme
36 leaves baby arugula
Balsamic Vinaigrette (see recipe)
seasonal baby lettuces (i.e., arugula, baby Swiss chard, and baby spinach)

Preheat oven to 350°. Cut eight 4-inch circles from each pastry sheet; then re-roll scraps to get 4 additional circles. Prick with fork or weigh down before baking and bake for 15 to 20 minutes until slightly golden. The base should be fairly flat, not puffed.

Mix cheeses in a food processor fitted with a paddle. Blend until cheeses are fluffy. Slowly add cream; then herbs, salt, and pepper. Taste. Add additional salt and pepper if necessary.

Cut vegetables into rounds. (You should end up with 40 rounds of each kind, so you'll have a few extras.) Combine olive oil, salt and garlic. Coat vegetables with oil and grill lightly.

Spread each pastry crust with approximately 1½ tablespoons of the cheese mixture. Arrange 1 slice of each vegetable in a ring on mixture, overlapping them so that they don't hang over the edge. Alternate colors so that it looks pretty. Garnish each crust with a sprig of thyme and a leaf of baby arugula.

Serve on a dinner plate with tart on one side and baby lettuces lightly tossed with balsamic vinaigrette on the other.

Serves 36

Balsamic Vinaigrette

1/2 large shallot
1¾ cups balsamic vinegar
1/8 cup Dijon mustard
1 tsp. minced peeled garlic
1/8 cup kosher salt
1¼ tsp. fresh cracked black pepper
1 splash Maggi (available at specialty shops or Oriental markets)
1/2 tsp. fresh oregano leaves
1 1/3 qts. extra virgin olive oil

Chop shallot in a food processor. Add all remaining ingredients, except the olive oil, and process; then add the olive oil very slowly.

Yields 1½ quarts

Portobello Pizza

Executive Chef David Leo Banks
Harry's Savoy Grill, Wilmington, DE

4 portobello mushrooms, 4 to 6 inches in diameter, stems removed
1/2 cup flour seasoned with salt and pepper
3 large eggs
1/8 cup water
1 cup cornmeal
1/4 cup olive oil
3 cups Tomato Coulis (see recipe)
1 cup grated fontina cheese, loosely packed
1 medium red onion, cut into rings and grilled
1/4 lb. serrano ham or proscuitto, julienned
16 fresh basil leaves
1/4 cup grated Pecorino Romano cheese

While the tomato coulis is simmering, you can begin to prepare the mushrooms. Preheat oven to 350°. You will need 3 shallow bowls, each big enough to hold a portobello mushroom in diameter. Dredge each mushroom through each bowl containing, in order, seasoned flour, egg wash, and cornmeal, being sure to coat the mushroom thoroughly in each stage.

In a sauté pan, cook the coated mushrooms in olive oil over medium heat, lightly browning each side. Once browned, remove the mushrooms from the oil and place on a shallow baking sheet. Fill each prepared mushroom with some tomato coulis, fontina cheese, grilled onion, and serrano ham or proscuitto. Place in oven for 5 to 7 minutes or until the cheese is thoroughly melted.

On warmed plates, pour a small pool of tomato coulis and place the portobello pizza in the center of the plate. Garnish with 4 basil leaves and a pinch of the pecorino Romano cheese.

Serves 4

Tomato Coulis

5 whole cloves garlic, peeled
1/8 cup pure olive oil
1 small carrot, peeled and diced
1 small white onion, diced
1 heart of celery with tops (approx. 3 stalks)
4 lbs. fresh Roma plum tomatoes or 4 cups canned whole peeled tomatoes
1/4 cup water
salt and white pepper to taste

In a medium saucepan, roast the garlic with the olive oil until lightly browned, then remove the garlic from the oil so it does not get bitter. Sauté carrots, onions, and celery until onions become transparent. Add the tomatoes, water, and roasted garlic and let simmer on low heat for 20 minutes, stirring occasionally. Add salt and pepper to taste.

Puree the sauce in a food processor until smooth; then return it to heat and let it simmer for 5 more minutes. Strain the sauce to remove any large lumps that may still exist in the sauce.

NOTE: This is a thin sauce so do not be surprised by its smooth and flowing texture.

Soups & Salads

New Jersey Clam Chowder 45

New Orleans Clam Chowder 46

Seafood Bisque 47

Roasted Vegetable Chowder with Curry 48

Cream of Pumpkin Soup 49

Billy Weaver's Cream of Mushroom Soup 50

Roasted Shallot and Wild Mushroom Soup 51

Sopa de Calabaza 52

Rasam Soup 53

Creamless Tomato and Fennel Soup with Crabmeat 54

Braised Lamb Shank Pot Au Feu 55

Halibut Pot Au Feu 56

Clear Tomato Gazpacho 57

Tropical Fruit Gazpacho 58

Prickly Pear and Pineapple Gazpacho 59

Sour Cherry Soup 60

Caren's Shrimp Salad 61

Mixed Tomato, Proscuitto and Mozzarella Salad 62

Asian Vegetable Salad 63

Quinoa Salad with Citrus Vinaigrette 64

Watercress and Bibb Salad and Pumpkin Seed Vinaigrette 66

Rococo Salad of Limestone and Tat-Soi 67

Thai Spiced Shrimp Salad Asian Greens and Pesto Dressing 68

Grilled Calamari with Cucumbers and Baby Greens 69

Sesame Crusted Tuna Loin with Ponzu-Wasabi Vinaigrette 70

Cabrales and Patria Chiles Viniagrette 71

Roasted Poblano Vinaigrette 71

New Jersey Clam Chowder

Executive Chef Luigi Baretto
Ram's Head Inn, Absecon, NJ

2 pints half-and-half
1 cup clam juice
1 medium onion, diced
1/2 tsp. chopped garlic
2 T. flour
10 oz. cream of asparagus soup (canned or your own recipe)
3 New Jersey tomatoes, cut and seeded
2 dozen New Jersey chowder clams, chopped
1 cup diced, precooked white potatoes
1 tsp. celery powder
1/2 tsp. pepper
1/2 tsp. paprika
1/2 tsp. thyme
1 cup New Jersey asparagus spears, precooked for garnish

Combine half-and-half with clam juice in a saucepan and bring to a boil. In a soup pot, sauté onion and garlic until golden. Add flour and stir. Add hot half-and-half mixture and whip until smooth. Add the cream of asparagus soup, tomatoes, clams, potatoes, and spices. Mix well. Bring to a boil, reduce, and let simmer for 10 to 15 minutes, stirring often. Additional clam base can be added to taste. Garnish with asparagus spears.

Serves 6

About the Chef

Name: Luigi G. Baretto

Education/Training: Italy

Inspirations/Influences: creating new tastes with both local and regional foods and produce

Hobbies: gardening   **Family:** married, one son   **Hometown:** Absecon, NJ

Favorite Food to Eat: Northern Italian dishes, seafood

Favorite Food to Prepare: Northern Italian dishes

Favorite Cookbook: Pellaprat and regional cookbooks

New Orleans Clam Chowder

Executive Chef Joe Stewart
GG's Restaurant, Doubletree Guest Suites, Mount Laurel, NJ

8 oz. bacon, diced
1 lb. andouille sausage
1 cup each: diced celery, onion, carrot, green pepper
2 T. tomato paste
1 T. chopped garlic
1½ tsp. paprika
1½ tsp. gumbo filé
1 T. fresh thyme
1/2 cup white wine
1 T. flour
1½ qt. chopped clams with juice
1 large potato, diced
1 qt. milk
1 qt. heavy cream

In pot, sauté bacon and sausage for 3 minutes. Add celery, onion, carrot, and pepper. Sauté until soft. Add tomato paste, garlic, and seasonings. Add white wine; cook 3 minutes. Add flour and stir until thickened. Add remaining ingredients and simmer for 45 minutes.

Serves 12

About the Chef

Name: Joseph F. Stewart

Education/Training: The Restaurant School

Inspirations/Influences: seasonal fresh ingredients

Hobbies: golf, spending time with family and friends

Family: married 20 years to Jane, two children — Jamie and Joe, Jr.

Hometown: Born in Philadelphia; moved to New Jersey six years ago

Favorite Food to Eat: duck foie gras, smoked salmon

Favorite Food to Prepare: seafood — so many variations and cooking techniques

Favorite Cookbook: *Larousse Gastronomique*

Seafood Bisque

Executive Chef Jason Ruch
New World Cafe, Cinnaminson, NJ

1/4 lb. butter
3 carrots, diced
1 bunch celery, diced
2 white onions, diced
1 bunch leeks, diced
1 T. fresh ground garlic
1/2 cup flour
1 cup white wine
4 cups shrimp stock
1 pinch saffron
1 T. cayenne pepper
salt and pepper
1/2 T. Worcestershire sauce
2 lbs. mussels, poached
1 lb. scallops, poached
1 lb. crabmeat, poached
1 lb. lobster meat, poached
2 cups heavy cream
1 bunch each: fresh parsley and dill, chopped

Sauté carrots, celery, onion, leeks, and garlic in butter until soft. Whisk in flour. Cook for 5 minutes, stirring constantly. Add white wine and cook for 2 minutes. Add stock, saffron, cayenne pepper, salt and pepper, and Worcestershire sauce. Cook until soup thickens. Add mussels, scallops, crabmeat, and lobster. Cook for another 5 minutes. Remove from flame. Add cream and herbs.

Serves 20

Roasted Vegetable Chowder with Curry

Executive Chef Mark Buker
The Inn at Sugar Hill, Mays Landing, NJ

⑥

1 large onion, diced
5 to 6 cloves garlic
3 stalks celery, diced
3 tomatoes, seeded and diced
2 carrots, diced
1 cup cauliflower
1 cup broccoli florets
4 ears of corn, kernels removed
1/4 cup olive oil
1/2 lb. bacon, diced
4 T. butter
6 T. flour
8 cups water or chicken stock
1 T. curry powder
1 14-15 oz. can creamed corn
3 red potatoes, diced
1½ to 2 cups milk
1/2 cup grated fontina cheese
salt and pepper to taste

Preheat oven to 425°. Toss first 8 ingredients with olive oil. Place in roasting pan and cook for 40 to 45 minutes or until vegetables just start to color. Set aside. In a heavy stock pot, sauté bacon until it just starts to crisp. Remove with slotted spoon and reserve. Add butter to pot and melt. Lower heat and add flour to form a roux (paste). Slowly whisk in water or stock. When all lumps are gone, add curry powder, creamed corn, potatoes, and milk. Cook for 20 to 30 minutes until potatoes are just tender. Add reserved vegetables, bacon, and fontina cheese. Season with salt and pepper.

Serves 10 to 12

Cream of Pumpkin Soup

Director of School Culinary Arts Michael Baskette
The Art Institute of Philadelphia, Philadelphia, PA

1 small onion, finely chopped
2 stalks celery, peeled and finely chopped
1 T. corn oil
1½ cups diced fresh pumpkin
1 tsp. ground cinnamon
1/4 tsp. ground nutmeg
1 tsp. salt
1 tsp. ground white pepper
2 cups chicken broth
1/2 cup sour cream

Sauté onions and celery in corn oil until tender but not brown. Add the pumpkin and spices and cook for 2 minutes. Add the chicken broth and simmer over medium heat for 30 minutes. Add sour cream and puree all ingredients together in a blender. Serve hot or cold.

Serves 8

NOTE: You can substitute any variety of winter squash, like butternut or acorn, for the pumpkin.

Billy Weaver's
Cream of Mushroom Soup

Billy Weaver
Friday Saturday Sunday Restaurant, Philadelphia, PA

"Don't worry if mushrooms are not 'brand new fresh.' All the better! Mushrooms that have browned slightly add color and taste to the soup."

1 lb. Kennett Square "cream" mushrooms, finely diced
1/2 stick butter
2 T. flour
1 qt. chicken stock
1 qt. heavy cream
cognac to taste
salt and white pepper to taste

Place mushrooms and butter in a large stock pot and sauté until most of the liquid from the mushrooms is "cooked off." Sprinkle flour over mushroom mixture. Stir while cooking for a few minutes; then add the chicken stock and mix well. Allow the mixture to reduce over a medium flame to 1/2 its original volume (about 1/2 hour). Refrigerate.

   Before serving, heat mixture while adding the heavy cream. Add cognac and salt and white pepper to taste.

Serves 6

Roasted Shallot and Wild Mushroom Soup

Executive Chef Trish Morrissey
Philadelphia Fish & Co., Philadelphia, PA

8 shallots, peeled and halved
2 tsp. olive oil
2 T. olive oil
1/2 lb. wild mushrooms (shiitakes, portobellos, or oyster mushrooms), sliced
1/2 lb. button mushrooms, sliced
2 Idaho potatoes, peeled, diced, and held in water
3 bay leaves
1 qt. chicken or vegetable stock
salt and pepper to taste

Preheat oven to 400°. Toss shallots with 2 teaspoons olive oil in an ovenproof pan, cover with foil, and roast for 15 minutes. Uncover. Continue to cook for 5 minutes. Remove from oven and set aside. Heat 2 tablespoons of olive oil in a soup pot, add mushrooms, and cook for 5 minutes, stirring often. Add shallots, potatoes, and bay leaves. Cook for 2 minutes, pour in stock, and bring to a boil. Reduce to a simmer for 30 minutes. Remove from heat, pull out bay leaves with a slotted spoon, and puree mixture in a blender or food processor. Season with salt and pepper and serve.

Serves 8

Sopa de Calabaza

South American Squash Soup

Executive Chef Guillermo Pernot
Vega Grill, Manayunk, PA

1 3-lb. calabaza, peeled and diced
1/4 tsp. ground allspice
1/4 tsp. ground cinnamon
1/4 tsp. ground cumin
1/4 tsp. ground coriander
1 Spanish onion, chopped
5 cloves garlic, chopped
salt and pepper to taste
2 qts. chicken stock
water if necessary
2 T. cilantro, julienned

Place the calabaza in a roasting pan and dust with the spices. Place in a 350°
oven and roast until golden brown.

In a large pot, heat calabaza, onions, garlic, salt and pepper, and chicken
stock and cook until tender. Puree mixture in a blender or food processor until
smooth. You may need to add water. Serve hot and garnish with cilantro leaves.

Serves 4

Rasam Soup

Executive Chef Daniel McConnell
Philadelphia Tea Party, Philadelphia, PA

2 qt. charcoal-filtered water
2 T. tamarind paste
4 Indian chile peppers (red)
4 curry leaves
1 T. curry powder
1 T. ground turmeric
1/2 cup soy bean oil
2 cups thinly cut leeks, cleaned
2 cups chopped carrots
4 cups baking potatoes, peeled and cut into 1/2-inch cubes
1 16-oz. package rice noodles
salt to taste

Combine water, tamarind paste, chiles, curry leaves and powder, and turmeric in a heavy saucepan. Stir well and bring to a boil; reduce to a simmer, stirring occasionally. In a separate saucepan, heat oil and gently sauté leeks, carrots, and potatoes until leeks become soft but not limp. Add stock to vegetables by pouring through a mesh strainer. Let simmer for about 15 minutes. Add salt to taste. Cook rice noodles in a pot of boiling salted water for 5 to 7 minutes. Drain and run under cold water. Serve the soup and noodles separately, adding noodles per bowl.

Serves 8

Creamless Tomato and Fennel Soup with Crabmeat

Executive Chef David Gottlieb
The Dilworthtown Inn, West Chester, PA

3 Spanish onions, sliced
3 bulbs fennel, sliced
1 bulb garlic, chopped
1 bunch leeks, sliced thin
10 lbs. plum tomatoes, sliced
1 bunch thyme, finely chopped
1 bunch basil, finely chopped
1 bunch parsley, finely chopped
salt and pepper to taste
1 lb. lump crabmeat, cleaned

Cook onions, fennel, garlic, and leeks in large sauce pot for approximately 10 minutes or until they are tender and clear but not brown. Add tomatoes and bring to a boil. Simmer for 30 minutes. (Tomatoes will release their own juices.)

Add herbs and salt and pepper. Puree soup with hand mixer or blender. Strain to remove seeds. Garnish with crabmeat.

Yields 6 pints

Braised Lamb Shank Pot Au Feu

Executive Chef Jim Coleman
Treetops Restaurant, Rittenhouse Hotel, Philadelphia, PA

"Lamb shank has always been a personal favorite at the Rittenhouse in one form or another. I love the rich and robust flavor of lamb and especially the intense flavors contained in the shank or foreleg. Because the shank contains thick muscle and connective tissue, it is tough unless braised slowly and for a long time, but prepared right, the meat falls off the bone and melts in the mouth. Pot au feu is the classic French preparation of meat and vegetables simmered slowly and gently in a broth. Traditionally, the broth is served as a soup before the meat and vegetables are enjoyed as the main meal."

1 T. olive oil
4 lamb shanks, about 6 oz. each, trimmed of all fat
1/2 cup red wine
5 cups low-sodium chicken stock
1 bay leaf
2 tsp. fresh rosemary
1 T. chopped garlic
3 carrots, sliced on the bias, 1/4-inch thick
1 white onion, quartered
1½ cups diced butternut squash
4 oz. button mushrooms
4 sprigs rosemary

Preheat the oven to 325°. Heat the olive oil in a large ovenproof sauté pan with a lid. When the pan is hot, sear the lamb shanks on all sides over high heat for 5 to 6 minutes or until golden brown. Deglaze the pan with the wine. Add the stock, bay leaf, and rosemary and bring to a boil. Cover with a lid and cook in the oven for 1 hour.

Remove the pan from the oven and add the garlic, carrots, onion, squash, and mushrooms. Cover with the lid and continue cooking in the oven for 30 minutes, until the lamb is completely tender.

Ladle the vegetables and broth into large serving bowl. Arrange the lamb shank in the center of the bowl and garnish with the rosemary sticking upright out of the bone.

Serves 4

Halibut Pot Au Feu

Sous Chef Brian W. Duffy
Big Fish Restaurant, Conshohocken, PA

C

1.5 oz. Thai cellophane noodles
6 7-oz. pieces halibut
Broth (see recipe)
24 pea pods
5 red peppers, julienned
20 shiitake mushrooms, sliced
1 lb. jicama, julienned
30 enoki mushrooms
6 T. chopped scallions
6 pinches cilantro

Soak noodles in warm water and set aside. Poach fish in broth for 6 to 8 minutes. Remove pin bones after cooking. Add pea pods, red peppers, shiitakes, and jicama to broth. Cook 30 seconds. Place broth into 6 bowls. Add cellophane noodles, pea pods, red peppers, shiitakes, jicama, enoki (save some for garnishing), and finally the halibut. Garnish with remaining enoki mushrooms, scallions, and cilantro.

Serves 6.

Broth

1 T. sesame oil
2 T. minced garlic
1 T. diced pickled ginger
1½ cups sake or white wine
1½ quarts clam juice or fish stock
1/4 cup soy sauce
1 T. chili oil

Sauté garlic and ginger (lightly) in sesame oil for 30 seconds. Add wine, clam juice, and soy sauce. Bring to boil. Take off heat and add chili oil.

Clear Tomato Gazpacho

Executive Chef Adam Sturm
Azalea Restaurant, Omni Hotel, Philadelphia, PA

4 lbs. beefsteak tomatoes
salt and pepper to taste
2 sprigs cilantro, roughly chopped
3 oz. lemon grass, roughly chopped
1/2 pint baby pear tomatoes, halved
1 bunch chives, minced
1 red pepper, finely diced
1 hothouse cucumber, peeled and diced

Puree the beefsteak tomatoes with salt and pepper to taste. (Tomatoes must be seasoned in order to assure the success of this recipe.) Line a large bowl with approximately 1 yard of cheesecloth. Pour in seasoned tomato puree. Bunch and tie the cheesecloth to form a "bag." Hang the tomatoes over the bowl for 30 minutes or until the tomatoes have been completely drained of their liquid. Reserve the tomato liquid.

Combine cilantro, lemon grass, and the reserved tomato liquid. Bring liquid to a simmer and strain. When the broth has cooled and has been chilled, garnish with baby pear tomatoes, chives, peppers, and cucumbers.

Serves 4

Tropical Fruit Gazpacho

Chef De Cuisine Andrew Berks
Founders, Park Hyatt Philadelphia at the Bellevue, Philadelphia, PA

1 pineapple
4 cups pineapple juice
1 mango, diced
1 jalapeño pepper, diced
1/2 cup diced red pepper
1/4 cup diced red onion
1/4 cup sliced scallion
juice of 1 lime
1 tsp. cumin
1/4 tsp. cracked black pepper
2 T. chopped cilantro

Peel pineapple and slice lengthwise. Grill until lightly charred. Puree half of the pineapple with the pineapple juice and mango. Dice the remaining half of the pineapple and add to puree. Add peppers, onions, scallions, and lime juice. Season with cumin and cracked pepper. If too thick, add more pineapple juice. Chill and serve garnished with cilantro.

Serves 6 to 8

NOTE: Grilling the pineapple is optional.

About the Chef

Name: Andrew Berks

Education/Training: The Restaurant School

Inspirations/Influences: new trends, customer feedback

Hobbies: food and wine

Family: married, one cat

Hometown: Mount Laurel, NJ

Favorite Food to Eat: risotto with morels

Favorite Cookbook: too many to mention

Prickly Pear and Pineapple Gazpacho

Executive Chef Chris Todd
Arroyo Grille, Manayunk, PA

1 red pepper, minced
1 yellow pepper, minced
1 red tomato, minced
1 yellow tomato, minced
1 cucumber, minced
3 stalks scallions, minced
1/2 cup prickly pear puree
1 qt. tomato juice
1/4 cup champagne vinegar
2 T. olive oil
1 pineapple, pureed
1 T. mint
1 T. cilantro
salt and pepper to taste

Combine peppers, tomatoes, scallions, cucumbers, and scallions in a large bowl. Add the prickly pear puree, tomato juice, vinegar, olive oil, and freshly pureed pineapple to the bowl. Mix in the mint and cilantro and add salt and pepper to taste.

Serves 6 to 8

Sour Cherry Soup

Executive Chef Ed Doherty
La Campagne, Cherry Hill, NJ

3 cups dry white wine
1/2 cup sugar
1 lb. sour cherries, pitted
2 T. kirsch
juice of 2 lemons
3 cups crème fraîche or sour cream

In a saucepan, combine wine and sugar. Bring to a simmer to dissolve sugar. Add cherries and simmer 2 to 3 minutes. Remove from heat and allow to cool. Puree in a blender or food processor, then work through a food mill or sieve. Whisk in kirsch, lemon juice, and 2 cups of crème fraîche. Chill thoroughly. Ladle into chilled bowls and garnish with dollops of remaining 1 cup of crème fraîche.

Serves 8

About the Chef

Chef: Edward J. Doherty

Education/Training: École de Cuisine La Varenne; B.A. Education from University of Delaware

Inspirations/Influences: retro-French, Provence, regional American

Hobbies: home improvement, golf, cooking at home with friends and family

Family: married, four kids (including twins)

Hometown: Merchantville, NJ

Favorite Food to Eat: pizza

Favorite Food to Prepare: BBQ - Mediterranean style

Favorite Cookbook: *Mastering the Art of French Cooking* by Julia Child

Caren's Shrimp Salad

Owner Howard Nutinsky
Corned Beef Academy, Philadelphia, PA

1 whole lemon, cut in half
1 to 2 bay leaves
1 tsp. paprika
2 lb. large shrimp
2 to 3 stalks celery, chopped
1 tsp. course ground pepper
1 tsp. Old Bay seasoning
3/4 tsp. celery seed
1 cup Russian dressing
salt to taste

Combine 2 quarts water, lemon, bay leaves, and paprika in a pot and bring to a boil. Add shrimp and cook until shrimp turn pink and start to "curl." Remove shrimp and wash in cold water to stop cooking. Peel, devein, and chop shrimp into large pieces. Mix chopped shrimp with celery, pepper, Old Bay seasoning, and celery seed. Add Russian dressing and mix well. Taste and correct seasoning with salt and pepper if needed. Serve in sandwiches or on chopped greens as a salad. Garnish with additonal lemon.

Serves 4 to 6

About the Chef

Name: Howard Nutinsky

Education/Training: over 15 years of practical on-the-job experience

Inspirations/Influences: my tastes and my customers' needs

Hobbies: golf, computers, cigars

Family: married 10 years to Caren, two children — Andrew (7) and Joey (2)

Hometown: Philadelphia, PA

Favorite Food to Eat: too many to list

Favorite Food to Prepare: too many to list

Favorite Cookbook: *Joy of Cooking*

Mixed Tomato, Proscuitto and Mozzarella Salad

Executive Chef Wendy Welcovitz
The Inn Philadelphia, Philadelphia, PA

10 oz. plum tomatoes, sliced into rounds
5 oz. yellow teardrop tomatoes, halved
6 oz. cherry tomatoes, halved
8 oz. small fresh mozzarella, sliced
3½ oz. finely sliced proscuitto
1 cup basil leaves, torn if large
Balsamic Dressing (see recipe)

Arrange the tomatoes, mozzarella, and proscuitto on 4 individual serving plates. Drizzle with dressing. Serve at room temperature.

Serves 4

Balsamic Dressing

1/2 cup extra virgin olive oil
2 T. balsamic vinegar
salt and freshly ground black pepper to taste

Whisk together oil and vinegar until well-blended. Season to taste with salt and pepper.

Asian Vegetable Salad

Executive Chef Jerry S. Truxell
Cedarbrook Hill Country Club, Wyncote, PA

1/2 cup snipped string beans
1 medium yellow squash, quartered and cut
1/4 cup shredded bok choy
1/2 cup snipped snow peas
1 medium zucchini, quartered and cut
1/4 cup diced plum tomatoes
1/4 cup diced red pepper
1/4 cup sesame oil
1/4 cup extra virgin olive oil
2 T. crushed garlic
2 T. chopped cilantro
2 T. chopped basil
salt and pepper to taste

Bring a large pot of salted water to a boil. Add string beans and cook for 3 to 4 minutes. Add squash and bok choy; cook for 3 to 4 minutes. Add snow peas and cook for 1 minute. Strain and cool vegetables in an ice bath. Drain well and toss <u>all</u> vegetables together with sesame oil, olive oil, garlic, and herbs. Season to taste with salt and pepper. Refrigerate and serve chilled.

Serves 4

Quinoa Salad with Citrus Vinaigrette

Chef Instructor Gerald Scanlon
The Restaurant School, Philadelphia, PA

2 quarts water
1/2 lb. quinoa, rinsed
1/2 cup chopped parsley
1/4 cup minced cilantro
1 tsp. minced garlic
2 scallions, sliced thin
1 red onion, diced and brunoised
1 green pepper, diced and brunoised
juice and zest of 2 oranges
juice and zest of 1 lemon
juice and zest of 1 lime
1/2 cup peanut oil
1/2 cup blended oil
dash of Worcestershire sauce
2 T. brown sugar, firmly packed
salt and pepper to taste
purple kale
2 oranges, segmented or 1 can mandarin oranges

Bring water to a boil. Add quinoa and cook for 6 minutes or until al dente. Drain and wash with cold water. Mix together all ingredients from parsley through brown sugar and toss with quinoa. Season to taste with salt and pepper and place in service platter. Garnish with purple kale and orange segments.

Serves 8

About the Chef

Name: Gerald J. Scanlan, C.E.C.

Education/Training: Culinary Institute of America

Inspirations/Influences: new and fresh ingredients

Hobbies: soccer, coaching, sports

Family: single father, two boys — Jerry and Brendan

Hometown: Washington Township, NJ

Favorite Food to Eat: Middle Eastern

Favorite Food to Prepare: American influenced

Favorite Cookbook: any book by James Beard

Watercress and Bibb Salad with Jicama and Pumpkin Seed Vinaigrette

Executive Chef Jim Coleman
Treetops Restaurant, Rittenhouse Hotel, Philadelphia, PA

"Watercress is a member of the mustard family and it provides a zippy contrast to the buttery, sweet Bibb. You can also substitute mustard greens or arugula for the watercress. Jicama is a root vegetable that is also known as the Mexican potato. It makes a great salad ingredient — it has a crisp, watery, and refreshing texture, rather like water chestnuts (which you can substitute if you'd like to add an Asian twist to this salad) and a slightly nutty flavor."

8 oz. Bibb lettuce
4 oz. watercress, leaves only
Vinaigrette (see recipe)
8 oz. jicama, peeled and julienned
2 T. pumpkin seeds, toasted

Arrange the Bibb lettuce on 4 salad plates. Toss the watercress with the vinaigrette and arrange on top of the Bibb lettuce. Arrange the jicama over the salad and sprinkle each salad with the pumpkin seeds.

Serves 4

Vinaigrette

1 tsp. minced garlic
1 tsp. minced shallot
2 T. canola oil
2 T. champagne vinegar
2 T. low-sodium chicken stock

Whisk all the vinaigrette ingredients together in a mixing bowl and set aside.

Rococo Salad of Limestone and Tat-Soi

Executive Chef Mustapha Rouissiya
Rococo, Philadelphia, PA

@

1 head Belgian endive, diced
1 cup limestone or Bibb lettuce
3 oz. tat-soi or spring salad mix
2 oz. Light Poppyseed Dressing (see recipe)
1 ounce Gorgonzola cheese
2 strawberries, diced

Mix endive, limestone or Bibb, and tat-soi together in a large bowl. Add light poppyseed dressing. Garnish with Gorgonzola and strawberries.

Serves 2

Light Poppyseed Dressing

3 T. sour cream
1 tsp. poppyseeds
1 T. white vinegar
2 T. honey
juice of 1/4 lemon
1/4 cup peanut oil
sea salt and pepper to taste

Combine all ingredients well. Chill.

Thai Spiced Shrimp Salad Asian Greens and Pesto Dressing

Chef/Owner Philippe Chin
Chanterelles, Philadelphia, PA

2 oz. cellophane noodles
1 cup coconut milk
1 T. red curry paste
1 T. fish sauce
1 small Thai red chili pepper
20 16-20-sized shrimp, peeled and deveined
1/2 lb. Asian greens
Pesto Dressing (see recipe)
2 T. chopped scallions
1 T. chopped cilantro

Place cellophane noodles into a bowl. Cover with warm water and set aside. Pour coconut milk into a pan and add curry paste, fish sauce, and the fresh chili. Slowly bring to a simmer. Add the shrimp and cook uncovered, stirring frequently, over low heat for about 8 minutes, then chill.

Strain the noodles and toss with a little of the pesto dressing. Strain the shrimp. Distribute the noodles equally in the center of 4 serving plates. Toss the greens with the pesto dressing; top the noodles with the greens. Place the shrimp around the greens. Drizzle the shrimp with remaining dressing. Sprinkle the plate with the chopped scallions and cilantro.

Serves 4

Pesto Dressing

1/4 cup Thai basil
1/4 cup toasted macadamia nuts
2 T. Chinese black vinegar
1/4 cup extra virgin olive oil
salt and pepper to taste

In a blender, combine the basil, macadamia nuts, and vinegar, adding the olive oil slowly. Salt and pepper to taste. Strain and set aside.

Grilled Calamari with Cucumbers and Baby Greens

Executive Chef Clark Gilbert
La Terrasse, Philadelphia, PA

8 small fresh squid, cleaned and rinsed
olive oil
salt and pepper
juice of 1 lemon
1 medium shallot, finely chopped
2 cloves garlic, finely chopped
2 T. capers, nonpareil
chopped fresh herbs
1 seedless cucumber
1 bag baby greens

Lightly toss calamari in olive oil and season with salt and pepper. Place on a very hot grill for 1½ to 2 minutes per side. Squid will blow up and become slightly translucent. Set squid aside and let it come to room temperature.

In a mixing bowl, add remaining olive oil, lemon juice, shallots, garlic, capers, and fresh herbs. Whisk to incorporate. Cut calamari into 1" cross sections and add to vinaigrette.

Slice cucumber thinly and fan around outside of plate within the rim. Take enough vinaigrette to lightly dress baby greens and place in center of plate surrounded by cucumbers. Divide the calamari evenly between all 4 plates and top with a little additional vinaigrette, making sure to utilize capers, shallot, and garlic.

Serves 4.

NOTE: Use any combination of herbs that you like. Chef Gilbert prefers parsley, basil, chive, and tarragon.

Sesame Crusted Tuna Loin with Ponzu-Wasabi Vinaigrette

Chef/Owner Philippe Chin
Chanterelles, Philadelphia, PA

1 1-lb. piece of sushi grade tuna loin, clean
2 T. black sesame seeds, toasted
2 T. white sesame seeds, toasted
1 tsp. olive oil
salt and pepper to taste
Ponzu-Wasabi Vinaigrette (see recipe)
1/4 lb. mixed greens

Season the tuna with salt and pepper on each side. Roll in mixed black and white sesame seeds. Lightly brush tuna with olive oil and sear in a large skillet for about 3 minutes each side.

Slice the tuna into 12 medallions. Serve immediately on plates drizzled with part of the vinaigrette. Serve with bouquets of mixed greens tossed with the remaining vinaigrette.

Serves 4

Ponzu-Wasabi Vinaigrette

1 T. ponzu (available in Asian food markets)
1 T. diluted wasabi
1/2 T. rice vinegar
1 T. extra virgin olive oil
1/2 T. sesame oil
1 T. water

In a mixing bowl, whisk together the ponzu, wasabi, and vinegar and slowly whisk in the oils. Add the water.

Cabrales and Patria Chiles Vinaigrette

Executive Chef Guillermo Pernot
Vega Grill, Manayunk, PA

4 T. cabrales cheese
5 cloves garlic, roasted
3 T. lime juice
1 patria (Anaheim) pepper, roasted, peeled, and seeded
3 T. red wine vinegar
1/2 cup olive oil
salt to taste

Process all ingredients in a blender until smooth.

Yields 1 cup

Roasted Poblano Vinaigrette

Executive Chef Guillermo Pernot
Vega Grill, Manayunk, PA

4 poblano peppers, roasted, seeded, and peeled
2 scallions
2 cloves garlic
1/2 cup cilantro leaves
2 T. lime juice
1/4 cup olive oil
pinch of sugar
1 cup lowfat buttermilk
salt and pepper to taste

Process all ingredients in a food processor or blender until smooth or semi-chunky (your preference).

Yields 1½ cups

Risottos & Pastas

Tomato Risotto 75

California Risotto 76

Melted Leek Potato Risotto.. 76

Squash Risotto 77

Tomato-Sweet Corn Risotto.. 78

Crabmeat Risotto with Fava Beans 79

Roasted Corn, Rock Shrimp and Basil Risotto 80

Lobster and Asparagus Risotto.. 81

Cappanata a la Luca.. 82

Penne with Sweet Roasted Pepper Sauce 83

Cavatelli with Sun-dried Tomato Pesto 84

Cavatelli alla Scarpinato's 85

Sonoma Shrimp Ravioli.. 86

Ravioli Polla Verda... 87

Three Cheese Gnocchi with Tomato Cream 88

Potato Basil Gnocchi with Tomato Olive Sauce 89

Scallops and Penne with Pesto and Cream 90

Shrimp Amelia... 91

Farfalle with Venison Sausage and Smoked Mozzarella............... 92

Asian Sesame Noodles... 93

Toasted Linguine with Julienned Chicken
    and Sun-dried Tomatoes 94

Tomato Risotto

Executive Chef Eric Hall
Circa, Philadelphia, PA

C

1 pt. chicken stock
1 cup whole peeled plum tomatoes, roughly pureed
2 T. olive oil
1 small white onion, diced
1 tsp. minced garlic
1/4 cup red wine
10 oz. Arborio rice
1 T. butter
1/4 cup heavy cream
1 T. grated Parmesan cheese
1/4 cup chopped fresh basil
1/4 cup chopped parsley
salt and pepper to taste
Red and Spicy Lobster (Recipe appears on page 101.)

Mix chicken stock and tomatoes. Reserve. In a 4-quart, heavy-bottomed sauce-pan, sauté the onion until translucent over medium-high heat, about 2 minutes. Add garlic and sauté 1 minute more. Deglaze pan with the red wine. Add rice and 1/4 of the chicken stock/tomato mixture. Stir continuously while cooking. As the rice absorbs the liquid, gradually add more of the stock, still stirring, until all of the liquid is incorporated. Add the butter, cream, Parmesan cheese, and chopped herbs and continue to stir. Taste a little and adjust the flavor with salt and pepper. Also, if you desire the risotto to be a bit softer, just add a little bit of water and continue to cook until you have reached the desired consistency. Serve with red and spicy lobster.

Serves 6

California Risotto

Chef/Owner Ian Friedman
Sage Cafe, Beach Haven, NJ

1 T. butter
1/2 onion, finely chopped
salt and pepper
2 cups risotto
3 cups chicken stock
1 T. toasted pine nuts
l T. finely chopped fresh basil

In a saucepan, sauté butter and onions and season with salt and pepper. Add risotto and continue to sauté. Add chicken stock, cover, and let simmer on low heat, checking frequently to make sure the risotto is not burning. Garnish with pine nuts and basil.

Serves 2

Melted Leek Potato Risotto

Executive Chef John Anderson
Husch Restaurant & Bar, Narberth, PA

2 Idaho potatoes, peeled and diced
1 leek, sliced
1 tsp. butter
1/2 cup heavy cream

Place potatoes in a pot of salted water and bring to a boil. Remove from heat, strain, and let cool. (They should not be fully cooked as they will be cooked again.)

Place leeks and butter in a pan over low heat. Cook slowly for 10 minutes. Add potatoes and cream and let the cream slowly evaporate while stirring occasionally. When the cream begins to bind the potatoes together, sprinkle cheese into risotto.

Serves 4

Squash Risotto

Chef/Owner Toby Weitzman
Creative Catering Company, Cherry Hill, NJ

1/2 stick unsalted butter
1 large onion, chopped
1½ cup peeled, diced butternut squash
6 cups chicken broth
1½ cups Arborio rice
1/2 cup dry white wine
1 T. butter
1/2 cup grated Parmesan cheese
1 T. chopped fresh parsley

Melt butter. Add onion and sauté until transparent. Add squash and 1/2 cup stock. Cover and cook until tender, about 12 minutes. Mix in rice. Add wine and stir until absorbed. Add remaining stock and simmer, uncovered, until absorbed (about 30 minutes), stirring occasionally. Melt butter and add to Parmesan cheese; then add cheese to rice mixture. Season with salt and pepper. Divide among bowls; sprinkle with parsley.

Serves 6

Tomato-Sweet Corn Risotto

Chef/Proprietor Kevin von Klause
White Dog Cafe, Philadelphia, PA

☺

"This is one of our favorite summer risottos. The opposing tanginess of the toma-toes and the sweetness of the corn is bridged by a large handful of chopped fresh basil. Served with a green salad, some crusty bread, and a crisp white wine, it is a heavenly meal. For the broth we use a quick and easy corn stock made by simmer-ing corn cobs and aromatics—it reinforces the sweet corn flavor."

2 T. extra virgin olive oil
1 cup diced leeks (white part only)
1 tsp. minced garlic
1½ cups Arborio rice
1/2 cup dry white wine
Corn-Tomato Stock (Recipe appears on page 234.)
1 cup finely diced fresh ripe tomato
1/2 cup chopped basil leaves
3/4 cup freshly grated Parmesan cheese
1/2 tsp. salt
1/2 tsp. freshly ground black pepper

In a nonreactive large saucepan set over medium heat, heat the olive oil until it shimmers. Add the leeks and cook until translucent, about 2 minutes. Add the garlic and cook for 1 minute. Add the rice, toss to coat with the oil, and cook until it exudes a nutty aroma, about 1 to 2 minutes. Continue stirring and add the wine. When the wine is absorbed, add enough of the corn-tomato stock to just cover the rice. Bring to a gentle simmer and stir. As the rice absorbs the liquid, add more stock, a ladleful at a time, stirring before and after each addition. (You might not use all of the broth.) After about 20 minutes, the rice should be tender but still firm in the center.

Stir in the reserved corn kernels and diced tomato. Taste the rice for doneness. If it is still starchy in the center, add a little more broth and continue to stir until the broth is absorbed. The rice should be tender yet firm, loose but not runny. Stir in the basil, Parmesan cheese, salt, and pepper. Taste for season-ing. Serve immediately.

Serves 4

Crabmeat Risotto with Fava Beans

Chef/Owner Bruce Lim
Ciboulette, Philadelphia, PA

1 medium Spanish onion, finely chopped
5 T. virgin olive oil
1½ cup Italian rice (Arborio)
1/2 cup white wine
salt and pepper
3 cups light chicken broth
3 T. butter
3 oz. Parmesan cheese
1 lb. jumbo lump crabmeat
1/2 cup fava beans, blanched

Sweat onion in olive oil. Slowly stir in rice. Add white wine and salt and pepper. Stir in light chicken broth slowly. Add butter, Parmesan cheese, crabmeat, and fava beans to cooked rice. Serve.

Serves 4.

About the Chef

Name: Bruce Lim

Education/Training: France

Inspirations/Influences: I love to cook.

Family: wife, two daughters

Hometown: Singapore; now resides in Cherry Hill, NJ

Favorite Food to Eat: chicken soup

Favorite Food to Prepare: raw fish

Favorite Cookbook: *Larousse Gastronomique*

Roasted Corn, Rock Shrimp and Basil Risotto

Executive Chef Louis Imbesi
Catelli Ristorante & Café, Voorhees, NJ

3 oz. extra virgin olive oil
1 cup diced onion
3 cloves garlic, minced
3 cups Arborio rice
4 tomatoes, peeled, seeded, and diced
8 cups chicken stock or light seafood stock
2 lbs. fresh rock shrimp, cooked
1½ cups roasted corn kernels
4 fresh basil leaves, roughly cut
2 oz. whole butter
salt and pepper to taste

Heat olive oil in a shallow, heavy-bottomed pot. Sauté onions until translucent. Stir in garlic and sauté 3 minutes. Add rice and stir until well coated, about 3 minutes. Add tomatoes and continue to cook for 3 minutes. Heat stock in a separate pan. Add 4 cups of stock to rice mixture and simmer over low heat for 8 minutes. Stir in remaining stock and simmer for 5 minutes. Add rock shrimp and corn; simmer for 3 minutes. Add basil, butter, and salt and pepper to taste. Stir together until well-incorporated. Serve immediately.

Serves 8

About the Chef

Name: Louis Imbesi

Education/Training: self-taught — have been working in restaurants and hotels since I was 15 years old

Inspirations/Influences: current food trends, seasonal availability

Hobbies: reading trade magazines and cookbooks, tennis, soccer

Family: I am a first-generation Italian American. **Hometown:** Cherry Hill, NJ

Favorite Food to Eat: seafood   **Favorite Food to Prepare:** exotic seafood

Favorite Cookbook: *Charlie Trotter's*

Lobster and Asparagus Risotto

Executive Chef Jim Coleman
Treetops Restaurant, Rittenhouse Hotel, Philadelphia, PA

"The very first risotto I ever ate was at a restaurant in New York, and yes, it contained lobster. I tasted it and fell in love. Risotto is a very adaptable and flexible medium; you can substitute tomato or even pineapple juice for the chicken stock and play with the combinations of flavors of the other ingredients. Some people are intimidated by risotto, as it has a reputation for having to be cooked just right, but it is not as hard to cook as most think. In this recipe, for example, you don't even have to stand over it — you finish it in the oven until the liquid has evaporated."

6 oz. lobster tail meat (about 1 or 2 tails), cut into 1/8 inch-thick pieces
1 T. minced garlic
2 T. minced shallots
1 red bell pepper, seeded and diced
6 T. white wine
2 cups Arborio rice
3 T. freshly squeezed lemon juice
4 cups low-sodium chicken stock
1 large tomato, blanched, peeled, seeded, and diced
12 asparagus spears, cut on the bias
1½ T. chopped fresh dill
1½ T. thinly sliced fresh basil
1 tsp. salt
4 sprigs fresh dill, for garnish

Preheat the oven to 400°. Coat a high-sided, oven-proof sauté pan or skillet with nonstick cooking spray and place over medium-high heat. Add the lobster, garlic, shallots, and red bell pepper and sauté for 1½ minutes or until the lobster is just cooked. Remove the lobster from the pan and set aside to cool.

Add the wine, rice, and lemon juice to the pan, stir together thoroughly, and cook for 2 minutes. Add 1 cup of the stock and continue cooking, stirring constantly, until the liquid has just evaporated. Add 1½ cups more of the stock and stirring constantly, allow the stock to evaporate again. Stir in the remaining 1½ cups stock, the tomato, asparagus, dill, basil, and salt. Transfer the pan to the oven and finish cooking for about 20 minutes until all the liquid has evaporated. Remove the pan from the oven and stir in the reserved lobster. Spoon the risotto onto the serving plates, arranging the lobster meat on top of the rice. Garnish with the dill sprigs and serve.

Serves 4

Cappanata a la Luca
Cold Tomato Salad Over Hot Pasta

Chef/Proprietor Luca Sena, padre
Assistant to Chef, Luca Sena, figlio
Panorama at the Penn's View Hotel, Philadelphia, PA

4 ripe salad tomatoes, chopped into 1/4-inch squares
1 onion, diced
1 cup extra virgin olive oil
salt and pepper
1 lb. pasta
4 large leaves fresh basil, chopped
Parmesan cheese
1 leaf fresh basil

Place tomatoes and onion in a bowl. Toss with extra virgin olive oil and salt and pepper. Cook pasta al dente and strain. Pour tomatoes over pasta. Season with chopped basil and Parmesan cheese. Garnish with basil leaf.

Serves 4

Penne with Sweet Roasted Pepper Sauce

Executive Chef David W. Brennan
DiLullo's, Philadelphia, PA

3 extra large sweet yellow peppers
3 extra large sweet red peppers
1/4 cup olive oil
3/4 cup minced red onion
2 cups Fresh Tomato Sauce (Recipe appears on page 231.)
1/4 cup fresh basil leaves, torn into thirds
1 lb. penne pasta
salt and freshly ground pepper to taste

Roast the peppers; remove stems, seeds, and skin. Cut peppers into 1-inch strips. Reserve.

In a large sauté pan, heat olive oil over medium heat and sauté onions until soft. Add the peppers, tomato sauce, and fresh basil. Simmer for 5 minutes.

Cook the pasta in lightly salted water. Drain and toss with pepper sauce. Finish with salt and freshly ground pepper.

Serves 8

About the Chef

Name: David W. Brennan

Education/Training: Culinary Institute of America, 1983

Hobbies: golf, tennis

Family: married, one son — Ryan, born 8/31/95

Hometown: Pottstown, PA

Cavatelli with Sun-dried Tomato Pesto

Executive Chef Francesco Martorella
Brasserie Perrier, Philadelphia, PA

3 cups flour
1 egg yolk
1 T. ricotta *impostata*
1 tsp. mascarpone cheese
2 cups sun-dried tomatoes
4 anchovy fillets
1 tsp. chopped garlic
1 cup basil
1/4 cup parsley
1/4 cup finely chopped tomato
1 tsp. grated Parmesan

Fold flour, egg yolk, ricotta, and mascarpone together using the "well method."
Knead and let rest for 1 hour.

If dried, reconstitute sun-dried tomatoes in hot water. Using a food processor, puree sun-dried tomatoes with anchovies, garlic, basil, and parsley to make pesto. Cut pasta into small bite-size pieces and cook in boiling salted water for approximately 1 to 2 minutes. Serve pasta topped with heated pesto and garnish with chopped tomato and Parmesan cheese.

Serves 4

About the Chef

Name: Francesco Martorella

Education/Training: Culinary Institute of America, sous chef at The Four Seasons, co-owner of Ciboulette, executive chef at Ritz-Carlton

Inspirations/Influences: summers spent in Italy as a child; farmers who grow the fruits and vegetables I cook with

Hobbies: cycling, being with my daughter, working in my English garden

Family: one daughter and another on the way. My father was a chef.

Hometown: Philadelphia, PA

Favorite Food to Eat: pasta, Chinese food   **Favorite Food to Prepare:** fish

Favorite Cookbook: *Charlie Trotter's* and *The Book of Alain Ducasse*

Cavatelli alla Scarpinato's

Executive Chef Vincenzo Scarpinato
Scarpinato's Ristorante, Blackwood, NJ

1 T. chopped garlic
3 T. olive oil
6 oz. hot or mild sausage (remove meat from casing)
1/2 cup sliced sun-dried tomatoes
1 hot pepper, sliced into 1/2" wheels (Anaheim, chili, or long hot is recommended)
1/4 cup white wine
1/2 cup sliced black olives
4 artichoke hearts, quartered
pinch of salt and fresh ground pepper
1/2 cup beef or veal stock
1 lb. cheese cavatelli, cooked al dente
1/2 cup grated Pecorino Romano cheese
1 bunch fresh parsley, finely chopped

In a large sauté pan, sauté garlic lightly in oil. Add sausage, sun-dried tomatoes, and hot pepper. When sausage is 3/4 cooked, add wine and reduce slightly. Add olives, artichokes hearts, and salt and pepper. Toss. Add stock and pasta. Let simmer and reduce. Serve garnished with grated cheese and parsley.

Serves 2 as entree
Serves 4 as pasta course

Sonoma Shrimp Ravioli

Executive Chef Don Paone
Sonoma Restaurant, Manayunk, PA

1 small onion, chopped
2 cloves garlic, chopped
1/4 lb. butter
3 slices stale white bread
3 egg whites
1 cup cream
1/2 cup grated Pecorino Romano cheese
1/4 cup chopped Italian parsley
kosher salt and cayenne pepper
4 sheets spinach pasta dough (available at your local pasta store)
Brandy, Basil, and Tomato Butter Sauce (Recipe appears on page 235.)

Sauté onions and garlic in butter until translucent. Add bread and cream and stir over high heat until cream is absorbed. Place mixture into a food processor and process until mixture is silky smooth. Add egg whites and shrimp; pulse until incorporated. (Shrimp should remain chunky but not too big as to poke holes in the ravioli.) Fold in parsley and cheese. Season with kosher salt and cayenne pepper. (Overcompensate on seasoning as weakly seasoned stuffing will not taste good in the ravioli against the blandness of the pasta dough.) Refrigerate.

Using a ravioli mold, lay out bottom sheet of pasta and spoon out 1 tablespoon of filling for each ravioli. Using a pastry brush or moist rag, moisten the edges of each individual mold so the top sheet will stick when applied. Apply top sheet and top with top part of ravioli mold. Press firmly and cut.

Cook ravioli in a pot of boiling salted water. Cook to desired doneness. Toss with shrimp butter sauce and serve.

Serves 8

NOTE: Ravioli may be cooked immediately or frozen for future use. If frozen, they will take a little longer to cook.

Ravioli Polla Verda

Chef/Owner John Cancelliere
Ristorante Volare, Philadelphia, PA

1/2 lb. spinach, cooked and chopped
1/2 lb. boneles chicken breasts, chopped
olive oil
1/4 large sweet onion, diced
salt and pepper to taste
1 tsp. garlic
pinch cumin
pinch dry mustard
1/2 cup Parmesan cheese
2 whole eggs
1 lb. fresh pasta dough or 1 lb. wonton wrappers

Sauté spinach and chicken breasts in olive oil for about 5 minutes. Add onion and spices and cook for 20 minutes. Remove from heat and cool 30 minutes. Puree the cooled mixture in a blender or food processor until completely smooth. Add cheese and eggs and mix well. Refrigerate 1 hour. Cut pasta into 3-inch squares and place a teaspoon of mixture onto each square. Fold into a triangle, moisten edges with water, and press with a fork to close. Boil ravioli for 3 minutes and serve with marinara sauce.

Serves 6

NOTE: John's recipe for marinara is very simple. Sauté fresh peeled and chopped tomatoes with garlic and Parmesan cheese. The amounts are up to you.

About the Chef

Name: John Cancelliere   **Education/Training:** Argentina Culinary Institute
Inspirations/Influences: family tradition since 1914
Hobbies: professional soccer player from 1967-1979; then restaurants
Family: wife Dora, son Paslual, daughter Monica, six grandchildren
Hometown: Longano, Italy
Favorite Food to Eat: pasta, seafood, grilled meats
Favorite Food to Prepare: mixed grilled meat
Favorite Cookbook: too many to mention

Three Cheese Gnocchi with Tomato Cream

Executive Chef John Anderson
Husch Restaurant & Bar, Narberth, PA

2 medium potatoes, skin on
1/2 cup grated Parmesan cheese
2 T. ricotta cheese
2 T. grated Asiago cheese
1 egg
salt and pepper
1 cup flour
1 tsp. butter
2 T. tomato paste
1 cup heavy cream
1 tomato, diced
1 T. sliced basil leaves

Boil the potatoes in water until a fork can be stuck into them easily. Remove the potatoes from the water and while they are still warm, peel and cut into pieces. Pass potatoes through a food mill into a pan. The trick is to move the food mill and not create a pile of potatoes. Place the pan in the refrigerator for 15 minutes until the potatoes are cool.

Transfer the potatoes to a cool workspace and form them into a circle with a hole in the center. Add all the cheeses, egg, and salt and pepper. Begin mixing the ingredients and slowly add the flour as you knead the dough for 8 to 10 minutes. You now should have a ball of dough. Cut the ball of dough into 4 pieces and roll each out into "snakes" of dough. Cut each section into 1-inch pieces and place on a tray.

Boil a pot of water and add the gnocchis a few at a time for cooking. Remove from the water when they are floating (they should be firm to the touch). Place them in a bowl of ice water to quickly cool them down.

Heat a sauté pan and add the butter. Add the gnocchis and tomato paste. When the tomato paste is heated through, add the heavy cream. Season with salt and pepper and place in bowls. Garnish with tomato and basil.

Serves 4

Potato Basil Gnocchi with Tomato Olive Sauce

Chef/Proprietor Ben McNamara
Isabella's, Philadelphia, PA

12 oz. Idaho potatoes, unpeeled
1 oz. unsalted butter
2 T. chopped fresh basil
1 egg
1 egg yolk
4 oz. flour
salt and pepper to taste
Tomato Olive Sauce (Recipe appears on page 231.)

Place potatoes in a large pot with cold water. Bring to a boil and cook until a pairing knife can be cleanly inserted into the center of potato. Drain and peel off skins with a pairing knife.

In a large bowl, rice (finely mash) potatoes with butter until the butter is melted. Add basil and mix well. Add egg and egg yolk and mix until just incorporated. Add flour and salt and pepper until incorporated. Cut the dough into 4 separate pieces. On a floured surface, roll the dough with fingertips to form 1/2-inch cylinders. Cut the rolled gnocchi dough into 1/2-inch pieces with a sharp knife.

Boil gnocchi in salted water until they all float to the surface for 1 minute. Drain and toss with tomato olive sauce.

Serves 4

Scallops and Penne with Pesto and Cream

Chef/Owner Michael Fortunato
Remi's Cafe, Haddonfield, NJ

1 T. olive oil
1 lb. scallops, 10-20 per lb.
1½ T. minced shallots
1 cup white wine
1/2 cup pine nuts
1 cup sliced sun-dried tomatoes
2 cups heavy cream
1/2 cup pesto
4 T. Parmesan cheese
1 lb. pasta (penne or bowtie)

In large sauté pan, sauté scallops in olive oil over medium-high heat for 4 to 5 minutes or until opaque. Remove scallops from pan and keep warm. Sweat shallots in pan until translucent. Deglaze pan with white wine and reduce until almost dry. Add pine nuts, sun-dried tomatoes, and heavy cream. Bring to a boil. Add pesto and Parmesan cheese. Toss with cooked pasta.

Serves 4.

Shrimp Amelia

Sous Chef Brian W. Duffy
Big Fish, Conshohocken, PA

20 oz. fresh pasta
20 jumbo shrimp
2 T. minced shallots
1½ cups sliced shiitake mushrooms
1½ cups diced tomatoes
2 tsp. minced garlic
2½ cups red wine
6 oz. butter, cut into pats
4 oz. flour
salt and pepper to taste
chopped parsley

Cook pasta and reserve. Sauté shrimp over medium heat. Add shallots, mushrooms, tomatoes, and garlic. Remove shrimp when fully cooked. Add wine and reduce. Roll butter pats in flour and then add to wine until sauce is thickened. Salt and pepper to taste. Toss pasta in sauce. Place pasta in center of plate, top with shrimp, and garnish with parsley.

Serves 4

About the Chef

Name: Brian W. Duffy

Education/Training: The Restaurant School

Inspirations/Influences: passion for food

Hobbies: rugby

Hometown: Bala Cynwyd, PA

Favorite Food to Eat: shellfish, wild game

Favorite Food to Prepare: fish, shellfish

Farfalle with Venison Sausage and Smoked Mozzarella

Executive Chef David Gottlieb
The Dilworthtown Inn, West Chester, PA

2 oz. crimini mushrooms, sliced
2 oz. shiitake mushrooms, sliced
2 oz. oyster mushrooms, sliced
2 oz. sun-dried tomatoes, julienned
4 oz. venison sausage, cooked and sliced on bias
4 tsp. finely chopped shallots
4 tsp. finely chopped garlic
2 cups chicken stock
4 dashes each salt and pepper
4 dashes fresh herb mix (thyme, parsley, and basil), finely chopped
4 T. butter
1 lb. farfalle pasta, cooked and drained
2 oz. smoked mozzarella (affumicata), sliced

Sauté mushrooms in a sauté pan. Add sun-dried tomatoes, venison sausage, shallots, and garlic, cooking until shallots are just translucent. Add chicken stock and reduce. Add salt and pepper, herbs, and butter. Toss in farfalle. Adjust seasonings; then toss in mozzarella. Serve in large pasta bowl.

Serves 4

Asian Sesame Noodles

Chef Mary Malasky Mules
Peachtree & Ward Catering, Willow Grove, PA

1 lb. Chinese egg noodle nests
1/2 cup sesame oil
3/4 cup soy sauce
1/3 cup balsamic vinegar
1 T. Chinese red pepper oil
1/4 tsp. black bean chile paste
1/3 cup granulated sugar
3 T. chopped scallions
3 T. chopped cilantro
1 tsp. chopped garlic
1/4 cup chopped ginger
3 oz. red and yellow peppers, julienned
1/2 lb. bitter greens, washed

Bring 8 quarts of water to a boil. Drop in Chinese egg noodle nests. Stir and cook for 6 to 8 minutes until done. (Fluff constantly with a fork to break apart nests.) Drain and rinse with cold water.

Mix the next 10 ingredients together in a bowl. Toss noodles with the mixture and garnish with peppers and bitter greens.

Serves 8

About the Chef

Name: Mary Malasky Mules

Education/Training: The Restaurant School

Inspirations/Influences: everything

Hobbies: skiing, cooking

Family: married

Hometown: Philadelphia, PA

Favorite Food to Eat: oysters

Favorite Food to Prepare: borscht

Favorite Cookbook: most

Toasted Linguine with Julienned Chicken and Sun-dried Tomatoes

Executive Chef Daniel Dogan
The Terrace at Greenhill, Wilmington, DE

2 T. olive oil
2 T. butter
2 T. minced shallot
1 tsp. minced garlic
6 oz. boneless chicken breast, cleaned and sliced into strips
flour
8 sun-dried tomatoes, julienned
4 shiitake mushroom caps, julienned
4 chanterelle mushrooms, halved
1 medium portobello mushroom, quartered
4 oz. white wine
4 oz. demi-glace
1 T. chopped fresh rosemary
1 T. chopped fresh sage
6 oz. toasted linguine*
1 sprig rosemary
3 fresh sage leaves

Heat olive oil and butter in sauté pan. Add shallots and garlic and sauté until translucent. Dredge chicken strips in flour and brown on each side over medium heat. Add sun-dried tomatoes and mushrooms. Add white wine and reduce liquid by 1/2. Add demi-glace, rosemary, and sage. Toss with pasta and plate. Garnish with fresh herbs.

Serves 2

*To toast pasta: Lay pasta on baking pan and sprinkle with olive oil, lightly coating pasta. Place in preheated 350° oven and brown. Let cool. Then cook al dente.

About the Chef

Name: Daniel Dogan

Education/Training: The Restaurant School

Inspirations/Influences: customer feedback, current trends, innovative products

Hobbies: hiking, reading, sky diving

Family: wife Kim

Hometown: Detroit, MI

Favorite Food to Eat: seared sweetbreads

Favorite Food to Prepare: game meat, exotic fish

Favorite Cookbook: *Thrill of the Grill*

Shellfish & Seafood

Roasted Maine Lobster 99

Sautéed Lobster with Ginger Basil Beurre Blanc 100

Red and Spicy Lobster with Tomato Risotto 101

Kevin and Sam Choy's Mussel and Lobster Stir-Fry 102

Mussels with Beer Sauce 104

Moules à la Marinière 105

Mescalero Mussels 106

Clams with Black Bean Cake and Tomatillo Salsa 107

South American Chocolate BBQ Shrimp 108

Shrimp Szechuan Style 109

Kapok Tree Coconut Fried Shrimp 110

Pan Seared Shrimp with Julienne Vegetables 111

Corn-Crusted Crab and Shrimp Cakes
   with Summer Herbs Sauce 112

Phoenix Crab Cakes 113

Crabcakes with Roasted Pepper and Corn Hash 114

Sautéed Soft Shell Crabs with Roasted Corn Salsa 116

Macadamia and Coconut Encrusted Scallops
   with Papaya Cilantro Sauce 117

Grilled Jumbo Scallops with
   Wild Mushroom Charred Tomato Essence 118

"Shellpile" Oyster Stew with Verbena 120

Cajun Bouillabaisse 122

Seafood Jambalaya 123

Beer Seafood Fest 124

Steamed Fish 125

Pan Seared Codfish with Caramelized Onions 126

– more –

Dover Sole 127

Mushroom-Crusted Fillet of Flounder 128

Fish Provencal 129

Brazilian Baked Monkfish 130

Panchetta Monkfish 131

Fire Grilled Pompano with Banana-Cilantro Salsa 132

Sautéed Red Snapper with Toasted Pecan/Pistachio Butter ... 133

Red Snapper with Four Vinegars............................. 134

Sautéed Rouget With Fava Beans, Asparagus
  and Red Wine Sauce 136

Ancho Honey Glazed Salmon 138

Barbequed Salmon with Crispy Yams 139

BBQ Salmon on Grilled Romaine with Tarragon Potatoes 140

Grilled Salmon with Tomato, Olive Oil, and Fresh Herbs 141

Pesto-Crusted Salmon with Roasted Tomato Oil 142

Salmon with Exotic Mushrooms 144

Roast Moroccan Salmon Fillet 146

Steamed Salmon with Ginger and Scallion Sauce 147

Pan Seared Citrus and Rum Chilean Sea Bass 148

Paupiette of Sea Bass with Sauce Provencale
  in Thin Potato Crust 149

Grilled Marinated Swordfish 150

Sautéed Trout with Corn-Peanut Crust
  and Bacon-Shallot Butter 152

Rainbow Trout 153

Asian Tuna with Wasabi Vinaigrette 154

Anise-Seared Tuna with Black Currant Balsamico 155

Foie Gras Stuffed Tuna Steak 156

Grilled Tuna with Caribbean Salsa 157

Tuna Puttanesca 158

Wasabi Crusted Tuna Steak 159

Roasted Maine Lobster

Executive Chef Dany Chevalier
Nicholas Nickolas, The Rittenhouse Hotel, Philadelphia, PA

(o)

2 2½ lb. lobsters
4 oz. vegetable oil
2 T. shallots
2 oz. brandy
4 oz. white wine
4 oz. clam juice
1 cup fresh corn kernels
16 spaghetti clams or any type of small clam
4 T. diced red pepper
1 cup fingerling potatoes or baby red bliss, sliced lengthwise and par-roasted
2 T. chopped cilantro
2 T. chopped chives
6 T. unsalted butter, softened
salt and pepper to taste

Take whole lobster, remove claws, and steam for 5 to 6 minutes. Cool, crack, and take out claw meat. Take the lobster body and split lengthwise with chef knife, cleaning the stomach area out. Remove lobster head with knife. Heat vegetable oil over medium heat in large sauté pan. Add the lobster, flesh side down, and roast in pan approximately 4 to 6 minutes until you have a nice caramelization effect. Once caramelized, turn lobster over to shell side in pan and add shallots. Deglaze with brandy. Cook brandy; add white wine, clam juice, corn, and baby clams. Cook until clams open up. Add red pepper, potatoes, herbs, and butter. Season with salt and pepper.

Serves 2

Sautéed Lobster
with Ginger Basil Beurre Blanc

Chef/General Manager Michael Pfeffer
Old Original Bookbinder's Restaurant, Philadelphia, PA

2 8-oz. lobster tails
flour
oil
1 tsp. minced shallots
2 tsp. minced fresh ginger
4 oz. white wine
1 T. chopped fresh basil
3 oz. butter
salt and pepper to taste

Dredge lobster tails in flour. Place in a hot sauté pan with enough oil to coat the bottom of the pan. Sauté lobster until golden brown on both sides. Remove lobster for pan and set aside. Drain any excess oil from pan. Add shallots and ginger. Sauté until shallots start to caramelize. Add wine and basil and reduce by 1/3. Pull pan off of heat and whisk in butter. Season to taste. Lace sauce over lobsters and serve.

Serves 2

Red and Spicy Lobster with Tomato Risotto

Executive Chef Eric Hall
Circa, Philadelphia, PA

3 1¼ lb. lobsters
1/4 cup olive oil
1 T. chopped garlic
1/2 tsp. crushed red pepper
2 T. chopped fresh basil
1 T. chopped fresh parsley
1/2 cup white wine
1/2 cup chicken stock
1 14 oz. can whole peeled plum tomatoes in juice, crushed by hand
salt and pepper to taste
Tomato Risotto (Recipe appears on page 75.)

Split the live lobster lengthwise and clean out the entrails, leaving in the coral and tomalley. Heat a large sauté pan over medium-high heat and add the olive oil. Place the split lobsters in the pan on the exposed side and cook for 2 to 3 minutes. Turn them over in the pan and add the garlic, red pepper, and herbs, cooking for 1 minute. Add the wine, chicken stock, and tomatoes. Turn the heat down to a simmer and cook covered for about 10 minutes more. Serve on a platter with tomato risotto.

Serves 6

Kevin and Sam Choy's Mussel and Lobster Stir-Fry

Chef/Owner Kevin Meeker
Philadelphia Fish & Co., Philadelphia, PA

1 T. vegetable oil
2 T. minced fresh garlic
red pepper flakes to taste
1 cup chicken stock
3 cups mussels, cleaned
2 1¼ lb. whole lobsters, cooked and cut into sections
1/2 can fermented black beans, rinsed and drained
corn starch mixed with water
4 T. unsalted butter, softened
1/2 cup cilantro, washed and chopped

Pour oil into a large skillet and warm over moderate heat. Add garlic and red pepper flakes and cook for about 1 minute. Slowly pour in chicken stock and bring to a simmer. Add mussels, lobster, and black beans. Cook for about 4 to 5 minutes. Thicken with corn starch. Add butter and cilantro and stir. Serve alone or over pasta.

Serves 6

NOTE: You may substitute 10 shrimp for lobster.

About the Chef

Name: Kevin Meeker

Education/Training: I opened my first restaurant in 1976 . . . been hooked ever since. In addition to Philadelphia Fish & Company, also co-owner of Cuvee Notredame and The Plough and the Stars Irish Restaurant.

Inspirations/Influences: influenced by chefs and people who are into food that I meet day to day and while traveling. Every one eats and everyone has a unique way of preparing certain foods. The more I taste, observe, smell, and listen to what others do, the more new ideas I get from them.

Hobbies: going on vacation to exotic places

Family: married to Janet, three children — Leigh (10) and twins Connor and Nolan (5)

Hometown: Haddonfield, NJ

Favorite Food to Eat: Indian, Asian, hard-shell crabs, all spicy foods

Favorite Food to Prepare: whole fish on the grill

Favorite Cookbook: *The Thrill of the Grill*

Mussels with Beer Sauce

Executive Chef/Owner Michel Notredame
Cuvee Notredame Restaurant, Philadelphia, PA

@

4 tsp. butter
1 cup julienned carrots
1 cup chopped onions
1 cup julienned celery
1 cup julienned leeks
2 cloves garlic, chopped
4 lbs. mussels
2 glasses strong dark beer
salt and pepper to taste

Melt butter in a large pot. Add veggies and garlic. Stir for 3 minutes. Add mussels, beer, and salt and pepper. Cover. When mussels are open, they are ready. Serve with a side of French fries and mayonnaise.

Serves 2

About the Chef

Name: Michel Notredame

Education/Training: law school

Hobbies: cooking

Favorite Food to Eat: every type of food that is fresh and well-prepared

Favorite Food to Prepare: Belgian

Favorite Cookbook: *Everybody Eats Well in Belgium Cookbook* by Ruth Van Waerebeek

Moules à la Marinière
"Boatman" Style Mussels Steamed in White Wine with Shallots and Herbs

Chef De Cuisine Fritz Blank
Deux Cheminées, Philadelphia, PA

"This recipe was first used at Deux Cheminées in 1979, and probably should not be called "a la Marinière" since the addition of fennel, hot pepper flakes, and a milk product deviates significantly from standard recipes."

1 quart dry white wine
2 T. freshly squeezed lemon juice
3 T. Pernod
1/2 cup fresh fennel bulb diced into 1/4-inch cubes
2 T. finely chopped fresh garlic
2 T. finely chopped fresh shallots
1 T. dried crushed hot red peppers
2 T. roughly chopped fresh parsley
2 tsp. freshly cracked black peppercorns
1 cup buttermilk (or half-and-half or heavy cream)
1/4 lb. butter cut into 1/2-inch cubes
18 to 24 large mussels

Mix first 11 ingredients together. Place the well scrubbed live mussels into a large accommodating sauce pot. Ladle 8 to 10 ounces of the mixture over the top of the mussels. Cover and place over high heat. Bring to a full boil, shaking occasionally, for a few minutes. As soon as all the mussels are opened, they are done. (Do not overcook!) Serve immediately in large bowls with crusty French bread on the side.

Mescalero Mussels

Executive Chef Curt Taylor
Los Amigos's "New Mexico Grille," Philadelphia, PA

2 oz. oil
4 doz. mussels, cleaned
2 oz. minced garlic
4 oz. gold tequila
3 oz. Tabasco sauce
8 oz. chicken stock
2 T. chopped cilantro
thick sliced bread
Salsa Fresca (Recipe appears on page 219.)

Heat the oil in a large sauté pan. Add the mussels and the garlic and cook over high heat for 2 minutes. Take the pan off the heat source; add tequila and flame. When the alcohol has burned off, add the Tabasco and incorporate well. Add the chicken stock and cilantro and cover. Cook over high heat for 5 minutes or until the mussels have opened. Pour into large bowl. Serve with toasted bread and salsa fresca.

Serves 4

About the Chef

Name: Curt Taylor

Education/Training: associate degree in Culinary Arts from Atlantic Community College

Inspirations/Influences: innovative chefs and restaurants

Hobbies: biking, hiking, martial arts

Family: married, three children

Hometown: Gibbsboro, NJ

Favorite Food to Eat: shad roe

Favorite Food to Prepare: chile

Favorite Cookbook: *Nuevo Latino* by Douglas Rodriguez

Clams with Black Bean Cake and Tomatillo Salsa

Executive Chef Chakapope Sirirathasuk
Friday Saturday Sunday Restaurant, Philadelphia, PA

1 lb. dried black beans
1/2 red onion, chopped
2 cloves garlic, minced
1/2 red bell pepper, seeded and chopped
1½ T. chopped fresh cilantro
2 tsp. ground cumin
1 T. breadcrumbs
salt and pepper to taste
olive oil
6 dozen littleneck clams, scrubbed clean
dry white wine
Tomatillo Salsa (Recipe appears on page 220.)

Place black beans in a pot and cover with water. (The water should be about 1 inch over the level of the beans.) Bring to a boil. Discard the water and add new. Simmer until beans are done (usually about 1½ hour). Allow to cool.

Mash about 1/3 of the beans to make a paste. (I use a potato masher.) Combine bean paste with remaining beans, onions, garlic, red pepper, cilantro, cumin, breadcrumbs, and salt and pepper. Form into 6 patties. Fry patties in olive oil in a sauté pan until brown.

Place 1 patty each into 6 shallow soup bowls. Keep bowls warm in a 200° oven. Place clams in a large covered pot with some dry white wine. Steam the clams open; then add tomatillo sauce and mix it into the clam broth. Serve each bean cake with 12 clams around it, spooning some broth over all. Garnish with additional chopped cilantro if desired.

Serves 6

South American Chocolate BBQ Shrimp

Chef Alan Lichtenstein
New World Cafe, Cinnaminson, NJ

🌀

1 lb. shrimp, peeled
1/4 cup vegetable oil
1 T. ground cumin seed, toasted
1 T. chopped garlic
2 T. chopped cilantro
salt and pepper
BBQ Sauce (Recipe appears on page 224.)
1/4 cup diced scallion
1/4 cup cooked corn kernels
1/4 cup diced mixed peppers
1 cup diced tomatoes

Marinate shrimp for 2 hours in oil, cumin, garlic, 1 tablespoon cilantro, and salt and pepper.

Sauté shrimp for 1 minute on high heat. Reduce heat to medium and add 1 cup BBQ sauce. Simmer 5 minutes. Toss with 1 tablespoon cilantro, scallion, corn, peppers, and tomatoes. Serve with prepared rice.

NOTE: Remaining BBQ sauce may be frozen or refrigerated for 3 weeks.

About the Chef

Name: Alan Lichtenstein

Education/Training: various restaurants, various chefs

Inspirations/Influences: exotic flavors

Hobbies: folk music

Family: single parent

Hometown: Philadelphia, PA

Favorite Food to Eat: sushi

Favorite Food to Prepare: authentic Mexican

Favorite Cookbook: *Thrill of the Grill*

Shrimp Szechuan Style

Chef/Owner Alex Long
Chrysanthemum, Cherry Hill, NJ

16 large shrimp (about 1 lb.), peeled and deveined
sesame oil
1 tsp. minced fresh garlic
1 slice fresh ginger, julienned
1 scallion, chopped
1/2 cup chopped water chestnuts
1 T. sugar
1/2 cup rice vinegar
1/2 cup chicken stock
1 T. Szechuan chili sauce
salt and pepper to taste
1 T. water
1 T. cornstarch

Sauté shrimp in oil until just pink. Remove shrimp from pan and set aside. Add garlic, ginger, scallion, and chestnuts to the pan and stir. Add next 5 ingredients to pan and stir until it boils. Combine water and cornstarch, add to pan, and stir until thick and bubbly. Add cooked shrimp and stir until heated through.

Serves 4

About the Chef

Name: Alex Long

Education/Training: assorted

Inspirations/Influences: contemporary Chinese cooking

Hobbies: going out to eat

Favorite Food to Eat: French

Favorite Food to Prepare: French, Chinese

Favorite Cookbook: *Local Flavor*

Kapok Tree Coconut Fried Shrimp

Chef/Owner Yudi Millan
The Pacific Grille, Mt. Laurel, NJ

2 cups flour
1/2 tsp. baking powder
1/2 cup plus 4 cups shredded fresh coconut
2 cups water
1 tsp. coconut extract
2 lbs. shrimp, tails left on
1 cup flour
peanut oil
3 T. orange liqueur
1½ cups orange marmalade

To prepare batter, combine the flour and baking powder; then sift. Add the 1/2 cup coconut, water, and coconut extract. Beat well. Dredge each shrimp in flour; then dip in the batter. (Let the excess batter drip off.) Roll the shrimp in the 4 cups shredded coconut. In a large, heavy skillet or pot, pour in 1 inch of peanut oil or enough oil to thoroughly immerse the shrimp. Heat the oil to 325°. Drop a few shrimp into the heated oil and fry until golden brown, about 3 minutes. If a fryer is used, fry no more than 6 shrimp at one time. Drain the shrimp on paper towels. Keep warm in a preheated 200° oven. Combine the orange liqueur and orange marmalade to create a dipping sauce. Serve the hot shrimp with the dipping sauce on the side.

Serves 6

About the Chef

Name: Yudi Millan

Education/Training: Busan University, Busan, Korea

Inspirations/Influences: dynamics of culture and food

Hobbies: gardening, travel   **Family:** married, three children

Hometown: Cherry Hill, NJ

Favorite Food to Eat: seasonal fruits

Favorite Food to Prepare: any dish involving fresh herbs and ingredients

Favorite Cookbook: the one I'm about to write

Pan Seared Shrimp with Julienne Vegetables in a Pernod Cream Sauce

Executive Chef David Gottlieb
The Dilworthtown Inn, West Chester, PA

1 oz. olive oil
15 jumbo shrimp
1 T. minced shallots
1 tsp. minced garlic
6 oz. Pernod
1 cup heavy cream
1 oz. chives, finely chopped
1 oz. parsley, chopped
salt and pepper to taste
Julienne Vegetables (Recipe appears on page 207.)

Add olive oil to a very hot sauté pan. Season shrimp with salt and pepper. Place shrimp into pan. In about 1 minute when shrimp start to curl up, flip them over. Toss in shallots and garlic and cook for about 30 seconds. Add Pernod. Reduce by about 2/3. Add heavy cream and reduce. Add salt and pepper; then toss in fresh herbs. When shrimp are fully cooked, take them out and finish reducing the sauce until it reaches nap consistency.

Place julienne vegetables, evenly divided, in the center of 3 plates. Place 5 shrimp per plate around vegetables and nap with sauce. Garnish with fresh herbs if desired.

Serves 3

Corn-Crusted Crab and Shrimp Cakes with Summer Herbs Sauce

Chef/Proprietor Kevin von Klause
White Dog Cafe, Philadelphia, PA

"We make our crab cakes only in the summertime when the New Jersey corn is at its best and the blue crabs from Maryland are sweet, plump, and plentiful. Served with the creamy herb-flecked sauce, these corn-crisped cakes are both tasty and the quintessence of summer."

8 oz. jumbo lump crabmeat, picked over
8 oz. shrimp, peeled, deveined, and roughly chopped
1 red bell pepper, finely diced
3 whole scallions, thinly sliced
1 celery rib, finely diced
1 cup fresh corn kernels
1/2 cup mayonnaise
3/4 cup dry bread crumbs
1 egg, whisked
1 tsp. salt
1½ tsp. Tabasco sauce
1 cup cornmeal
1/4 cup olive oil
Summer Herbs Sauce (Recipe appears on page 229.)

Combine the crabmeat, shrimp, bell pepper, scallions, celery, corn, mayonnaise, bread crumbs, egg, salt, and Tabasco in a large bowl; mix well. Place the cornmeal in a shallow dish. Shape the crab and shrimp mixture into 8 equal cakes. Dredge each cake in the cornmeal to coat both sides well. In a large skillet set over medium-low heat, heat the oil until it shimmers. Carefully add 4 of the crab cakes and cook until golden brown and cooked through, about 4 minutes on each side. Cook the remaining cakes, adding more oil if necessary. Serve warm with summer herbs sauce.

Serves 4

Phoenix Crab Cakes

General Manager Francis Hannan
Phoenix Restaurant, Garden State Park, Cherry Hill, NJ

2 lb. jumbo lump crabmeat
2 eggs, beaten
1/2 cup mayonnaise
1/4 cup cubed white bread
2 T. minced red pepper
1/4 tsp. hot sauce
2 T. Worcestershire sauce
1 tsp. garlic powder
1 tsp. Old Bay seasoning
salt and white pepper to taste
oil
fresh parsley
lemon slices

Mix all ingredients together well except parsley and lemon slices. Form into 8 cakes, each 1/2-inch thick. Heat 1/2-inch oil in a skillet and fry crabcakes about 4 minutes on each side until golden brown and crispy. Remove from pan and drain on absorbent paper. Garnish with fresh parsley and lemon slices. Serve with tartar sauce if desired.

Serves 4

Crabcakes with Roasted Pepper and Corn Hash

Chef Kimberly Quay
Roscoe's Kodiak Cafe, Manayunk, PA

C

2 eggs
1/3 cup heavy cream
3/4 cup finely ground fresh breadcrumbs
1 red pepper, roasted, peeled, seeded, and diced
1 green pepper, roasted, peeled, seeded, and diced
1 lb. lump crabmeat, picked through for shells
1 bunch scallions, thinly sliced, white part only
1/8 tsp. nutmeg
1/8 tsp. cayenne pepper
1 tsp. salt
1/2 bunch basil, finely chopped
2 T. olive oil
Roasted Pepper and Corn Hash (Recipe appears on page 202.)
Avocado Puree (see recipe)
Zucchini Crisps (see recipe)
1 bunch chives, chopped

In a large bowl, combine eggs and heavy cream; whisk until smooth. Add bread crumbs and mix thoroughly. Let sit for 5 minutes so that crumbs soak up the egg mixture. Fold in roasted peppers, crabmeat, scallions, and seasonings, mixing just to combine. Do not overmix or the crabmeat will break into shreds.
Chill for approximately 30 minutes. Shape into cakes, each 3½ ounces, pressing together firmly. Chill again until ready to pan fry.

Preheat oven to 350°. Heat olive oil in a nonstick skillet until hot but not smoking. Carefully place crabcakes in the pan and fry until browned on one side. Place in oven for 8 to 10 minutes, until crabcakes are heated through.

Spoon hash on plate and place hot crabcakes on top. Spoon dollops of the avocado puree around the plate and top with a few zucchini crisps. Garnish with the chopped chives.

Serves 4

Avocado Puree

1 ripe avocado
juice of 1 lime
1/3 cup sour cream
salt and pepper

Blend all ingredients together in a blender or food processor. Season with salt and pepper. Chill.

Zucchini Crisps

1 zucchini, ends trimmed
3 cups oil
1/2 cup flour
salt and pepper

Cut zucchini on a mandoline or vegetable slicer approximately 1/8-inch thick. Heat oil to 350° in a heavy, medium-sized sauce pot. Dust zucchini slices with flour, shaking off any excess. Drop in the hot oil and fry until golden and crispy. Do not add too many at one time or the slices will not get crispy. Drain on paper towels. Season with salt and pepper.

Sautéed Soft Shell Crabs with Roasted Corn Salsa

Chef/General Manager Michael Pfeffer
Old Original Bookbinder's Restaurant, Philadelphia, PA

4 soft shell crabs, cleaned
flour
3 oz. olive oil
2 T. minced garlic
salt and pepper to taste
3 oz. white wine
Roasted Corn Salsa (Recipe appears on 219.)

Dredge crabs in just enough flour to coat. Heat oil in hot sauté pan. Add crabs and cook approximately 2 to 3 minutes on each side or until golden brown. Drain excess oil. Add garlic and cook until garlic is golden. Add wine and salt and pepper. Place 2 on each plate and top with roasted corn salsa.

Serves 2

Macadamia and Coconut Encrusted Scallops with Papaya Cilantro Sauce

Executive Chef Luigi Baretto
Ram's Head Inn, Absecon, NJ

16 large sea scallops
1 tsp. chopped cilantro
salt and white pepper to taste
juice of 1 lime
5 oz. macadamia nuts, chopped
5 oz. shredded coconut
Papaya Cilantro Sauce (Recipe appears on page 226.)
cilantro leaves
kiwi slices

Place scallops in a bowl. Sprinkle with cilantro, salt and pepper, and the lime juice. Marinate in refrigerator for 1 hour.

Preheat oven to 350°. Mix together chopped macadamia nuts and shredded coconut. Drain scallops from marinade and coat them thoroughly in the mixture.

Arrange scallops in a casserole dish. Cover with aluminum foil and bake for 10 minutes. Uncover casserole and bake for an additional 10 minutes until golden brown in color.

Heat papaya sauce over low heat until it starts to boil. Remove from fire. Spoon sauce on dish and arrange scallops on top. Garnish with cilantro leaves and slices of kiwi.

Serves 4

Grilled Jumbo Scallops with Wild Mushroom Charred Tomato Essence

Chef/General Manager Michael Pfeffer
Old Original Bookbinder's, Philadelphia, PA

2 lbs. jumbo scallops, 10-20 per lb.
vegetable oil (to coat)
salt and pepper to taste
2 cups water
1 cup long-grain white rice
1 tsp. salt
Wild Mushroom Tomato Essence (see recipe)
1 sprig fresh rosemary

Skewer scallops onto metal or bamboo skewers, coat with oil, and season with salt and pepper. Boil water. Add rice and salt and cook until al dente. Drain excess water, set rice aside, and keep it warm. Quickly grill the scallops until cooked through. Place rice in center of plate. Top with scallops napped with tomato essence. Garnish with rosemary sprig.

Wild Mushroom Charred Tomato Essence

3 large, vine ripened tomatoes
oil (corn, seed, or peanut)
salt and pepper to taste
2 oz. crimini mushrooms, sliced
2 oz. shiitake mushrooms, sliced
2 oz. chanterelle mushrooms, sliced
2 cloves garlic, minced
1/2 cup dry white wine
1½ cups clam juice
1 oz. Pernod
8 to 12 oz. chorizo sausage, cut into thin rounds
2 sprigs fresh thyme

Destem and remove core from tomatoes. Coat with oil and season with salt and pepper. Place over open grill/flame and char skin on all sides until blackened. Place in a preheated 350° oven and continue to cook until tender. Remove from oven and run through food mill, extracting as much juice as possible. Discard seeds, skin, and set essence aside.

In a 14-inch skillet or large sauce pan, heat oil until very hot, but not smoking. Add mushrooms and garlic. Sauté lightly, do not brown. Add wine and clam juice and tomatoes. Reduce 10 minutes on simmer. Add Pernod and chorizo sausage; continue cooking. Add fresh thyme and adjust seasoning.

Serves 6

"Shellpile" Oyster Stew
with Verbena

Chef/Owner Tony Clark
Tony Clark's, Philadelphia, PA

4 T. butter
2 slices bacon, diced
1 medium onion, diced
1/4 cup cognac
3 medium potatoes, peeled and diced
1 cup clam juice
1½ cups heavy cream
1/4 tsp. cayenne pepper
1 tsp. chopped verbena
20 oysters, liquid rescued
salt and fresh pepper to taste

Place butter and bacon in a medium sauce pot over low heat and allow butter to melt and bacon to render. Add onion and cook slowly until onion is translucent and soft. Add cognac and cook until dry.

Add potatoes, clam juice, reserved oyster liquid, and heavy cream. Bring to a simmer and cook until potatoes are tender. Add cayenne pepper and verbena and bring back to a simmer. Add oysters and salt and pepper to taste. Cook 2 minutes and serve.

Serves 4

About the Chef

Name: Tony Clark

Education/Training: Culinary Institute of America; 13 years at Four Seasons Hotel; began working in restaurants at age 14

Inspirations/Influences: It is very rewarding to teach and to work with people who have the same passion for cooking that I have. Like me, they are not happy unless a meal is perfect.

Hobbies: cooking for my four children. I often visit their schools and teach cooking classes. The children also frequent the kitchen at the restaurant.

Family: married to Doreen, four children

Hometown: South Jersey native living in Washington Township, NJ

Favorite Food to Eat: everything but Asian Durade

Favorite Food to Prepare: can not be limited to one type. I am as passionate about the egg as I am about the truffle.

Favorite Cookbook: I have many favorite cookbooks. Anything from Auguste Escoffier keeps me interested.

Cajun Bouillabaisse

Executive Chef Chef Trish Morrissey
Philadelphia Fish & Co., Philadelphia, PA

8 large scallops
1 lb. catfish, cut into 4 oz. pieces
1/2 lb. andouille sausage, cut into 1 oz. slices
2 T. vegetable oil
2 tsp. minced garlic
2 scallions, sliced
1 medium onion, 1/2 diced and 1/2 sliced
1 medium green pepper, 1/2 diced and 1/2 sliced
2 ribs celery, 1 diced and 1 sliced on the bias
2 T. Pernod
1½ cups crushed tomatoes
3/4 cup clam juice
1 tsp. Worcestershire sauce
Tabasco sauce to taste
salt and pepper to taste
Cajun Roasted Potatoes (Recipe appears on page 203.)

Spray a heavy frying pan with cooking spray and heat over medium heat for 2 to 3 minutes. Sprinkle the scallops and catfish with salt and pepper; place in fry pan with sausage. Sear quickly on both sides. Remove from heat and set aside.

In a large saucepan, heat 1½ tablespoons oil over medium heat. Add garlic, scallions, diced onion, diced pepper, and diced celery. Sauté for 5 minutes or until softened. Add Pernod and sauté for 2 minutes. Add crushed tomatoes and clam juice; bring to a boil. Reduce heat to low and simmer for 15 minutes. Add the Worcestershire and Tabasco sauces and season with salt and pepper to taste. Remove from heat. Puree the mixture in a blender until smooth and set aside.

In a medium-sized pan, heat the remaining oil over medium heat. Add the sliced onions, peppers, and celery. Cook until slightly softened, then add the catfish, scallops, and sausage mixture. Simmer for 5 to 10 minutes or until the fish is cooked through. Serve with Cajun roasted potatoes.

Serves 4

Seafood Jambalaya

Executive Chef Jeffrey Devine
The Mansion, Voorhees, NJ

3/4 cup diced onions
1/4 cup julienned celery
1/8 cup julienned green pepper
2 T. butter
1 T. chopped garlic
8 oz. tomatoes, peeled, seeded, and chopped
8 oz. ham, diced
1½ T. tomato paste
1/2 T. chopped parsley
1/4 tsp. thyme
1/4 tsp. red pepper
1/8 tsp. black pepper
4 oz. chicken stock
1/2 cup uncooked rice
4 oz. shrimp 16-20 count, peeled, deveined, and cut in half
4 oz. raw lobster meat, diced
4 oz. bay scallops

Sauté onions, celery, and peppers in butter until tender. Add garlic and sauté briefly. Add tomatoes, ham, tomato paste, seasonings, and stock and bring to a boil. Reduce heat to low and simmer for 10 minutes. Preheat oven to 300°. In a separate pan, sauté rice in additional butter until rice is opaque but not brown. Add to vegetable mixture. Cover and bake for 12 to 15 minutes. Add seafood during the last 3 minutes of cooking.

Serves 4

About the Chef

Name: Jeffery J. Devine, C.E.C.

Education/Training: Culinary Institute of America

Inspirations/Influences: happy brides and grooms

Hobbies: fishing, hot air ballooning **Family:** married to Gail Devine

Hometown: Cape May, NJ **Favorite Food to Eat:** Philadelphia cheesesteaks

Favorite Food to Prepare: anything with seafood

Favorite Cookbook: *The New Professional Chef*

Beer Seafood Fest

Chef/Owner Olivier De Saint Martin
Dock Street Brewery & Restaurant, Philadelphia, PA

"All in one dish! The best accompaniments for beer are potatoes, shellfish, fatty fish, meaty fish, spices, asparagus. A uniquely light, flavorful, delicate, plain, and simple natural dish!"

12 oz. sea bass fillet, skin on (any kind of bass)
12 oz. salmon fillet, skin on
4 russet potatoes, peeled and cut into ovals
1 lb. asparagus tips
8 oysters in shell, brushed and cleaned
1½ cups Pilsner (Bohemian), crisp, well-balanced lager
1/4 tsp. caraway seed
1/2 lb. mussels, cleaned
3 oz. cold butter
2 T. chopped parsley
salt and pepper to season

Cut each fish fillet into 4 slices and season with salt and pepper. Cook the potatoes completely in salted water. Cook the asparagus al dente in salty water; then refresh in iced water. Butter the bottom of a large sauce pan. Add the fish pieces plus the 8 oysters. Pour the beer on top and sprinkle the caraway seeds. Bring to a boil, cover, and reduce the heat. After 2 minutes, add the potatoes, asparagus, and mussels. Let simmer (covered) until the mussels open.

Remove fish, shellfish, potatoes, and asparagus from pot and place on a deep serving plate. Bring the juice to boil and whisk in the cold butter little by little. Pour the sauce over the seafood and sprinkle with fresh parsley.

Serves 4

About the Chef

Name: Olivier De Saint Martin

Education/Training: classic French   **Inspirations/Influences:** my mother

Hobbies: travel, sports   **Family:** married, one daughter

Hometown: Cherry Hill, NJ   **Favorite Food to Eat:** home food

Favorite Food to Prepare: all   **Favorite Cookbook:** *Taste of France*

Steamed Fish

Chef/Owner Joseph Poon
Joseph Poon, Philadelphia, PA

C

1 lb. whole striped bass, sea bass, tilapia, grouper, or a salmon fillet
1/2 tsp. salt
pinch of ground white pepper
2 T. shredded ginger
1 T. shredded scallions
3 T. light soy sauce
1/2 T. sugar
1/2 T. chicken base (paste or powdered bouillon)
1/2 cup chicken broth
2 T. heated vegetable oil

Clean the fish and sprinkle salt and white pepper inside the cavity and on the skin.

To make your own steamer, place a shallow stoneware bowl or other heat-tempered bowl in the center of a wok or a deep skillet. Fill the wok or skillet with 4 to 6 cups of water, just enough to surround the **outside** of the bowl with 1 to 2 inches of water. Top bowl with a platter large enough to accommodate the fish and fit in the wok or skillet. Place half the ginger and scallions on the plate and put the fish on top. Sprinkle remaining ginger and scallions over fish. Cover with a lid. Using high range-top heat, steam fish about 10 to 15 minutes.

While fish is cooking, combine the soy sauce, sugar, chicken base, and broth and mix. Before serving, drizzle the hot vegetable oil and sauce over fish.

Serves 2

Pan Seared Codfish with Caramelized Onions

Chef/Owner Olivier De Saint Martin
Dock Street Brewery & Restaurant, Philadelphia, PA

"At Dock Street we pair this wonderful dish with a medium body lager such as a Bohemian Pilsner."

4 codfish steaks, skin on
4 onions, sliced
2 cups red wine
2 cups red wine vinegar
1/3 cup honey
2 oz. butter
salt and pepper to taste
Sorrel Sauce (see recipe)

Preheat oven to 400°. In a large pot, combine onions, red wine, red wine vinegar, and salt and pepper. Cook over medium heat until all liquids are evaporated. Add the honey and cook until caramelized. Remove from heat and add butter. Pan sear the cod in olive oil until skin side is golden brown. Turn steaks over and finish in oven for 5 to 8 minutes. Plate the fish on onions and top with sorrel sauce.

Serves 4

Sorrel Sauce

3/4 cup white wine
3/4 cup dry vermouth
2 shallots, chopped
1 cup cream
1/2 lb. cold butter
4 oz. sorrel, sliced
salt and pepper to taste

In a medium-sized pan, heat the wine, vermouth, and shallots until liquid is reduced by half. Add the cream and after boiling for 2 minutes, whisk in the cold butter. Salt and pepper to taste and add the sorrel just before serving.

Dover Sole

Chef/Owner Luca Sena
La Famiglia Ristornate, Philadelphia, PA

4 fresh Dover sole
1½ lbs. tomatoes, crushed
1 cup extra virgin olive oil
1/2 cup chopped parsley
3½ oz. capers, soaked in vinegar
salt and pepper to taste

Preheat oven to 300°. Rinse Dover sole with water to clean. Slit the tail at each end and lift the skin toward the head to remove the skin. Place the fish in a casserole dish and pour the tomatoes and olive oil on top of the fish. Add parsley, capers, and salt and pepper. Bake for 35 minutes.

Serves 4

Mushroom-Crusted Fillet of Flounder

Chef/Owner Philippe Chin
Chanterelles, Philadelphia, PA

ⓖ

2 T. olive oil
1/2 cup mushroom puree
1 shallot, chopped
1 clove garlic, chopped
1 cup breadcrumbs
1 tsp. mushroom powder
salt and pepper to taste
4 6-oz. flounder fillets
1 T. chopped chives

In a large skillet, heat 1 tablespoon olive oil and sauté mushroom puree for 5 to 8 minutes. Add the shallot and garlic and cook for another 10 minutes over low heat until dry. Remove from heat and chill.

In mixing bowl, combine chilled mushroom mixture, breadcrumbs, mushroom powder, remaining olive oil, and salt and pepper.

Season both sides of the flounder fillets with salt and pepper. Oil a cookie tray and lay the fillets flat. Top with the mushroom crust mixture. Bake for 6 minutes in a preheated 375° oven. Garnish with chives. Serve immediately.

Serves 4

Fish Provencal

Chef/Owner Kevin Meeker
Philadelphia Fish & Co., Philadelphia, PA

2 ripe tomatoes, peeled, seeded, and diced
1 medium sweet yellow onion, diced
1 green pepper, diced
1/4 cup capers, rinsed and drained
1/4 bunch fresh thyme, finely chopped
1/4 bunch fresh rosemary, finely chopped
1/2 cup tomato juice
1/4 cup white wine
1/4 cup olive oil
3 cloves fresh garlic, minced
salt and pepper to taste
4 8-oz. halibut, scrod, or other mild fish fillets
4 pieces parchment cooking wrap
4 T. sweet butter

Combine tomatoes, onion, and green pepper in a large mixing bowl. Add the capers, thyme, rosemary, tomato juice, wine, olive oil, and garlic, mixing it together. Add salt and pepper to taste and refrigerate.

Preheat oven to 350°. Lay 1 fish fillet on each piece of parchment paper and place 1/4 of Provencal mixture on each fillet. Top with a pat (1 T.) of butter and wrap tightly. Bake for 10 minutes.

Serves 4

NOTE: Tomatoes, onions, and green pepper should all be diced the same size.

Brazilian Baked Monkfish

Executive Chef Craig Wilson
The Five Spot, Philadelphia, PA

"Quick, low-fat, elegant, and tasty!"

12 oz. monkfish fillet, cut into 1-inch thick medallions
1 cup cornmeal
1 tsp. garlic powder
1 tsp. sugar
1 tsp. salt
1 tsp. pepper
olive oil
10 whole cloves garlic, roasted
1/2 red onion, shaved
oil and vinegar

Preheat oven to 325°. Combine cornmeal, garlic powder, sugar, salt, and pepper. Dredge monkfish medallions in corn meal mixture. Heat olive oil in sauté pan. Skillet brown monkfish on both sides and then transfer to oven. Bake for 7 to 10 minutes or until fish is soft in the middle. Put on 2 serving plates. Top with roasted garlic, onion, and a few dashes each of oil and vinegar.

Serves 2

Panchetta Monkfish

Chef Steven Ward
BLT's Cobblefish, Philadelphia, PA

2 6-oz. monkfish fillets, pounded
2 tsp. chopped garlic
2 T. chopped leek (white)
2 T. chopped onion
8 oz. escarole, blanched and chopped
salt and pepper to taste
2 tsp. vinegar
4 oz. panchetta, sliced 1/8-inch thick
4 T. white wine
2 T. herb pesto
2 tsp. butter
squeeze of lemon

Place monkfish between plastic wrap and pound. Sauté garlic, leeks, and onion until tender. Add escarole and sauté lightly. Season with salt and pepper; then deglaze pan with vinegar. Place half of mixture on each monkfish. Roll; then wrap with panchetta. Sear on one side and then the other. Place in preheated 400° oven and bake 7 to 10 minutes or until done. Remove from oven and deglaze baking dish with wine. Add pesto, butter, and squeeze of lemon. Divide sauce between 2 plates, top with fish, and serve.

Serves 2

About the Chef

Name: Steven Ward

Education/Training: Culinary Institute of America

Inspirations/Influences: Southern chefs, mothers

Hobbies: dog training, roller blading, summer activities

Family: a brother and a sister

Hometown: Glenside, PA

Favorite Food to Eat: ribs, jambalaya, olives

Favorite Food to Prepare: fish, cheesesteaks

Favorite Cookbook: Dooky Chase and Graham's

Fire Grilled Pompano with Banana-Cilantro Salsa

Executive Chef/Owner Bill Beck
Pompano Grille, Philadelphia, PA

1 to 1½ lb. whole pompano, cleaned and gutted
1 T. olive oil
salt and pepper to taste
Banana-Cilantro Salsa (Recipe appears on page 217.)

Rub fish with oil and salt and pepper. Char-grill over medium to low flame about 7 minutes on each side. Enjoy clean flavor with banana-cilantro salsa.

Serves 1

About the Chef

Name: Bill Beck

Education/Training: self-taught

Inspirations/Influences: tropical island flavors, Asian, French

Hobbies: walking, reading, travel

Family: Wendy, business partner and wife; daughter Kimber (6)

Hometown: Glenside, PA

Favorite Food to Eat: any kind of seafood

Favorite Food to Prepare: exotic fishes and shellfish

Favorite Cookbook: *Charlie Trotter's Seafood*

Sautéed Red Snapper with Toasted Pecan/Pistachio Butter

Chef/Owner Gerard P. Gehin
Beau Rivage Restaurant, Medford, NJ

1/2 cup flour
1/4 tsp. cayenne pepper
2 tsp. garlic powder
1/4 tsp. ground thyme
4 tsp. paprika
1½ tsp. salt
4 red snapper fillets (1 to 1½ lbs.)
1/2 cup milk
1/4 cup peanut oil
Toasted Pecan/Pistachio Butter (see recipe)

Mix first 6 ingredients in a medium bowl to make a seasoned flour. Dip each red snapper fillet in milk; then dredge in the seasoned flour.

Heat oil in a large skillet. Add snapper fillets; sauté, turning once until golden brown, about 6 minutes. Remove snapper fillets; cover and keep warm.

To serve, transfer a snapper fillet to each warmed dinner plate and spoon a portion of the toasted pecan/pistachio butter over each fillet.

Serves 4

Toasted Pecan/Pistachio Butter

1/3 cup pecans
1/3 cup shelled pistachios
1/8 tsp. ground white pepper
1/8 tsp. cayenne
4 T. butter
1 T. lemon juice
2 T. minced parsley

Sprinkle pecans and pistachios with white and cayenne peppers. Heat butter in skillet. Add pecans and pistachios; sauté until lightly browned, about 3 minutes. Remove from heat and stir in lemon juice and parsley.

Red Snapper with Four Vinegars

Executive Chef Frederick Vidi
Frederick's Regional Italian Cuisine, Philadelphia, PA

4 cups julienned seedless cucumber
1 cup julienned red bell pepper
1 T. chopped fresh scallion
1 tsp. grated fresh ginger
1 tsp. minced fresh garlic
1 tsp. chopped fresh flat-leaf parsley
2 T. granulated sugar
1/2 cup white wine vinegar
4 6- to 8-oz. red snapper fillets, skin on
1/4 cup extra virgin olive oil
salt and pepper to taste
1 cup pure olive oil
1/2 cup white balsamic vinegar
1/2 cup raspberry vinegar (see recipe)
1/2 cup kiwi vinegar (see recipe)
1/2 cup blackberry vinegar (see recipe)
4 rosemary sprigs
8 fresh chives

Combine cucumber, red bell pepper, scallion, ginger, garlic, parsley, 1 teaspoon granulated sugar, and white wine vinegar in a bowl. Let mixture marinate for 2 hours.

Score skin on fish fillets in a crisscross pattern (to prevent fish from curling). Rub each fillet with extra virgin olive oil and salt and pepper. Sear fillets in a very hot sauté pan, coated with pure olive oil, until golden. Heat to desired temperature.

Arrange cucumber mixture (at room temperature) on 4 plates and top with fillets. Spoon white balsamic vinegar and fruit vinegars separately on each plate and drizzle small amount on each fish fillet. Garnish with a fresh rosemary sprig and 2 crisscrossed chives.

Serves 4

Fruit Vinegars

1/2 cup fruit
4 T. pure olive oil
4 T. white wine vinegar
1 tsp. granulated sugar

Combine ingredients in a food processor. Blend, strain, and chill.

About the Chef

Name: Frederick Vidi

Education/Training: self-taught

Inspirations/Influences: Italian culture

Hobbies: interior design, fishing

Family: married to Diane, daughter Dianna

Hometown: Philadelphia, PA

Favorite Food to Eat: Asian influenced foods

Favorite Food to Prepare: ossobuco Milanese

Favorite Cookbook: Beautiful Foods of Italy

Sautéed Rouget With Fava Beans, Asparagus and Red Wine Sauce

Executive Chef Jean-Marie Lacroix
Four Seasons Hotel Philadelphia, Philadelphia, PA

2 T. olive oil
4 3-oz. fillet of rouget or red snapper
salt and pepper
2 T. butter
1 lemon
12 asparagus spears (green, pencil thin)
4 oz. fava beans
2 pinches chopped garlic
2 tsp. chopped shallot
1 T. chicken stock
2 tsp. chopped basil
Red Wine Sauce (Recipe appears on page 227.)

Pour 1 tablespoon olive oil in a non-stick pan. Heat until oil gives off a haze. Lightly dust rouget with salt and pepper. Place fillet, skin side down, into the pan. Cook for 2 minutes. Flip to other side, add 1 tablespoon butter and brown. Nap the butter over the fish for 2 minutes. Squeeze lemon over fish. Remove fish from pan and place on towel to dry excess fat.

Blanch asparagus and fava beans in boiling salted water. Cook asparagus for 2 minutes and fava beans for 1 minute. Remove from water and place in ice bath for 3 minutes. Remove and place on a towel.

Warm a sauté pan. Cook garlic and shallots in remaining olive oil until the onions start to turn translucent. Add the vegetables and cook slowly for 1 minute. Add salt and pepper, chicken stock, and remaining butter. Cook for 1 minute; finish with basil.

Place the vegetables in the center of plate and place fish on top. Pour red wine sauce around plate.

Serves 2

About the Chef

Name: Jean-Marie Lacroix

Education/Training: Thonon les Bains in France

Inspirations/Influences: fresh local ingredients

Hobbies: gardening

Family: married 30 years to Vivienne, two daughters, four grandchildren

Hometown: Epinal in France's Franche-Compte region

Favorite Food to Eat: well-prepared soups, simple and tasty dishes

Favorite Food to Prepare: terrines, fish and shellfish, meat casseroles, stews

Favorite Cookbook: my first — my mother's recipe box; *Larousse Gastronomique*

Ancho Honey Glazed Salmon

Executive Chef/Owner Bill Beck
Pompano Grille, Philadelphia, PA

8 oz. salmon, fillet cut
1 tsp. olive oil
juice of 1/2 lemon
salt and pepper to taste
Ancho Honey Glaze (see recipe)

Rub fillet with oil, lemon juice, and salt and pepper. Char-grill over low to medium flame about 3 to 4 minutes on each side or pan sear in sauté pan until crispy on both sides, about 1½ to 2 minutes per side. (This will be medium rare.) Drizzle with sauce on one side when 30 seconds away from desired temperature. (Do this with either cooking procedure.)

Serves 2

Ancho Honey Glaze

8 oz. honey
1 cup orange juice
2 T. lime juice
2 T. lemon juice
1/2 whole dried ancho pepper
1/4 whole habañero pepper, diced

Combine all ingredients in a saucepan. Reduce at a simmer until the sauce returns to the consistency of honey. Strain through fine mesh strainer. Leftover sauce will keep indefinitely in refrigerator.

Barbequed Salmon with Crispy Yams

Executive Chef James McGill
Jake's Restaurant, Philadelphia, PA

4 cups apple cider
1-2/3 cups soy sauce
8 T. unsalted butter
1 tsp. chopped garlic
2 T. arrowroot, diluted in 3 T. water
4 7-oz. salmon fillets with skin
2 yams, peeled and julienned
vegetable oil

In a medium saucepan, combine the apple cider, soy sauce, butter, and garlic and simmer for a few minutes. Bring to a boil. Reserve 1/3 for the marinade. Thicken the remaining to create the barbeque sauce by whisking in arrowroot over a simmering heat. Strain through a fine strainer over a small saucepan and reserve.

Marinate the salmon fillets, skin side up, in the 1/3 reserved marinade in a flat glass dish covered with plastic wrap. Refrigerate overnight or up to 2 days.

When ready to prepare meal, soak yams in water for 2 to 3 minutes. Heat the vegetable oil for approximately 20 minutes until it reaches 350°. Fry the yams until golden brown. Remove and drain on paper towels.

Remove the salmon fillets from the marinade. Heat and oil a grill and cook salmon for approximately 5 minutes to desired doneness.

To serve, ladle barbeque sauce into the middle of each dish, making a pool. Place the salmon fillet on top, leaning at an angle. Place the yams behind the sauce using prongs to create height. As a side dish, serve each person 1/2 cup steamed vegetables such as broccoli, cauliflower, julienned carrots, and pea pods.

Serves 4

NOTE: Arrowroot has more protein and is a more effective thickening agent than cornstarch.

BBQ Salmon on Grilled Romaine with Tarragon Potatoes

Chef Paul Simon
Jake and Oliver's House of Brews, Philadelphia, PA

4 medium Idaho potatoes, sliced into 3/4-inch thick rounds
Tarragon Vinaigrette (see recipe)
4 6-oz. salmon fillets
salt and pepper to taste
BBQ sauce of your choice
2 heads romaine lettuce, washed and towel dried

Preheat oven to 400°. Toss sliced potatoes in 2 tablespoons of the vinaigrette. Bake in oven until golden brown. Keep warm.

Preheat grill. Season salmon with salt and pepper. Brush with oil. Grill on one side for approximately 2 minutes. Flip and glaze with BBQ sauce. Cook to desired doneness.

Toss romaine in enough of the vinaigrette to coat. Grill until just wilted. Serve with BBQ sauce, the remaining vinaigrette, potatoes, and a cold Pilsner or lager style beer.

Serves 4

Tarragon Vinaigrette

1 bunch tarragon, chopped
1 bunch thyme, chopped
juice of 2 lemons
4 cloves garlic, chopped
2 cups olive oil
salt and pepper to season

Combine herbs, lemon juice, and garlic in a mixing bowl. Slowly whisk in oil. Season with salt and pepper.

Grilled Salmon with Tomato, Olive Oil, and Fresh Herbs

Chef/Owner Jean Francois Taquet
Restaurant Taquet, Wayne, PA

"This is a very nice item to serve in the summertime. Fresh vegetables such as zucchini, eggplant, fennel, or leeks may be grilled along with the salmon to compliment this dish. (Due to the full flavor of the fresh herbs, salt is not needed.)"

1 large ripe Jersey tomato, diced
2 T. extra virgin olive oil
juice of 1 lime
1 tsp. chopped fresh basil
1 tsp. chopped fresh tarragon
1 tsp. chopped fresh dill
1 tsp. chopped fresh coriander
1/4 tsp. ground black peppercorn
4 5-oz. Norwegian salmon fillets

Combine tomato, olive oil, lime juice, fresh herbs, and ground black peppercorn. Keep the preparation refrigerated. (This sauce may be prepared up to 2 hours before serving). Grill the salmon on both sides for 2 minutes. Place it on plate and top with tomato sauce.

Serves 4

Pesto-Crusted Salmon with Roasted Tomato Oil

Executive Chef Mark Buker
The Inn at Sugar Hill, Mays Landing, NJ

☉

1 cup fresh basil leaves
2 to 3 cloves garlic
2 T. Parmesan cheese
3 T. roasted pecans
extra virgin olive oil
plain bread crumbs
4 6-to 8-oz. salmon fillets
salt and pepper to taste
Roasted Tomato Oil (see recipe)

In food processor, blend basil, garlic, Parmesan cheese, and pecans to form a dry paste. Add enough olive oil to produce a runny paste. Scrape into bowl and add bread crumbs until crust has a slightly moist crumb texture. Set aside.

Preheat oven to 375°. Season salmon with salt and pepper. Apply a thin (about 1/8 inch) coat of crust to meat side of each fillet. Place salmon in baking dish and drizzle with olive oil. Bake until desired doneness, about 8 to 10 minutes per inch of thickness of fish. Place fillets on plates. Drizzle with tomato oil.

Serves 4

Roasted Tomato Oil

3 ripe plum tomatoes, halved and seeded
salt and pepper to taste
2 cloves garlic
1 cup extra virgin olive oil

Roast tomatoes in a 400° oven until dry and starting to char. Let cool somewhat. Place in blender with remaining ingredients and puree.

About the Chef

Chef: Mark Buker

Education/Training: The Restaurant School, The Four Seasons, Jack's Firehouse

Inspirations/Influences: cravings

Hobbies: brewing beer, flying remote-control airplanes

Family: wife Debbie, and golden retriever Dakoda

Hometown: Williamstown, NJ

Favorite Food to Eat: ethnic — Thai, Mexican/Southwestern, Indian, North Italian, and South American

Favorite Food to Prepare: same as above

Favorite Cookbook: *All Around the World* by Shelia Lukins

Salmon with Exotic Mushrooms

Executive Chef John Anderson
Husch Restaurant & Bar, Narberth, PA

4 7-oz. salmon fillets
salt and pepper
oil
3 tsp. butter
1 lb. exotic mushrooms, quartered
8 oz. asparagus, cut into 1-inch pieces
Sauce (see recipe)
Melted Leek Potato Risotto (Recipe appears on page 76.)

Season all sides of the fish with salt and pepper. Place the oil in a medium-heated sauté pan. Place the salmon fillets in the pan and sauté the fish until golden colored, about 2 minutes; then turn the fish over and place in the oven for 3 to 5 minutes. Check the fish for doneness. (Cut open a piece in the center and look at fish or feel it.) If the fish is soft to the touch, it is rare: the firmer it becomes, the more well-done it is.

While the fish is in the oven, heat another pan until smoking hot and add the butter. Add mushrooms and season with salt and pepper. Add the asparagus. Sauté until the mushrooms and asparagus have softened.

To serve, place melted leek potato risotto in the center of 4 plates. Place salmon and vegetables on top. Drizzle the sauce around the plate and over the mushrooms and asparagus. Enjoy.

Serves 4

NOTE: Be sure to use a reputable fish butcher when purchasing your fish. To get 4 nice fillets, it will be close to a side of salmon. The sauce for this recipe is a sweet reduction of balsamic vinegar that is thickened with butter to give a velvety texture.

Sauce

1 cup balsamic vinegar
1 cup butter, cubed
salt and pepper to taste

Pour the balsamic vinegar in a pot and heat under a low heat until the vinegar evaporates down to a glaze. Be careful not to let it reduce all the way as it will burn. Remove from the heat and whisk in butter. Season with salt and pepper.

About the Chef

Name: John L. Anderson

Education/Training: Culinary Institute of America; also trained under Edward Brown and Daniel Boulud

Inspirations/Influences: interesting product, cookbooks, and seasonal vegetables

Hobbies: collector of baseball cards and view masters, computer geek

Family: My wife Liane is an attorney, and we have a two year old son, Danny.

Hometown: New York City, NY

Favorite Food to Eat: I love sushi!

Favorite Food to Prepare: French and American dishes

Favorite Cookbook: *Charlie Trotter's*

Roast Moroccan Salmon Fillet with Sun-dried Cranberry Couscous

Executive Chef Mustapha Rouissiya
Rococo, Philadelphia, PA

4 8-oz. salmon fillets, small bones removed
olive oil
salt and pepper to taste
Saffron Honey Sauce (Recipe appears on page 227.)
1/2 lb. baby zucchini
1/2 lb. baby yellow squash
1/2 lb. baby carrots
Charmoula (see recipe)
Sun-dried Cranberry Couscous (Recipe appears on page 209.)
preserved lemon

Preheat oven to 450°. Place the salmon in an ovenproof dish. Brush with olive oil and sprinkle with salt and pepper. Roast salmon for 7 minutes. While salmon is cooking, heat 1 cup of saffron honey sauce. Simmer the baby vegetables in sauce until tender.

Remove salmon from oven and coat the fillets with charmoula and keep warm. Divide the couscous between serving bowls. Center the salmon fillet over the couscous. Surround the couscous with baby vegetables. Spoon the saffron honey sauce into the bowl. Garnish salmon with preserved lemon if desired.

Serves 4

Charmoula

4 cloves garlic, finely minced
2 tsp. ground cumin
1 tsp. paprika
1/2 tsp. cayenne pepper
6 T. olive oil
3 T. lemon juice
1/4 cup chopped fresh cilantro
1/4 cup chopped Italian parsley

Place all the ingredients into a bowl and whisk together. Can be made in advance and stored in refrigerator until needed.

Steamed Salmon with Ginger and Scallion Sauce

Chef/Owner Patrick Lee
Joe's Peking Duck House, Marlton, NJ

2 6-oz. salmon fillets, rectangularly shaped
2 oz. shredded ginger
3 oz. shredded scallion
2 T. vegetable oil
3 T. low sodium soya
4 oz. fresh broccoli, blanched

Place fillets on a plate and top with ginger. Fill steamer with water. Wait until the water starts to boil and then carefully put the plate into the steamer and cook for 15 minutes. Remove fish platter and drain the condensed water. Sprinkle shredded scallion evenly over the fish. Heat the oil and pour it over the fish. Add soya and garnish with broccoli.

Serves 2

Pan Seared Citrus
and Rum Chilean Sea Bass

Chef/Owner Bill Beck
Pompano Grille, Philadelphia, PA

"You will find Chilean sea bass to be firm and meaty, yet light and slightly sweet."

1/2 tsp. minced fresh garlic
1 T. white rum
juice of 1/2 lemon and 1/2 lime
zest from 1/4 lemon and 1/4 lime
pinch of orange zest
salt and pepper to taste
1½ T. olive oil
2 8-oz. portions Chilean sea bass

Combine the first 7 ingredients. Rub the fish with the mixture and marinate in the refrigerator for up to 4 hours.

Preheat oven to 350°. In a preheated, lightly oiled pan, sear the fish on each side for about 2 minutes. Finish in oven for about 10 minutes.

Serves 2

Paupiette of Sea Bass with Sauce Provencale in Thin Potato Crust

Chef/Owner Trzeciak Francis
Provence, Haverford, PA

4 5-oz. sea bass fillets, skinned and boned
salt
freshly ground pepper
3 sprigs thyme, chopped
2 tsp. black olive puree
2 very large baking potatoes, peeled
extra virgin olive oil
Sauce Provencale (Recipe appears on page 228.)
thyme leaves (optional)

Shape each fillet into a rectangle. Sprinkle fillets with salt, pepper, and fresh thyme. Spread olive puree on each fillet.

Peel potatoes and cut each one lengthwise into 16 long thin slices with a vegetable slicer or mandoline. (You will need 8 slices per fillet.) Do not rinse potatoes. Place the first potato slice perpendicular to the fillet, starting on the left side. Place the second slice to overlap the first. Continue in this manner until the fillet is covered. Gently lift fillet with a spatula, folding the ends of the potatoes underneath. Place finished fillet to one side. (Can be made up to 1 hour in advance.)

Preheat oven to 425°. Heat oil in sauté or nonstick pan over high heat. When oil is hot, sauté paupiettes until golden brown, about 1 or 2 minutes per side. Remove from pan. Place in a baking pan and finish cooking in oven for 5 minutes.

Remove fish from oven. Pour sauce onto each plate. Place 1 fillet in center of plate on top of sauce. Garnish with thyme leaves if desired.

Serves 4

Grilled Marinated Swordfish

Chef Patrick Allen
Napoleon Restaurant-Bar, Philadelphia, PA

2 shallots, chopped
4 cloves garlic, chopped
5 tsp. chopped cilantro
1/2 cup champagne vinegar
1/2 cup olive oil
salt and pepper to taste
juice of 1/2 lime
4 8-oz. center cut swordfish steaks
Olive and Roasted Pepper Compote (see recipe)
Tomato Vinaigrette (see recipe)

Combine first 6 ingredients and squeeze lime juice into marinade; then place the lime into the marinade. Marinade fish for at least 3 hours or up to 6 hours.

Heat BBQ grill or broiler until very hot. Remove swordfish from the marinade 10 minutes before grilling. Grill fish for 4 minutes, flip and cook for 4 to 5 minutes longer. Swordfish should spring slightly.

Spoon olive and roasted pepper compote into center of 4 warm plates and top with grilled fish. Spoon the tomato vinaigrette onto the fish.

Serves 4

About the Chef

Chef: Patrick Allen

Education/Training: self-taught

Inspirations/Influences: seasonal produce

Hobbies: golf, music, theater

Family: married, two children

Hometown: Philadelphia, PA

Favorite Food to Eat: seafood

Favorite Food to Prepare: seafood

Favorite Cookbook: *Master Class* by Diane Holuigue

Olive and Roasted Pepper Compote

1 red pepper
1 melon pepper
1 green pepper
olive oil
1 8-oz. jar stuffed Greek olives
4 shallots, sliced
2 tsp. chopped flat-leaf parsley
juice of 1/2 lemon
1/8 cup extra virgin olive oil
salt and pepper to taste

Preheat oven to 400°. Rub peppers with oil and roast until skins are charred. Remove from oven and place in a Ziploc bag. Let peppers steep in bag for 10 to 12 minutes. Remove from bag. Peel charred skin from peppers, remove stems and seeds, and chop. Roughly chop olives. Combine peppers and olives in a mixing bowl. Add remaining ingredients. Serve at room temperature.

Tomato Vinaigrette

4 large plum tomatoes, peeled, seeded, and diced
2 cloves garlic, finely chopped
2 shallots, finely chopped
2 tsp. chopped flat-leaf parsley
juice of 1/2 lemon
1/4 cup olive oil
salt and pepper to taste

Combine all ingredients in bowl and keep at room temperature.

Sautéed Trout with Corn-Peanut Crust and Bacon-Shallot Butter

Chef/Owner Michael McNally
London Grill, Philadelphia, PA

1 cup cornmeal
1/2 cup chopped peanuts
salt and pepper to season
flour
2 eggs, beaten
1/4 cup olive oil
4 rainbow trout, boned
Bacon-Shallot Butter (see recipe)

Preheat oven to 350°. Mix together the cornmeal, peanuts, and salt and pepper. Dredge the trout in flour, coat with beaten eggs, and then coat in cornmeal/peanut mixture. Heat olive oil in a non-stick pan and sauté trout 4 to 5 minutes on each side. Finish cooking in oven for about 7 minutes. Garnish with bacon-shallot butter.

Serves 4

Bacon-Shallot Butter

1 lb. sweet butter, softened
2 large shallots, chopped
4 strips bacon, cooked and chopped
juice of 1/2 lemon
salt and pepper to taste

Mix all ingredients by hand or in processor. Chill.

About the Chef

Name: Michael McNally   **Education/Training:** self-taught

Inspirations/Influences: seasonal ingredients   **Hobbies:** running, sports

Family: co-owner with wife Terry, two kids   **Hometown:** Philadelphia, PA

Favorite Food to Eat: fish   **Favorite Food to Prepare:** Italian

Favorite Cookbook: anything by Madeleine Kamman

Rainbow Trout

Chef Stephen Timlin
Clubhouse Restaurant, Garden State Park, Cherry Hill, NJ

4 8-oz. boneless rainbow trout fillets, butterflied
salt and pepper
1/2 cup flour for dusting
3 T. clarified butter
2 T. canola oil
1 small red onion, julienned
1 large Jersey tomato, seeded and diced
1 tsp. minced fresh garlic or 1/2 tsp. granulated garlic
8 oz. fresh spinach leaves, stems off
1 cup white wine

Season fillets with salt and pepper and dust with flour. Heat butter and oil in large sauté pan over medium heat. Add fillets. Sauté for 3 minutes on each side or until golden. Transfer trout to serving plate. Add onion and tomato to pan and sauté 1 minute. Add garlic and spinach and immediately deglaze pan with white wine. Cook for approximately 30 seconds, being careful not to overcook spinach. Top each trout fillet with tomato-spinach mixture and the remaining liquid.

Serves 4

Asian Tuna
with Wasabi Vinaigrette

Executive Chef Joe Stewart
GG's Restaurant, Doubletree Guest Suites, Mt. Laurel, NJ

4 6-oz. tuna steaks
1 tsp. minced garlic
1 T. light soy sauce
1/4 cup extra virgin olive oil
1/4 cup sesame seeds
4 1-oz. bunches mesculin greens
Wasabi Vinaigrette (see recipe)
1 lb. udon noodles, cooked
1 lb. mixed baby vegetables

Marinate tuna in garlic, soy, and olive oil for 30 minutes. Coat tuna with sesame seeds. Sauté tuna in very hot pan, 1 minute each side. Slice on the bias and fan on greens. Top with vinaigrette and serve with noodles and vegetables.

Serves 4

Wasabi Vinaigrette

1/4 cup sesame seeds
2 cups rice vinegar
1/2 cup soy sauce
1/4 cup honey
2 T. wasabi
2 T. sweet chili sauce
1/4 cup chopped cilantro
1/4 cup chopped chives
1 tsp. pared and minced garlic
1 tsp. pared and minced ginger root

Sauté sesame seeds until golden. Combine remaining ingredients. Add hot sesame seeds and mix well.

Local Flavor

Anise-Seared Tuna with Black Currant Balsamico

Chef/Proprietor Kevin von Klause
White Dog Cafe, Philadelphia, PA

☉

"Made from concentrated white Trebbiano grape juice and aged in wooden barrels, balsamic vinegar has a natural sweetness and velvety texture that has been revered for centuries. Its full-bodied complex flavor is so rich and meaty that sometimes we use it as a substitute for veal demi-glace. In this recipe, we treat tuna as a red meat and top it with a mouth-watering sauce of caramelized shallots, currants, and balsamic vinegar."

1/4 cup dried black currants
1/2 cup good-quality balsamic vinegar
4 yellowfin tuna steaks, each about 6 oz.
salt and freshly ground black pepper
aniseeds
3 T. olive oil
2 large shallots, peeled and cut into thin rings, about 1/4 cup
4 cloves garlic, thinly sliced
1 T. fresh thyme leaves
2 bunches arugula, leaves washed
1/4 cup roughly chopped walnuts, toasted

Soak the currants in the vinegar in a small bowl for 1 hour. Sprinkle both sides of each tuna steak with salt, pepper, and a heavy coating of aniseeds. In a nonreactive large skillet set over high heat, heat 1 tablespoon of the oil until it shimmers. Add the tuna steaks and sear for about 3 minutes on each side or cook to the desired doneness. Remove the fish to a plate and keep warm.

Turn the heat to medium-high and add the remaining 2 tablespoons oil to the pan. Add the shallots and sauté until browned and crisp, 3 to 5 minutes. Add the garlic and cook until golden, about 2 minutes. Add the thyme leaves and the currants and balsamic vinegar mixture. Bring to a boil and simmer for 1 minute.

Arrange the arugula over 4 warmed plates. Place 1 tuna steak on each plate; top the fish with the balsamic sauce and sprinkle with the toasted walnuts.

Serves 4

Foie Gras Stuffed Tuna Steak

Executive Chef David R. Grear, Jr.
Paradigm, Philadelphia, PA

2 6-oz. tuna steaks
1/2 oz. foie gras
4 cups Swiss chard
1 oz. red onion, julienned
1 oz. golden raisins
2 oz. honey
4 oz. Beurre Blanc (Recipe appears on page 224.)
2 oz. Port Wine Reduction (see recipe)

Cut the tuna steaks half-way down the center, creating a pocket. Stuff with foie gras. Grill on all sides for approximately 1½ to 2 minutes for rare to medium rare. Sauté Swiss chard, onion, golden raisins, and honey until Swiss chard is just wilted. Divide mixture between 2 service plates and top with tuna. Drizzle buerre blanc around the bottom of the plate and on top of tuna. Drizzle port reduction on top of beurre blanc.

Serves 2

Port Wine Reduction

16 oz. port wine
4 bay leaves
10 peppercorns

Heat all ingredients until liquid is reduced to 2 ounces.

Grilled Tuna with Caribbean Salsa

Chef/Owner Michael Tarzy
Just Between Friends Restaurant and Catering, Tabernacle, NJ

1 (6 oz.) can mandarin oranges with juice
2 mangos, diced
1/2 fresh pineapple, diced
1 red onion, finely diced
3 green onions, white part only, chopped
1/2 cup white wine vinegar
3 T. chopped fresh cilantro
2 T. sesame seeds, toasted
salt and pepper to taste
6 6-oz. tuna fillets

Mix all ingredients except tuna in a bowl. Cover and refrigerate for 2 hours.

Preheat grill to medium. Grill fillets for 3 to 4 minutes per side or until desired doneness. Top with salsa.

Serves 6

About the Chef

Chef: Michael Tarzy

Education/Training: small restaurants

Inspirations/Influences: cultural traditions and current trends

Hobbies: travel, the beach, and, of course, eating out

Family: single

Hometown: Marlton, NJ

Favorite Food to Eat: Ben & Jerry's Vanilla Chocolate Chunks (which was discontinued)

Favorite Food to Prepare: meatloaf and mashed potatoes

Favorite Cookbook: CIA textbook

Tuna Puttanesca

Chef/Owner Ian Friedman
Sage Cafe, Beach Haven, NJ

2 T. olive oil
2 6-oz. fillet of tuna*
salt and pepper
Puttanesca (see recipe)
California Risotto (Recipe appears on page 76.)

Preheat a sauté pan with olive oil until you can barely see the heat rise from the pan. Season the tuna on both sides with salt and pepper. Gently place the fish in the hot pan, searing both sides to the desired temperature.

Place 1 fillet on each plate and top with puttanesca sauce. Serve with risotto.

Serves 2.

* You may substitute any firm fish fillet.

Puttanesca

1 red pepper, diced
1/2 red onion, diced
1 T. chopped garlic
1/2 cup olive oil
1/2 cup white wine
1/4 cup sugar
10 pitted calamata olives
1/4 cup capers
1 tsp. red pepper flakes
2 lbs. tomatoes, peeled, diced, and stewed
1/2 cup chicken stock

In a saucepan, sauté pepper, onion, and garlic in olive oil until translucent. Add the white wine and reduce 3/4 of the way. Combine sugar, olives, capers, pepper flakes, tomatoes, and chicken stock and add to mixture in pan. Simmer for 20 minutes on low flame, stirring often.

Wasabi Crusted Tuna Steak

Executive Chef Jerry S. Truxell
Cedarbrook Hill Country Club, Wyncote, PA

2 8-oz. tuna steaks
1/4 cup mushroom teriyaki sauce
olive oil
2 T. wasabi powder
Asian Vegetable Salad (Recipe appears on page 63.)
1/2 cup chopped scallions

In a shallow bowl, toss tuna with teriyaki to coat. Refrigerate for 20 minutes.

Coat a heavy skillet with oil and heat until smoking. Dust tuna evenly with wasabi on both sides and sear about 2 minutes per side. Tuna will be medium rare.

To serve, place an even portion of vegetable salad on 4 plates. Slice tuna on a bias and top salad with an even number of slices of fish. Garnish with chopped scallions.

Serves 4

Meats, Game & Poultry

෧

Filetto Di Manzo Alla Barolo 165

Filet Ricardo 166

Coffee Mop Steak 167

Beef Medallion and Seafood Combo 168

London Broil Jack Daniel's 170

Grilled Veal Chop with Exotic Mushroom Sauce 171

Vitello Alla Principessa 172

Roasted Pork Tenderloin with Roasted Corn Polenta 173

Escalopes de Porc aux Cœurs de Celeris 174

Pork Loin with Pistachios 175

Apricot Chipotle Glazed Roast Pork Tenderloin 176

Grilled Tenderloin of Pork with Papaya Salsa 177

Honey-Grilled Lamb Chops with Jalapeño Pepper Puree 178

Lamb Racks Au Jus with Pureed Sweet Potatoes 179

Fire-Grilled Rack of Baby Lamb 180

Roast Duckling with Blueberry Sauce 181

Roasted Sage-Rubbed Cornish Game Hens 182

Roasted Pheasant Breast with Cranberry Compote 183

Smothered Chicken and Onions 184

Chicken Breast Au Poirve with Roasted Pepper Bruschetta 185

Chicken Dijon 186

Grilled Lemon Chicken 187

Grilled Tandoori Chicken Breast with Mint Raita Sauce 188

Curried Chicken with Orange, Grapes and Star Fruit 189

Chicken and Shrimp Sante Fe 190

Pan Roasted Chicken with Maine Lobster
   and Lump Crab Stuffing 191

෧

Filetto Di Manzo Alla Barolo

Executive Chef Frederick Vidi
Frederick's Regional Italian Cuisine, Philadelphia, PA

4 center cut filet mignons (8- to 9-oz. each)
1/2 cup pure olive oil
salt and pepper to taste
1/2 cup balsamic vinegar
4 portobello mushroom caps, no stems
8 green asparagus spears
4 white asparagus spears (optional)
8 chippolini onions, peeled
1 T. each: chopped fresh rosemary and basil
2 T. chopped fresh flat-leaf parsley
2 tsp. granulated sugar
1/4 cup chopped garlic
1/4 cup chopped shallot
1/4 cup chopped fresh scallion
4 T. butter, lightly salted
1 cup Barolo wine
2 cups demi glacé (beef gravy)
4 cups julienned vegetables (leeks, carrots, and scallions)
8 roasted pepper strips (preferably red)
4 fresh rosemary sprigs

Rub filet with olive oil and sprinkle with salt and pepper. Grill or pan sear to desired temperature. Mix remainder of olive oil with balsamic vinegar in a shallow pan. Put mushrooms, asparagus, and chippolini onions in marinade. Sprinkle with 1/2 tablespoon rosemary, 1 tablespoon basil, 1 teaspoon parsley, 1 teaspoon sugar, and 1/8 cup chopped garlic. Marinate 2 hours, turning every 1/2 hour. Grill or cook in a preheated 350° oven for at least 15 to 20 minutes or until desired doneness.

Combine remainder of rosemary, basil, parsley, and garlic plus shallot, scallion, and 2 tablespoons of butter in pan and sauté until tender. Add remainder of sugar, Barolo wine, and demi glacé. Reduce by half and strain through sieve. Put remaining butter in hot pan and sear julienned vegetables until tender.

Arrange vegetables over 4 plates. Pour 1/4 of sauce on each plate. Place filet on sauce. Place mushroom on filet. Arrange asparagus, onions, and roasted pepper strips on plates equally. Garnish with a fresh rosemary sprig.

Serves 2

Filet Ricardo

Sous Chef Brian W. Duffy
Big Fish, Conshohocken, PA

6 6-oz. filet mignons
1/2 cup diced shiitake mushrooms
1/2 cup diced portobello mushrooms
1 tsp. minced garlic
1 T. chopped scallion
1 T. diced shallots
1/4 cup diced tomatoes
1/4 cup feta cheese
oregano to taste
salt and pepper to taste
3/4 cup roughly chopped rock shrimp

Make an incision in each filet to hold the stuffing. Sauté mushrooms, garlic, scallion, shallots, and tomatoes over medium heat. Add feta cheese, oregano, and salt and pepper. Let liquid reduce; then add shrimp. Remove mixture from heat and let cool.

Fill each filet with cooled stuffing. Grill to desired temperature/doneness and serve.

Serves 6

Coffee Mop Steak

Executive Chef George Crea
Hilton at Cherry Hill, Cherry Hill, NJ

1 cup Worcestershire sauce
4 cups tomato puree
2 cups coffee
1 T. kosher salt
1/2 T. ground black pepper
1 lb. unsalted butter, cubed
4 10-oz. New York Strip steaks

In a thick-bottomed pot, bring Worcestershire sauce, tomato puree, coffee, salt, and pepper to a boil. Reduce heat and simmer 5 minutes. Add butter to pot, stirring until melted. Remove from heat and cool marinade in an ice bath until it reaches 40°. Reserve half the mixture for basting and marinate steaks in the remaining half for 1½ hours.

Charbroil steaks to desired temperature, basting often with marinade. Serve immediately.

Serves 4

About the Chef

Name: George Crea

Education/Training: Johnson & Wales University

Inspirations/Influences: the seasonal regional fare of today

Hobbies: weightlifting, classic cars

Hometown: Monessen, PA

Favorite Food to Eat: a New England lobster feast, fried whole belly clams

Favorite Food to Prepare: traditional and unique smoked barbecue

Favorite Cookbook: *The New Texas Cuisine* by Stephen Pyles

Beef Medallion and Seafood Combo

Executive Chef Charles Pineiro
Martini Cafe, Philadelphia, PA

4 medium potatoes, peeled and quartered
2 oz. plus 4 tsp. olive oil
2 tsp. capers
2 tsp. fresh rosemary
2 tsp. anchovy (optional)
4 3-oz. beef medallions
2 3-oz. lobster tails, butterflied
2 oz. scallops
2 oz. large tiger shrimp
1 cup sliced button mushrooms
1/2 cup chicken stock or broth
1/2 cup Worcestershire sauce
6 oz. butter
1/2 cup chopped tomatoes
2 tsp. chopped herbs of your choice

Boil potatoes until fork tender and then mash. Add 2 oz. olive oil, capers, rosemary, and anchovy and form into 2 cakes.

Season beef with 2 teaspoons oil and set aside. Sear all seafood in sauté pan for 2 to 3 minutes. Put aside. Add 2 teaspoons oil to the same pan and sauté mushrooms until lightly browned. Add chicken stock and Worcestershire sauce and reduce by half. Add seafood and cook for 2 minutes on medium heat. Add butter; when melted, remove pan from heat and set aside.

Pan fry potato cakes until browned on both sides. Cook beef to desired doneness.

To serve, place 1 cake in center of each plate; top with 2 beef medallions. Arrange seafood around the edges and pour sauce all over. Garnish with chopped tomatoes and herbs.

Serves 2

About the Chef

Name: Charles Pinieró

Education/Training: The Restaurant School, Founders at the Bellevue Hotel

Inspirations/Influences: making everything from scratch

Hobbies: antique shopping, flamenco music, cooking

Family: single; from a family of four

Hometown: Philadelphia, PA

Favorite Food to Eat: ethnic foods, spicy Asian foods

Favorite Food to Prepare: Spanish, French (Mediterranean influenced)

Favorite Cookbook: *The Food and Wine of Spain* by Penelope Casas

London Broil
Jack Daniel's

Chef/Owner Tony Daggett
Daggett's Catering, Washington Township, NJ

3 lbs. top round London broil
olive oil
cracked black peppercorns
1/2 tsp. cayenne pepper
1 medium onion, finely diced
chopped fresh parsley
splash of Kentucky Bourbon (pretend it's vinegar for a salad)

Rub meat with olive oil and coat with remaining ingredients. Marinate meat overnight in baking dish, turning a few times. Grill on high heat to sear in juices; turn and sear other side. Lower flame to medium. Baste with juices from marinade. Cook about 10 minutes on each side or to desired doneness. Slice at an angle across the grain.

Serves 10

NOTE: Serve with crusty rolls and horseradish or Boursin cheese.

Grilled Veal Chop with Exotic Mushroom Sauce

Executive Chef William Fischer
Caffé Aldo Lamberti, Cherry Hill, NJ

1 cup Demi-Glace (Recipe appears on page 225.)
4 14-oz. center cut veal loin chops
salt and pepper to season
1/4 cup minced shallots
1/2 cup button mushrooms
1/2 cup shiitake mushrooms
1/2 cup oyster mushrooms
1/2 cup portobello mushrooms
1/4 cup porcini mushrooms
1/4 cup sun-dried tomatoes
2 T. butter
2 T. brandy

Prepare the demi-glace in advance. Dry the chops and season with salt and pepper. Grill until medium-well. Meanwhile, sauté the shallots, mushrooms, and sun-dried tomatoes in the butter. Deglaze the skillet with brandy and flambé. Add the demi-glace and reduce until the sauce is thick enough to coat the back of a spoon. Position the chops in the center of each of 4 warm plates and top with mushroom sauce.

Serves 4

Vitello Alla Principessa

Head Chef Antonio Cardillo
Tulipano Nero, Mt. Laurel, NJ

12 oz. veal (6 pieces, 2 oz. each)
olive or vegetable oil
2 oz. Chablis wine
6 oz. asparagus spears
12 oz. crabmeat
6 thin slices fontina cheese
12 oz. Demi-Glace (Recipe appears on page 225.)

Preheat oven to 375°. Sauté veal in oil until brown. Add wine to pan. Sauté asparagus with veal and wine until wine evaporates. Place asparagus spears on top of veal. Add 2 ounces of crabmeat to top of each piece of veal/asparagus. Place 1 slice of cheese per portion on top of crabmeat. Add hot demi-glace. Bake 4 to 5 minutes.

Serves 2

Roasted Pork Tenderloin with Roasted Corn Polenta

Executive Chef Don Paone
Sonoma Restaurant, Manayunk, PA

1/2 cup balsamic vinegar
1/2 cup brown sugar
1/4 cup olive oil
3 cloves garlic
1 T. thyme
1 8-oz. pork tenderloin
Sun-dried Marmalade (Recipe appears on page 233.)
Roasted Corn Polenta (Recipe appears on page 211.)

Combine vinegar, brown sugar, olive oil, and garlic. Marinate loin in mixture for 1 day.

Roast loin in a preheated 400° oven for 5 to 10 minutes or until desired doneness. Top with sun-dried marmalade and serve with roasted polenta.

Serves 2

Escalopes de Porc aux Cœurs de Celeris

Pork Medallions with Braised Celery Hearts

Chef De Cuisine Fritz Blank
Deux Cheminées, Philadelphia, PA

⊚

"Served with a small portion of pasta — perhaps spätzle — and a garnish of a few sautéed cherry tomatoes, this simple, "lite," quick, and uncomplicated dish can be a gastronomic sensation on anyone's table."

6 medallions of boneless pork loin, each slice 3/4-inch thick
salt and freshly ground pepper
1/2 cup all-purpose flour
2 T. shortening or cooking oil (Lard is suggested for best flavor and digestibility.)
Braised Celery Hearts, 4 pieces plus reserved juice (Recipe appears on page 199.)
1/2 cup dry white wine or vermouth
1/2 cup cooking juices from the celery
4 T. Dijon-style mustard
2 T. butter at room temperature

Season the pork medallions with salt and pepper and dust lightly with the flour. Heat the lard in a skillet and sauté the pork medallions in batches until they are browned and just done, about 3 minutes on each side. Place the pork onto a serving plate and keep warm. Arrange 2 pieces of the braised celery on each plate. Discard any grease from the pork skillet and deglaze over high heat with the vermouth and the reserved cooking juice from the celery. Reduce by 1/2. Add the mustard and season with salt and pepper. Finish with the butter and serve the sauce over the pork and celery.

Serves 2

⊚

Pork Loin
with Pistachios

Chef John Vannoy, C.E.C.
The Restaurant School, Philadelphia, PA

1½ lbs. boneless pork loin, trimmed of fat
1 oz. brandy
1 oz. balsamic vinegar
8 oz. pistachios, chopped
pinch of salt and white pepper
zest of 1 orange
ground anise
1 tsp. breadcrumbs
pinch of olive oil

Preheat oven to 325°. With a sharpening steel, make a center hole into the pork loin. Drizzle the brandy and balsamic vinegar into the hole; then force in pistachios and salt and white pepper. Combine orange zest, ground anise, and breadcrumbs and rub the outside of the pork loin. Roast the pork for approximatelty 25 minutes or until the temperature of the pork reaches 150°. Rest and hold warm until ready to serve.

Serves 4

Apricot Chipotle Glazed Roast Pork Tenderloin

Executive Chef David Bennett
Kansas City Prime, Manayunk, PA

1 cup roughly chopped rock shrimp
1/2 cup diced tasso ham
1 cup diced cornbread
2 eggs
1/2 tsp. salt
1/2 tsp. pepper
1 14-oz. pork tenderloin
Chipotle Glaze (see recipe)
Red Onion Marmalade (Recipe appears on page 234.)
chopped hazelnuts

Combine shrimp, ham, cornbread, eggs, salt, and pepper in a bowl; then set aside. Trim pork tenderloin of silver skin and butterfly. Pound flat and season both sides with salt and pepper. Place stuffing mix in center of tenderloin and spread evenly over surface, leaving a 1/2-inch border on all sides. Roll tenderloin up and secure with butcher's twine. Refrigerate.

Sear pork on all sides and place in a 400° preheated oven. Cook to medium (about 8 to 10 minutes), brushing with glaze halfway through. Rest pork for 2 minutes after removing from oven. Slice pork into 10 pieces. Place 5 pieces in the center of each plate in a circular pattern. Spread marmalade around pork sparingly. Drizzle remaining glaze over plate and garnish with chopped hazelnuts.

Serves 2

Chipotle Glaze

2 cups port wine
6 plums, pitted, quartered, and peeled
1 chipotle pepper in adobo (available canned in specialty stores)
1/2 cup sugar
salt and pepper to taste

Combine first 4 ingredients in a saucepan and reduce by half. Puree, strain, and season with salt and pepper.

Grilled Tenderloin of Pork with Papaya Salsa

Executive Chef Lynn Buono
Feast Your Eyes Catering, Philadelphia, PA

1/2 tsp. virgin olive oil
3/4 tsp. chipotle powder
1 tsp. paprika
1/2 cup fresh coriander leaves
1/8 tsp. fresh thyme
1/2 tsp. grated orange rind
juice of 1 lime
1/2 tsp. kosher salt
2 cloves garlic, roasted and sliced
1 16-oz. tenderloin of pork
Papaya Salsa (Recipe appears on page 218.)

Grind first 8 ingredients in blender or food processor to create a seasoned rub. Stud loin with sliced roasted garlic; then coat with rub. Grill 10 to 15 minutes on a hot grill or until internal temperature is 150°. Slice on a bias and serve with papaya salsa.

Serves 4

Honey-Grilled Lamb Chops with Jalapeño Pepper Puree

Chef/Owner Susanna Foo
Susanna Foo Chinese Cuisine, Philadelphia, PA

5 T. olive oil
8 rib lamb chops, trimmed (total weight about 2 lbs.)
1/4 cup soy sauce
1 T. honey
2 T. Dijon mustard
1 T. Asian sesame oil
2 T. Jalapeño Pepper Puree (Recipe appears on page 222.)
1 T. chopped fresh rosemary or 1 tsp. crumbled dried rosemary
1 T. finely chopped lemon grass

Brush a grill with 1 tablespoon of the oil. Preheat grill with rack 4 to 6 inches from the heat source.

Place the lamb chops on a plate large enough to hold them in a single layer. Combine the remaining oil and the remaining ingredients in a medium-sized bowl and mix thoroughly. Pour this sauce over the lamb and marinate at room temperature for 30 minutes, turning once.

Remove the chops from the marinade and grill for 3 to 4 minutes. Turn the chops and continue cooking for 3 to 4 minutes more for medium-rare.

Serves 4

Lamb Racks Au Jus
with Pureed Sweet Potatoes

Executive Chef Tom Hannum
Hotel Dupont, Wilmington, DE

1 whole lamb rack, split and Frenched (have your butcher do this)
salt and pepper to taste
Sauce (see recipe)
Pureed Sweet Potatoes (see recipe)
rosemary sprigs

Season rack with salt and pepper. Sear well and roast in 350° oven for approximately 35 minutes or until it is medium rare. Cut into chops. Serve lamb racks with sauce and sweet potato puree. Garnish with rosemary sprigs.

Serves 6

Sauce

3 to 4 lbs. lamb bones and trimmings (available at butcher shop), roasted
1 lb. mirepoix
3 to 4 cloves garlic
2 gallons water
1 cup red wine
3 to 4 shallots
2 sprigs rosemary

Simmer roasted lamb bones and trimmings with mirepoix, garlic, and water for 1 to 2 hours until liquid is reduced to 1/2 gallon. Strain and adjust seasoning. In another pan, reduce wine, shallots, and rosemary by 3/4. Add lamb jus and reduce by 1/2. Strain.

Pureed Sweet Potatoes

2 sweet potatoes
2 to 3 oz. maple syrup

Peel and cook sweet potatoes. Puree with maple syrup until desired consistency. Add salt and pepper to taste.

Fire-Grilled Rack of Baby Lamb with Mint Peppercorn Vinaigrette

Executive Chef Mustapha Rouissiya
Rococo, Philadelphia, PA

6

"The mixed peppercorns called for in the sauce, a combination of black, white, green, and pink peppercorns, are usually available in stores. You can make your own mix with whatever whole peppercorns you have on hand."

4 8-oz. rack of lamb, cut into chops
1/2 lb. each: baby zucchini, baby yellow squash, baby carrots
1 T. butter
salt and pepper to taste
Mint Peppercorn Vinaigrette (see recipe)
Roast Corn and Scallion Mashed Potatoes (Recipe appears on page 205.)

Grill the lamb chops to preference (5 minutes per side for medium-rare; add 2 minutes for each additional degree of doneness). Simmer the baby vegetables in lightly salted water until tender. Strain and toss with butter and salt and pepper to taste.

Warm mint peppercorn vinaigrette. Spoon mashed potatoes into the middle of 4 plates. Divide the chops between the plates, leaning them upright against the mashed potatoes. Spoon the vinaigrette over the lamb. Arrange the vegetables on the plate on the other side of the lamb.

Serves 4

Mint Peppercorn Vinaigrette

2 T. honey
1 T. Dijon mustard
2 T. red wine vinegar
1/2 bunch mint, chopped
2 T. mixed peppercorns
1/2 tsp. hot chili sauce
1/2 cup oil (i.e., olive, canola, etc.)

In a bowl, combine all ingredients except oil. Whisk the oil in a slow stream until combined. The completed vinaigrette can be made in advance and stored in refrigerator until needed.

Roast Duckling with Blueberry Sauce

Executive Chef Luigi Baretto
Ram's Head Inn, Absecon, NJ

2 5-lb. ducks
salt, black pepper, and rosemary to season
1 cup Blueberry Sauce (see recipe)

Preheat oven to 375°. Clean ducks and season cavity with salt, black pepper, and rosemary. Place ducks, breast side up, on a rack in a roasting pan. Pierce the breast several times with a fork to allow the fat to drain during cooking. Roast about 1½ hours or until they are done. Remove ducks from pan, drain juices from cavity, and cut in half. Bone and serve with blueberry sauce.

Serves 4

Blueberry Sauce

1 cup water
1/2 pint blueberries (fresh or frozen)
2 oz. light brown sugar
1/2 oz. blackberry brandy
salt and black pepper to taste
1 tsp. corn starch
1 oz. butter (cut in cubes)

Puree blueberries with water. In a sauce pan, combine puree with sugar, brandy, and salt and pepper. Bring to a boil until reduced to about half its original volume. Skim as needed. Thicken sauce with corn starch; whip in butter until it is dissolved.

Roasted Sage-Rubbed Cornish Game Hens

Chef/Owner Toby Weitzman
Creative Catering Company, Cherry Hill, NJ

1/3 cup current jelly
1/4 cup sweet dessert wine
1½ tsp. dried sage
1½ tsp. dried thyme
1½ lb. Cornish hen, split, back discarded
salt and pepper
2 tsp. olive oil

Preheat oven to 450º. Heat current jelly, wine, 1/2 teaspoon sage, and 1/2 tea-spoon thyme in saucepan until jelly dissolves. Allow glaze to reduce, about 3 minutes. Season hens with remaining sage, thyme, and salt and pepper. Place hens, skin side up, on baking rack set on a baking sheet. Brush with olive oil. Cook for approximately 25 minutes or until cooked through, basting frequently with glaze. Spoon remaining glaze over and serve.

Serves 2

Roasted Pheasant Breast with Cranberry Compote

Executive Chef Tom Hannum
Hotel Dupont, Wilmington, DE

3 pheasants
oil
salt and pepper to taste
Cranberry Compote (see recipe)
Wild Rice (Recipe appears on page 213.)

Preheat oven to 350°. Rub pheasants with oil and salt and pepper to taste. Roast for approximately 25 minutes; do not overcook. Let rest; then carve and serve breasts. Serve with heated compote and wild rice on the side.

Serves 6

Cranberry Compote

1 bag fresh cranberries
1 cup sugar
1 cup port wine
zest and juice of 2 oranges

Gently cook cranberries, sugar, wine, and juice together for approximately 10 minutes or until cranberries open.

Smothered Chicken and Onions

Director of School of Culinary Arts Michael Baskette
The Art Institute of Philadelphia, Philadelphia, PA

2 whole chickens, quartered
2 T. virgin olive oil
1 large onion, sliced
1 leek, sliced into thin circles with green tops removed
2 tsp. chopped fresh garlic
2 tsp. ground pepper
1 T. dried marjoram leaf (not ground)
2 bay leaves
4 oz. dry white wine

Brown chicken pieces in hot oil until well browned; remove them from the pan. Cook onion and leek in same pan until they start to turn brown. Add garlic and spices and cook for another 2 minutes. Return chicken to pan and heat everything together. Add the white wine. Cover the pan and finish cooking it in a preheated 350° oven for 1 hour. Remove cooked chicken, season sauce to taste, and pour over pieces before serving.

Serves 8

Chicken Breast Au Poirve with Roasted Pepper Bruschetta

Executive Chef Edwin Hepner
River City Diner, Philadelphia, PA

⊚

4 10- to 12-oz. skinless, boneless chicken breasts
2 red bell peppers
2 yellow bell peppers
2 poblano chiles
salt and pepper
4 oz. extra virgin olive oil
8 oz. peppergrass (curly cress)
1 head frisee, cut into 4 inch leaf strands
1 baguette, 1/4-inch thick bias cut, 4 inches in length
4 oz. Telicherry peppercorns, roughly cracked
4 oz. white truffle oil
1 bunch opal basil, chiffonaded

Clean the chicken breasts so that they are free of all fat and sinew. Split the breasts down the middle and pound flat to a thickness of ¼ inch. Return breasts to refrigerator.

On a grill, roast peppers until they are slightly charred on the outside. Remove from the grill and place in a covered bowl so that the peppers steam. This will help loosen the skins. Once the peppers are cool, peel and cut them into long julienne strips. Return peppers to the bowl and season with salt and pepper and 1 ounce of olive oil. Reserve.

In a separate bowl, combine the peppergrass and frisee. Lightly toast the baguette pieces on a grill until brown and crisp.

Press the peppercorns into the flesh of the chicken breasts. Don't use too much of the peppercorns or they will become overpowering. In a very hot skillet, sear the breasts until lightly browned and cooked through. Quickly toss the mixed greens with the remaining olive oil and place about 3 to 4 ounces in the centers of the 4 plates. Place 2 half breasts on each plate; one at 12 o'clock and the other at 6 o'clock. Top bread slices with roasted peppers; place 2 slices on top of greens on each plate. Finish by drizzling the plate with the white truffle oil and a sprinkling of opal basil.

Serves 4

Chicken Dijon

Executive Chef Chakapope Sirirathasuk
Friday Saturday Sunday Restaurant, Philadelphia, PA

2 to 3 lbs. skinless, boneless chicken breasts
1 cup milk
1 egg
2 cups breadcrumbs
2 T. chopped fresh tarragon
1 T. chopped fresh parsley
1 cup flour
butter, melted
Dijon Sauce (see recipe)

Trim off all fat from chicken breasts. Place milk and egg in a large bowl and whisk to combine. In a separate bowl, mix together breadcrumbs, tarragon, and parsley. Place flour in a third bowl. Coat each breast with flour, dip in milk mixture, and then coat with breadcrumbs. (You will find breading easier if you use one hand to dip the chicken into the milk and the other hand to do the flour and breadcrumb coating.)

Preheat oven to 375°. Butter a baking sheet. Lay the breasts on the sheet and drizzle with melted butter. Bake for 25 minutes or until cooked through. Serve with Dijon sauce.

Serves 8 to 10

Dijon Sauce

3 cups heavy cream
1 tsp. salt
pinch of pepper
1 tsp. chopped fresh parsley
1 tsp. chopped fresh thyme
1/4 cup Dijon mustard

Put all ingredients except mustard in a saucepan or small pot. Stir to keep it from burning. Bring it to a boil; then simmer for about 15 minutes. Add Dijon mustard. Bring to a boil again. Serve over the baked chicken breasts.

Grilled Lemon Chicken

Executive Chef Wendy Welcovitz
The Inn Philadelphia, Philadelphia, PA

1/2 cup fresh lemon juice
1/2 cup fresh orange juice
2 cloves garlic, minced
1 T. grated fresh ginger
1 T. chopped fresh tarragon
1/2 tsp. salt
1/4 tsp. freshly ground pepper
6 skinless, boneless chicken breast halves

In a small bowl, stir together the lemon juice, orange juice, garlic, ginger, tarragon, salt, and pepper. Arrange the chicken breasts in a shallow glass pan and pour the lemon juice marinade over them. Marinate in the refrigerator, turning occasionally, for 2 to 3 hours.

Remove the chicken from the marinade and pat it dry with absorbent paper towels; reserve the marinade. Put the chicken on a hot grill. While grilling, turn the chicken 2 or 3 times, brushing with reserved marinade, until chicken is cooked and not pink, about 15 to 20 minutes.

Serves 6

Grilled Tandoori Chicken Breast with Mint Raita Sauce

Executive Chef Daniel McConnell
Philadelphia Tea Party, Philadelphia, PA

8 6-oz. boneless chicken breasts
1/2 cup vegetable oil
2½ T. salt
2½ cups chopped Spanish onions
3 T. chopped fresh garlic
1½ T. hot chile powder
1½ T. ginger powder
1/2 T. coriander powder
2 T. Spanish paprika
1/4 cup lemon juice
2½ cups plain yogurt
2 T. garam masala
1/2 cup chopped cilantro
1/4 tsp. red food dye
Mint Raita Sauce (see recipe)

Clean and pound chicken breasts. Put remaining ingredients, except mint raita sauce, in blender and puree until smooth. Pour over chicken, cover, and refrigerate for 24 hours.

When ready to prepare, grill chicken until desired doneness. Chicken will turn a bright red color on the outside and be juicy and spicy on the inside. Pour mint raita sauce over hot chicken.

Serves 4

Mint Raita Sauce

1/2 cup chopped cilantro
1/2 cup chopped Spanish onion
1 T. salt
1/2 T. cumin powder
1/2 cup lemon juice
2 T. fresh mint
1 cup yogurt

Place all ingredients in blender and puree until smooth.

Curried Chicken with Orange, Grapes and Star Fruit

Chef/Owner Tony Daggett
Daggett's Catering, Washington Township, NJ

3 to 4 lbs. chicken, quartered
3 T. curry powder
1 T. Thai seasoning
1/2 lb. green seedless grapes
1/2 lb. red seedless grapes
3 oranges, each cut into 8 sections, peels intact
2 star fruit, cut into 1/4-inch slices

Preheat oven to 350°. Dry rub chicken with curry powder and Thai seasoning. Place in roasting pan and surround with fruit. Bake for 1 hour, basting often.

Set grill for medium heat. Remove chicken from oven and pour fruit and juices into saucepan. Place chicken, bone side down, on grill and cook until done. Meanwhile, heat pan juices and fruit on medium high heat until thick and sauce-like. Season with additional curry if desired and pour over chicken.

Serves 8 to 10

Chicken and Shrimp Sante Fe

Chef Annemarie Phifer
Loose Ends Restaurant, Haddon Heights, NJ

4 skinless, boneless chicken breasts, pounded
12 large shrimp, peeled and deveined
salt and pepper
flour
2 to 4 oz. oil (as needed)
1/4 cup tequila
1/3 cup chicken stock
Black Bean Salsa (Recipe appears on page 217.)

Season chicken and shrimp with salt and pepper. Dredge in flour. Heat oil in a large sauté pan and sauté chicken until golden brown on both sides. Remove from pan. Add shrimp and more oil if needed. Cook shrimp for 2 to 3 minutes until firm. Place chicken back in the pan. Remove pan from heat — VERY IMPORTANT! Add tequila.

Return pan to heat. (It should flame up a bit.) Cook for 1 minute. Add chicken stock and simmer a few minutes until the chicken is cooked through and the liquid has reduced and thickened. Season to taste with salt and pepper. To serve, place a chicken breast on each plate, place 3 shrimp on top, and spoon on the sauce. Serve with black bean salsa.

Serves 4

About the Chef

Name: Annemarie Phifer

Education/Training: technical

Inspirations/Influences: fresh and new ingredients

Hobbies: photography, pets, stenciling

Family: married, three children

Hometown: Haddon Heights, NJ

Favorite Food to Eat: sushi, Thai, Korean

Favorite Cookbook: *Moosewood* books

Pan Roasted Chicken with Maine Lobster and Lump Crab Stuffing

Chef/Proprietor Ben McNamara
Isabella's, Philadelphia, PA

C

1 1¼-lb. live Maine lobster
salt and pepper
4 oz. unsalted butter
4 oz. white wine
3 T. lemon juice
1/4 lb. jumbo lump crabmeat, picked clean
1 large red pepper, roasted, peeled, seeded, and diced
4 scallions, coarsely chopped
4 large basil leaves, julienned
4 skinless, boneless chicken breast halves
1 oz. clarified butter

Remove arms, claws, and tails from lobster. Boil arms and claws until cooked through; then chill in ice water. Split tail lengthwise and season with salt and pepper. Sauté with 1 ounce butter in a small skillet until just cooked. Remove from pan and refrigerate immediately.

Add white wine to the pan and allow liquid to reduce by 1/3. Add lemon juice and remaining butter. When melted, remove from heat and let cool.

Once all lobster parts are cooled, remove meat from shells. Mix together crabmeat, roasted pepper, scallions, basil and butter wine mixture in a bowl. Cut lobster meat into large chunks and add to crab mixture. Refrigerate 1 hour.

Place chicken breasts on a clean surface. Remove the tenders and pound flat. Make 2 incisions — from the center of the breasts lengthwise to the outside of the breast — and open cavity as wide as possible. Place 1/4 of crab stuffing in center of each breast. Cover lobster and crab mixture with pounded chicken tender. Fold the 2 flaps over the tender to seal and roll onto tender side.

Preheat oven to 500°. In a heavy skillet, heat clarified butter until almost smoking. Dredge stuffed breasts in flour, shaking off the excess. Sear breasts in butter, tender-side down, until golden brown; then turn breasts over to brown. Finish cooking in oven 7 to 8 minutes or until firm. Serve with lemon sauce or any sauce desired.

Serves 4

Sides

Grilled Jumbo Asparagus with Truffles and Morels 195
Roasted Beets with Gorgonzola
    and Orange Rosemary Vinaigrette 196
Lucskos Káposziá 198
Braised Celery Hearts 199
Garden Green Bean Salad 200
Five Mushroom Ragout 201
Roasted Pepper and Corn Hash 202
Cajun Roasted Potatoes 203
Alo Gohbi 204
Roast Corn and Scallion Mashed Potato 205
Fried Yuca con Mojo Criollo 206
Julienne Vegetables 207
Vegetable Strudel 208
Sun-dried Cranberry Couscous 209
Grilled Polenta 210
Roasted Corn Polenta 211
Nicola Shirley's Rice and Beans 212
Wild Rice 213

Grilled Jumbo Asparagus with Truffles and Morels

Chef Adam Sturm
Azalea Restaurant, Omni Hotel, Philadelphia, PA

20 spears jumbo asparagus
1/2 lb. large morels*
4 shallots, minced
3 oz. olive oil
salt and pepper to taste
1 bunch chervil (reserve 4 spigs for garnish), chopped
2 oz. black summer truffles*
1 oz. white truffle oil
1 oz. aged balsamic vinegar

Peel and blanch asparagus in boiling salted water for 5 minutes. Refresh in ice water. Wash morels in cold water. In a large skillet, sauté morels and shallots in half of the olive oil until tender. Season to taste. With a very sharp knife, shave the truffles into thin slivers. Brush the asparagus with the remaining olive oil and grill. Warm morels and shallots and truffles together, add chopped chervil, and spoon on top of asparagus. Sprinkle with truffle oil and vinegar. Garnish with chervil sprigs.

Serves 4

* You may substitute any exotic mushroom.

Roasted Beets with Gorgonzola and Orange Rosemary Vinaigrette

Chef/Proprietor Kevin von Klause
White Dog Cafe, Philadelphia, PA

C

"If you like beets—and from what I see at the Cafe, many people do—you will love this sweet-tart starter. The combination of flavors and textures can't be beat, no pun intended. When peeling the roasted beets, be sure to wear gloves or rub the still slightly warm beets with an old, clean dish towel so the skins will easily slip off without coloring your hands. The beets and the vinaigrette can be prepared 1 day in advance if you wish and will stay fresh-tasting for days in the refrigerator."

2 red beets, about 12 oz.
1 bunch watercress or young spinach leaves, washed, dried, and stemmed
1 Orange-Rosemary Vinaigrette (see recipe)
4 oz. Gorgonzola, crumbled
1/4 cup pine nuts or walnuts, toasted
freshly ground black pepper

Preheat the oven to 400°. Place the beets in a nonreactive deep baking dish and add 1 inch of water. Tightly cover the dish with foil. Bake for 45 minutes or until the beets are tender enough to be pierced with a fork. Remove the foil and let the beets cool to room temperature. Rub off the beet skins with an old kitchen towel or peel with a paring knife. Cut the beets into 1/2-inch slices.

Arrange some of the watercress on each chilled salad plate. Top with 1/4 of the beets; spoon some of the vinaigrette over the beets, letting a bit of it pool on the plate. Crumble the Gorgonzola over the beets. Sprinkle with the toasted nuts and a grind of black pepper.

Serves 4

Orange-Rosemary Vinaigrette

1 cup fresh orange juice
1/2 tsp. minced orange zest
1 tsp. chopped rosemary leaves
1 tsp. minced shallots
2 tsp. champagne vinegar
1/4 tsp. sugar (optional, depending on the sweetness of the orange juice)
1 tsp. olive oil
pinch of salt
pinch of freshly ground black pepper

Whisk together all the ingredients in a large bowl. Set aside at room temperature for at least 30 minutes to allow the flavors to meld; then cover and refrigerate for up to 1 week.

About the Chef

Name: Kevin von Klause
Education/Training: Culinary Institute of America
Inspirations/Influences: farm fresh organic ingredients
Hobbies: mountain biking, reading, travel
Family: single
Hometown: Borger, TX
Favorite Food to Eat: mac and cheese
Favorite Food to Prepare: savory soups and stews
Favorite Cookbook: *White Dog Cafe Cookbook* (due Spring '98)

Lucskos Káposziá

Chef De Cuisine Fritz Blank
Deux Cheminées, Philadelphia, PA

"This Hungarian style 'slushy' cabbage — sometimes known as 'night-of-the-howling-wolf cabbage' — demonstrates the natural affinity certain herbs have for cabbage. Rather than merely seasoning our noble vegetable, the four herbs used here combine and actually marry with the cabbage to create a brand-new flavor which is distinct from any of the individual components. When this dish is made without meat, a cleaner taste results which I prefer to serve as a side vegetable rather than the traditional *Eintopf* with its ears and tails."

2 to 3 strips of bacon (optional)
2 to 3 T. lard or goose fat
1 large head green (white) cabbage
1 to 2 lbs. fresh pork shoulder, spare ribs, or pigs tails and ears (optional)
1 to 2 tsp. dried tarragon
1 to 2 tsp. dried summer savory (Hungarian = *csombor* ["tsom-boor-r-r"])
1 to 2 tsp. caraway seeds
1 to 2 tsp. dill seed
1 bay leaf, preferably fresh
1/4 cup white wine vinegar to taste
1 T. sugar to taste
water to cover cabbage
2 T. cornstarch in 1/4 cup water prepared into a slurry
2 cups sour cream or sour cream mixed with buttermilk or yogurt

Place bacon pieces and lard or goose fat into a large pot and melt over a medium-high flame. Halve cabbage head. Remove and discard the core. Slice each half into 1-inch wide slices and then each slice into 1-inch "cubes." Place into the pot and sauté until cabbage is coated with the cooking fat and wilted. *Do not brown.* Add the fresh pork, spices, vinegar, sugar, and sufficient water to cover the cabbage. Bring to a boil; then reduce heat and simmer for 2 to 3 hours until cabbage is very tender. Adjust seasonings and thicken with the cornstarch/water slurry. Finish with sour cream or a mixture of sour cream and buttermilk. Serve with roasted pork and/or sausages.

Braised Celery Hearts

Chef De Cuisine Fritz Blank
Deux Cheminées, Philadelphia, PA

6 whole heads of celery with tight, firm stalks
1/4 cup shortening
2 cups rich chicken or pork stock
2 cups dry white wine
salt and freshly cracked black pepper

Cut the bottom 4 inches off the celery and reserve the tops for future use. Trim the butts of each celery bottom and rinse well. Dry each carefully, then cut lengthwise in half or into quarters, depending on the size of the celery head. The stalks should remain together, joined by the butt. Heat the shortening in an accommodating braising pan and place the split celery bottoms into the pan and sauté over medium heat, turning occasionally, until nicely browned. Add the chicken or pork stock and white wine to the pan. Bring to a boil; then reduce to a simmer. Cover and cook for about 10 minutes until the celery is tender and easily pierced with a fork. Remove the celery and keep warm; season each with salt and pepper.

NOTE: If serving with Escalopes de Porc (page 174), reduce the cooking juices to about 2 cups. Pour into a small sauce pan and set aside.

Serves 12

About the Chef

Name: Fritz Blank

Education/Training: *Grossmutti's Küchen* (in my grandmother's kitchen)

Hobbies: collector of culinary ephemera, menus, and memorabilia; also interested in food history and the evolution of ethnographic cuisines; marine aquaculture, land agriculture, and animal husbandry; and public health current events

Hometown: Pennsauken, NJ

Favorite Food to Eat: authentic Chinese (which I purposefully have never learned to cook)

Favorite Food to Prepare: anything and everything, especially ethnographic and regional American (NOT concocted or fusioned, but honest as-you-find-it on the table), French, Austrian, Italian, or European in general

Favorite Cookbook: culinary bibliophile with over 7,00 volumes in my personal library

Garden Green Bean Salad

Owner Diana Melchiorre
Garden of Eden Natural Foods and Country Kitchen, Mt. Laurel, NJ

⊚

1 lb. fresh green beans, snapped or cut into 1- to 2-inch pieces
1 small red onion, thinly sliced
1 T. plus 1/4 cup canola oil
1 (4-oz.) jar pimentos
1/4 cup apple cider vinegar
2 T. Florida Crystals sugar*
1 tsp. sea salt

Place green beans in a saucepan, cover with water, and bring to a boil. Reduce heat to low. Cover and cook beans until tender-crisp. Do not overcook. Drain and set aside.

Combine onions and 1 tablespoon oil in a frying pan. Cook over medium heat until onions are translucent, stirring frequently so that onions do not brown or burn. Cut pimentos into thin strips and set aside. Reserve liquid.

In medium bowl, mix 1/4 cup oil, vinegar, sugar, salt, and 2 tablespoons of pimento liquid. Stir in pimentos, cooked onions, and green beans. Toss and coat with dressing. Cover and refrigerate 2 hours. Stir before serving.

Serves 8

*Florida Crystals sugar is unrefined sugar available in health food stores.

Five Mushroom Ragout

Executive Chef Liz Huffman
Buckley's Tavern, Centreville, DE

1/2 cup olive oil
2 T. chopped fresh garlic
2 T. chopped fresh shallots
2 T. chopped fresh thyme
1/4 lb. crimini mushrooms, quartered
1/4 lb. domestic mushrooms, quartered
1/4 lb. portobello mushroom caps, sliced
1/4 lb. shiitake mushrooms, stems removed
1/4 lb. oyster mushrooms, stems removed
salt and black pepper to taste
1 cup Merlot (use something good that you would drink!)

In a large pot, heat olive oil and quickly sauté garlic and shallots. Add thyme
and mushrooms. Season with salt and pepper to taste. Sauté mushrooms
until they begin to release their juices but are still firm. Add Merlot and
reduce liquid by 1/2. Adjust seasonings.

Serves 4 to 6

About the Chef

Name: Liz Huffman
Education/Training: on the job
Inspirations/Influences: fresh, seasonal
produce and visits to local farms
Hometown: Kansas City, MO
Favorite Food to Eat: greens: collards, swiss
chard, spinach
Favorite Food to Prepare: fruit-based salsas
and chutneys
Favorite Cookbook: *Salsas, Sambals, Chut-
neys, and Chow Chow*

Roasted Pepper and Corn Hash

Chef Kimberly Quay
Roscoe's Kodiak Cafe, Philadelphia, PA

1 red onion, diced
4 T. olive oil
4 ears corn, husked and kernels removed from cob
salt and pepper
1 red pepper, roasted, peeled, seeded, and diced
1 green pepper, roasted, peeled, seeded, and diced
1/2 bunch basil, finely chopped
4 red bliss potatoes, diced and held in water
1/3 cup chicken stock or water
3 T. butter

Sauté red onion in 2 tablespoons olive oil until just soft. Add the corn, tossing to mix with the onion. Sauté until the corn is cooked through. Season with salt and pepper. Add the roasted peppers and basil, tossing to incorporate.

Heat 2 tablespoons oil in a nonstick sauté pan. Add potatoes (water drained) to pan. (Be careful not to splash the hot oil.) Sauté until potatoes are cooked through and browned on all sides, about 5 to 7 minutes. Season with salt and pepper and drain on paper towels. When cooled, add to the pepper and corn mixture.

When ready to serve, heat corn, potato, and pepper hash in a sauté pan with chicken stock or water. When heated through, add butter, tossing to coat the hash. If the hash looks soupy, cook over low heat for another 5 minutes to reduce the liquid and evenly coat the vegetables.

Serves 4

Cajun Roasted Potatoes

Executive Chef Trish Morrissey
Philadelphia Fish & Co., Philadelphia, PA

1 lb. small potatoes, scrubbed well
2 tsp. Cajun seasoning
1 tsp. salt
vegetable oil to coat

Preheat oven to 375°. Toss together all ingredients in a bowl; then spread out on a baking sheet. Bake for 40 minutes and serve hot.

Serves 4

About the Chef

Name: Trish Morrissey

Education/Training: Drexel University; The Restaurant School

Inspirations/Influences: every season, my mom and grandmother

Hobbies: tennis, reading, painting

Hometown: Mclean, VA

Favorite Food to Eat: fish, real Northern Italian

Favorite Food to Prepare: family recipes from Italy

Favorite Cookbook: *The Splendid Table*

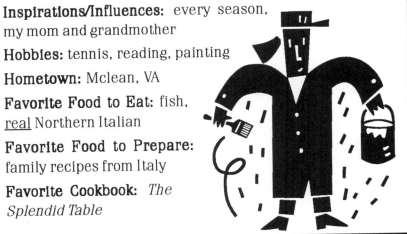

Alo Gohbi

Executive Chef Daniel McConnell
Philadelphia Tea Party, Philadelphia, PA

3 cups vegetable oil
6 medium baking potatoes, peeled and cut into 1/2-inch cubes
2 heads cauliflower, cut into florets
2 cups finely diced fresh ginger, peeled
1/4 cup coriander powder
1/4 cup cumin
1 T. hot chile powder
1 T. salt
1/4 cup chopped cilantro

Heat 2 cups oil in skillet. Cook potatoes and cauliflower until golden brown. Drain off oil, remove potatoes and cauliflower, and reserve. Heat remaining oil in same skillet. Add ginger, coriander powder, cumin, hot chile powder, and salt. Cook on medium heat for about 10 minutes, stirring constantly so not to let ginger stick to pan. Toss together with potatoes and cauliflower. Sprinkle cilantro on top when serving.

Serves 8

About the Chef

Name: Daniel McConnell

Education/Training: mainly practical and New School for Social Research

Inspirations/Influences: seeing people enjoying my art

Hobbies: photography, bowling, sight-seeing

Family: single (for now); family in NJ. Father was a chef in NYC.

Hometown: Hoboken, NJ

Favorite Food to Eat: simple Asian rice and vegetable dishes

Favorite Food to Prepare: Asian influenced

Favorite Cookbook: *Gastronomique*

Roast Corn and Scallion Mashed Potato

Executive Chef Mustapha Rouissiya
Rococo, Philadelphia, PA

1 lb. Yukon gold potatoes
1 T. salt
1 cup white or yellow corn kernels
4 T. butter
1 cup buttermilk (approximate)
4 scallions, chopped
salt and pepper to taste

Peel potatoes and cut them into similar-sized pieces. Place them in a large saucepan and cover with cold water. (The water should be about 1 inch over the level of the potatoes.) Season the water with salt. Place over medium-high heat, bring to boil, and cover. Cook until potatoes are tender, approximately 7 to 10 minutes.

While the potatoes are cooking, preheat broiler. Spread the corn kernels out over a lightly-oiled baking sheet. Broil the corn until golden brown. Remove from oven and let cool.

Place butter and buttermilk in a saucepan and warm to melt the butter. Remove potatoes from heat, drain, and return the potatoes to the pot. Lower heat and stir potatoes to cook off any extra water that might be remaining from cooking. Mash the potatoes, whipping in the melted butter/buttermilk mixture until light and fluffy. Stir in roasted corn and chopped scallions. Season to taste with salt and pepper.

Serves 4

Fried Yuca con Mojo Criollo

Executive Chef Guillermo Pernot
Vega Grill, Manayunk, PA

2 large yuca roots (about 2 lbs.)
water to cover
1 cup white vinegar
3 T. salt
8 cups vegetable oil
salt and pepper
Mojo Criolla (Recipe appears on page 226.)

Cut yuca in half, lengthwise; then with a sharp knife, peel off the thick skin and hold yuca in water. Take each half and cut it into quarters to obtain sticks 1 inch in diameter and 6 inches long. Place yuca in a pot with enough water to cover by 1 inch above the vegetable. Add vinegar and salt. Boil until yuca becomes translucent; then remove immediately and run cold water until cool.

Bring oil to 375° and fry several yuca sticks at a time. Cook until golden brown. Drain on paper towel and dust with salt and pepper. Keep warm. Repeat process until all yuca has been fried. Arrange on serving plate, drizzle with mojo criollo, and serve immediately.

Serves 4

Julienne Vegetables

Executive Chef David Gottlieb
The Dilworthtown Inn, West Chester, PA

1 bunch asparagus, cut on a bias
1 bulb fennel, julienned
1 red pepper, julienned
1 oz. olive oil
1 T. minced shallots
1 tsp. minced garlic
salt and pepper to taste
1 oz. chopped parsley
1 oz. chopped basil

In a warm sauté pan, cook vegetables in olive oil for about 2 minutes. Add shallots and garlic and cook for about 30 seconds. Season with salt and pepper and toss in fresh herbs. Cook until vegetables are tender.

Serves 3

Vegetable Strudel

Executive Chef Luigi Baretto
Ram's Head Inn, Absecon, NJ

4 sheets phyllo dough
melted butter
fresh garlic
1 lb. fresh spinach, blanched for 1 minute
salt, pepper, and Parmesan cheese to season
1 eggplant, skinned and sliced in ¼-inch thick pieces
2 carrots, peeled, julienned, and blanched for 3 minutes
2 zucchini, julienned
2 yellow squash, julienned
8 oz. sliced shiitake mushrooms
1 portobello mushroom, sliced
3 red peppers, roasted, skinned, and julienned
1 sheet puff pastry dough
egg wash

Preheat oven to 350°. Brush each layer of phyllo dough with melted butter and rub with fresh garlic. Place blanched spinach atop the stacked phyllo dough and season with salt, pepper, and Parmesan cheese. Add the remaining vegetables and season again with salt, pepper, and Parmesan cheese. Roll the phyllo dough to hold all the vegetables inside and place on top of puff pastry sheet. Brush the top with egg wash. Bake 20 to 30 minutes or until golden brown. Slice into 1-inch thick pieces.

Serves 8

Sun-dried Cranberry Couscous

Executive Chef Mustapha Rouissiya
Rococo, Philadelphia, PA

2 cups couscous
1/4 lb. sun-dried cranberries
2½ cups water or chicken stock
1 tsp. salt
2 T. unsalted butter or olive oil
pinch ground cinnamon
pinch ground ginger
pinch ground cumin
pinch freshly ground pepper

Place the couscous and sun-dried cranberries into a medium-sized bowl. In a saucepan, combine water or stock, salt, butter or oil, and spices. Bring to a boil. Remove from heat and pour over the couscous. Stir well and cover bowl with aluminum foil. Let rest 10 minutes; then fluff with fork.

Serves 4

About the Chef

Name: Mustapha Rouissiya

Education/Training: France, Morocco, Italy, and USA

Inspirations/Influences: timeless classic cuisine

Hobbies: traveling

Family: single, but looking (looking HARD!)

Hometown: Casablanca, Morocco

Favorite Food to Eat: Italian, Moroccan

Favorite Food to Prepare: all foods

Favorite Cookbook: *Romanogli's Table*

Grilled Polenta

Executive Chef Wendy Welcovitz
The Inn Philadelphia, Philadelphia, PA

3 cups water
1 tsp. salt
2 T. unsalted butter
3/4 cup polenta or yellow cornmeal
3/4 cup freshly grated Parmesan cheese
1/4 tsp. cayenne pepper
olive oil

Combine the water, salt, and butter in a medium saucepan and bring to a boil. Gradually add the polenta or cornmeal, whisking constantly so that it doesn't lump. Lower the heat and continue cooking for 10 to 15 minutes, stirring frequently until quite thick. Remove from heat and stir in cheese and cayenne.

Line a 9-inch pie plate with plastic wrap, letting it extend over the edges. Spread the polenta evenly over the plastic wrap and smooth the top with a spoon. Cover tightly with plastic wrap and chill until firm, at least 1 hour.

Prepare a grill fire. Apply olive oil to the grill rack and position it 4 to 6 inches above the fire. Invert the pie plate to unmold the polenta. Peel off the plastic wrap. Cut the polenta into 6 pie-shaped wedges. Brush each wedge lightly on both sides with olive oil. Arrange the polenta wedges on the rack. Grill about 10 minutes until golden, turning 2 or 3 times.

Serves 4 to 6

Roasted Corn Polenta

Executive Chef Don Paone
Sonoma Restaurant, Manayunk, PA

2 ears corn
oil
salt and pepper
2 cups milk
1 cup water
2 cups chicken stock
4 oz. butter
2 cups corn meal
1 cup Parmesan cheese
1 tsp. salt

Preheat oven to 400°. Brush corn with oil and salt and pepper. Roast for 10 minutes. When cool, remove kernels from cob.

Combine all liquid ingredients and butter. Slowly bring to a boil. Add corn meal, stirring constantly until all corn meal is incorporated. Add corn, Parmesan cheese, and salt. Turn heat down. Allow mixture to simmer 5 minutes. Remove from stove and spread a 1-inch layer onto cookie pan. Refrigerate until firm.

To serve, cut polenta into squares or other desired shapes and pan fry until crispy.

Serves 4

Nicola Shirley's Rice and Beans

Chef/Owner Nicola Shirley
Jamaican Jerk Hut, Philadelphia, PA

3 cups dried kidney beans
12 cups water
1 medium yellow onion, coarsely chopped
1 cup coarsely chopped scallions
1 Scotch Bonnet pepper
4 tsp. fresh thyme or 2 tsp. dried thyme
1/4 cup butter
1/2 block coconut cream
2 tsp. minced garlic
10 pimento seeds
6 cups rice

Soak beans for several hours or overnight in enough water to cover. Drain and rinse. Place beans and 12 cups water in large pot and bring to a boil. Cook at a medium boil for at least 1 hour or until beans are tender but still firm. Add remaining ingredients except rice. Return to boil. When coconut cream is dissolved, add rice and stir. Cook until water line is level or just below the rice line. Cover and reduce heat. Cook about 25 minutes until rice is still firm but cooked through.

Serves 6

NOTE: Look for Grace Brand Coconut Cream in supermarkets and gourmet food stores.

About the Chef

Name: Nicola Shirley
Education/Training: Johnson & Wales University
Inspirations/Influences: Caribbean background
Hobbies: studying herbs, badminton
Hometown: Kingston, Jamaica
Favorite Food to Eat: grapes, figs, cheese
Favorite Food to Prepare: jerk chicken
Favorite Cookbook: *Silver Palate*

Wild Rice

Executive Chef Tom Hannum
Hotel Dupont, Wilmington, DE

2 cups steamed wild rice
3 T. honey
1/4 cup diced dried fruits
1/4 cup diced walnuts
cracked black pepper

Preheat oven to 350°. Combine cooked rice, honey, dried fruits, and walnuts. Season with cracked pepper. Place in timbale molds and bake approximately 30 minutes in water bath to heat. Carefully unmold onto serving plates when ready to serve.

Serves 6

Salsas, Sauces & Such

Banana-Cilantro Salsa 217
Black Bean Salsa..217
Salsa Cruda 218
Papaya Salsa 218
Roasted Corn Salsa 219
Salsa Fresca...219
Tomatillo Salsa 220
Serrano's Five Pepper Hot Sauce 221
Jalapeño Pepper Puree 222
Basic Cream Sauce...223
Dijon-Dill Sauce 223
BBQ Sauce 224
Beurre Blanc 224
Demi-Glace 225
Mojo Criollo 226
Papaya Cilantro Sauce 226
Red Wine Sauce 227
Saffron Honey Sauce 227
Sauce Provencale 228
Summer Herbs Sauce 229
Salsa di Pomodoro..230
Fresh Tomato Sauce 231
Tomato Olive Sauce 231
Sweet Basil Pesto...232
Corn-Tomato Stock 233
Sun-dried Marmalade 233
Red Onion Marmalade 234
Garlic Butter 234
Brandy, Basil and Tomato Butter 235

Banana-Cilantro Salsa

Executive Chef/Owner Bill Beck
Pompano Grille, Philadelphia, PA

2 T. diced red bell pepper
1 T. scallion, cut on the bias
1 T. tamarind puree
1 T. diced poblano
1 T. fresh cilantro, chiffonaded
salt to taste
2 bananas, cut into 1/4-inch circular slices

Mix first 6 ingredients together. Add bananas, tossing gently with rubber spatula so as not to break them. Refrigerate for at least 2 hours so flavors marry.

Black Bean Salsa

Chef Annemarie Phifer
Loose Ends Restaurant, Haddon Heights, NJ

1 lb. black beans, cooked, rinsed of starch, and drained
1/4 cup each: diced red, yellow, and green bell peppers
1/2 small jalapeño pepper, minced
1/4 cup minced red onion
1 tsp. minced garlic
1/2 tsp. cumin
1/2 tsp. chili powder
1/4 tsp. cayenne
juice of 1 lime
1 T. red wine vinegar
2 T. olive oil
salt and pepper to taste

Mix all ingredients together. Chill. (Can be made 1 day ahead.) Bring to room temperature for best flavor. Serve with chicken and shrimp.

Salsa Cruda

Kitchen Staff
Zocalo, Philadelphia, PA

1 cup finely chopped tomato
1/3 cup finely chopped white onion
2 serrano chiles, minced
1/4 cup fresh cilantro
salt to taste

Combine all ingredients in a bowl and mix thoroughly. Serve chilled or at room temperature.

Papaya Salsa

Executive Chef Lynn Buono
Feast Your Eyes Catering, Philadelphia, PA

1/2 cup jalapeño pepper jelly
1 ripe papaya, diced
1/4 cup finely chopped red onion
1 T. finely chopped yellow pepper
1 T. finely chopped red pepper
2 T. chopped fresh cilantro
2 T. chopped fresh mint
1 T. fresh lime juice
zest of 1/2 lime, finely chopped

Heat jelly until melted. Remove from heat. Add remaining ingredients. Let stand at least 1 hour. Refrigerate to store.

Roasted Corn Salsa

Chef/General Manager Michael Pfeffer
Old Original Bookbinder's Restaurant, Philadelphia, PA

4 ears roasted corn, kernels removed
2 cups diced shiitake mushrooms
1/2 cup diced red bell pepper
1/2 cup chopped red onion
1 T. minced garlic
3 T. chopped cilantro
1 cup olive oil
1/3 cup balsamic vinegar
1 tsp. cumin
salt and pepper to taste

Combine all ingredients and mix thoroughly. Chill for approximately 1 hour to blend the flavors.

Salsa Fresca

Executive Chef Curt Taylor
Los Amigos's "New Mexico Grille," Philadelphia, PA

4 plum tomatoes, diced
1 jalapeño chili pepper, minced
1 T. diced red onion
1 T. chopped scallions
1 clove garlic, minced
1 T. chopped basil
1 tsp. balsamic vinegar
1 tsp. lime juice
1 tsp. olive oil
salt to taste

Combine all ingredients in a bowl and mix well.

Tomatillo Salsa

Executive Chef Chakapope Sirirathasuk
Friday Saturday Sunday Restaurant, Philadelphia, PA

4 tomatillos, seeded and minced
1 tomato, seeded and chopped
juice of 4 limes
1 tsp. granulated white sugar
2 cloves garlic, minced
2 cloves shallots, minced
1½ T. chopped fresh cilantro
1 T. olive oil
1 tsp. pepper flakes
salt and pepper to taste

Combine all ingredients and mix well. Add cayenne pepper for more heat if desired.

About the Chef

Name: Chakapope Sirirathasuk

Education/Training: community college; self-taught

Inspirations/Influences: being at Friday Saturday Sunday Restaurant for so long and still liking it; my mother's cooking

Hobbies: sports, music, TV

Family: married, four kids

Hometown: Thailand and Upper Darby, PA

Favorite Food to Eat: fried rice, chicken béarnaise

Favorite Food to Prepare: Thai curry

Favorite Cookbook: *Food & Wine Magazine, Bon Appetit*

Serrano's Five Pepper Hot Sauce

Chef Jospeh E. Shilling C.E.C.
Serrano Restaurant, Philadelphia PA

"Great with roasted chicken or grilled meats."

6 serrano peppers, seeded
6 jalapeño peppers, seeded
3 Anaheim chili peppers
1 tsp. red pepper seed
1 tsp. cayenne pepper
1 large white onion, skinned and quartered
1 T. sugar
1 cup red wine vinegar
1 cup water

Combine all ingredients in a saucepan. Bring to a boil and simmer 15 minutes.
Puree mixture in a blender. Refrigerate for best shelf life.

Jalapeño Pepper Puree

Chef/Owner Susanna Foo
Susanna Foo Chinese Cuisine, Philadelphia, PA

"I developed this pungent marinade over the years, using a combination of pureed jalapeño and garlic. In the recipe the seeds are pureed as well, for they contribute heat and flavor. It's delicious with grilled meat, game, and seafood. I prefer the jalapeño pepper to all other varieties because of its meaty texture, its balanced yet distinct flavor with a subtle hint of sweetness, its consistent level of heat, and its year-long availability."

1 lb. jalapeño peppers with seeds, stems removed
1 large head garlic, cloves separated and peeled (10 to 15 cloves)
1/2 cup olive oil
2 tsp. coarse or kosher salt

Preheat oven to 350°. Place the jalapeño peppers and garlic cloves in a shallow baking pan in a single layer. Spoon the oil over all and turn to coat. Roast for 30 minutes. Turn and roast for an additional 30 minutes or until the peppers and garlic are very soft. Cool.

Transfer to a food processor and puree, adding the salt. Spoon the puree into a jar with a tight-fitting lid. Cover and refrigerate up to 1 month or freeze up to 6 months.

Yields about 1½ cups.

Basic Cream Sauce

Chef William Love
Country Club Restaurant, Philadelphia, PA

2 T. flour
2 T. melted butter
2 cups milk
1/2 cup heavy cream
1/2 tsp. ground coriander
1/4 tsp. ground nutmeg
pinch of cayenne
salt and pepper to taste

Create a roux by combining flour and butter and cooking over moderate heat for 10 minutes, stirring occasionally. Meanwhile, scald milk, cream, and spices. Whisk roux into heated milk until smooth. Bring to a boil over low heat.

Dijon-Dill Sauce

Chef William Love
Country Club Restaurant, Philadelphia, PA

1 bunch scallions, sliced
1 bunch dill, chopped
1 T. butter
2 T. Dijon mustard
juice of 1 lemon
Basic Cream Sauce (see recipe)

Sweat scallions and dill in the butter until bright green. Stir scallions, dill, Dijon mustard, and lemon juice into cream sauce.

BBQ Sauce

Chef Alan Lichtenstein
New World Cafe, Cinnaminson, NJ

1 onion, diced
1 T. chopped garlic
1 cup red wine vinegar
1/2 cup brown sugar
1 cup ketchup
1 cup brewed coffee
1 cup diced tomatoes
1/4 cup honey
6 oz. unsweetened chocolate
1 T. cocoa powder
1 T. diced habañero or jalapeño pepper
1 T. ground cumin seed, toasted
1/4 cup Worcestershire sauce

Sauté onion with garlic for about 3 minutes. Add remaining ingredients and simmer for 10 minutes.

Beurre Blanc

Executive Chef David R. Grear, Jr.
Paradigm, Philadelphia, PA

2 6-oz. cans pineapple juice
4 bay leaves
1 shallot, sliced
4 peppercorns
12 oz. heavy cream
8 oz. unsalted butter, chilled and diced

Heat pineapple juice, bay leaves, shallot, and peppercorns until liquid is reduced and only 2 ounces remain. Add heavy cream and reduce again so that only 8 ounces remain. Remove from heat. Slowly add butter a little at a time, whisking to incorporate.

Demi-Glace

Executive Chef William Fischer
Caffé Aldo Lamberti, Cherry Hill, NJ

C

5 lbs. veal bones
1 lb. calves' feet
2 T. vegetable oil
3/8 cup tomato paste
1 celery stalk, chopped
2 carrots, chopped
2 cups chopped onions
1/2 clove garlic, chopped
3/8 cup burgundy wine
bouquet garni (thyme, bay leaves, and peppercorns)

Preheat oven to 500°. Toss the bones and calves' feet with the oil, coating them evenly. In a roasting pan, roast bones until golden brown. Remove and coat evenly with the tomato paste. Return to oven and roast again until lightly browned. Add the chopped vegetables and garlic and continue roasting until they are well browned.

Place the bones in a large stock pot. Add cold water, covering the bones with 5 inches of water. Deglaze the roasting pan with wine and add it to the stock. Add the bouquet garni, bring to a boil, and simmer until reduced by 49%.

Mojo Criollo

Executive Chef Guillermo Pernot
Vega Grill, Manayunk, PA

5 cloves garlic, minced
1 Spanish onion, minced
1/2 cup fresh lime juice
1 cup fresh orange juice
1/2 cup extra virgin olive oil
3 T. chopped parsley
salt and pepper to taste

In a saucepan, place garlic, onions, lime juice, and orange juice and bring to a boil. Reduce heat and simmer until onions are tender.

    In another saucepan, heat oil to the smoking point and add to the vegetable reduction. Simmer for 5 minutes and remove from heat. Add parsley and salt and pepper. Serve over any choice of vegetable.

Papaya Cilantro Sauce

Executive Chef Luigi Baretto
Ram's Head Inn, Absecon, NJ

1 medium fresh papaya, peeled and seeded
1/4 cup water (approximate)
1/2 tsp. chopped cilantro
juice of 1/2 lime
1/2 tsp. chopped jalapeño chile
1/4 tsp. ginger powder
1 oz. dark rum
salt and white pepper

Puree papaya in food processor, adding water. Pour into a saucepan and add remaining ingredients. Slowly bring to a boil over low heat. Serve hot.

Red Wine Sauce

Executive Chef Jean-Marie Lacroix
Four Seasons Hotel Philadelphia, Philadelphia, PA

2 T. chopped shallots
4 T. butter
2 cups red wine
1 cup fish fumet
2 sprigs thyme
2 T. olive oil
salt and pepper to season

In a pan, sweat the shallots in 1 tablespoon butter until tender. Add red wine and reduce by 2/3. Add fumet and reduce by 1/2. Add thyme and olive oil and simmer for 15 seconds. Slowly whip in remaining butter and season with salt and pepper.

Saffron Honey Sauce

Executive Chef Moustapha Rouissiya
Rococo, Philadelphia, PA

1 medium onion, peeled and cut into chunks
1 T. olive oil
1 tomato, seeded and cut into chunks
1 tsp. ground cinnamon
1 cinnamon stick
1 tsp. ground allspice
few threads of saffron
1 T. honey
2 T. chopped fresh cilantro
salt and pepper to taste
2 cups water

In a medium-sized saucepan, sauté onion in olive oil over medium heat until translucent. Add the tomato and continue cooking until the tomato softens. Add the spices, honey, cilantro, and salt and pepper. Add water and bring entire mixture to a boil. Reduce heat and simmer for 5 minutes. Sauce can be made in advance and stored in refrigerator until needed.

Sauce Provencale

Chef/Owner Trzeciak Francis
Provence, Haverford, PA

3 shallots, chopped
3 medium-sized cloves garlic, chopped
extra virgin olive oil
1 yellow pepper, diced
1 red pepper, diced
1 glass dry white wine (4 to 6 oz.)
1 tsp. unsalted butter
fresh thyme to taste

Sauté shallots and garlic in oil over medium heat for approximately 2 minutes. Add yellow and red peppers; stir and continue cooking. Add wine, reduce heat, and simmer. When mixture is reduced by half, add butter and fresh thyme.

About the Chef

Name: Trzeciak Francis
Education/Training: École Hoteliere, Paris, France, 1976-1979
Inspirations/Influences: Provencale, Mediterranean
Hobbies: fishing, gardening, eating
Family: married to Brenda; three children ages 5, 7, and 8
Hometown: Avignon, France
Favorite Food to Eat: fish, game, pasta
Favorite Food to Prepare: fish, game, pasta
Favorite Cookbook: Books by Jean Louis Palladin and Daniel Boulud

Summer Herbs Sauce

Chef/Proprietor Kevin von Klause
White Dog Cafe, Philadelphia, PA

"In the summer, it is impossible to turn away any of the fragrant organic herbs brought to our door by the farmers who supply our kitchen, so we must be especially creative in making use of their abundance. In this recipe we chose basil, dill, cilantro, chives, and tarragon for their combination of sweet and savory qualities, but you can substitute any verdant, fresh herbs with great success."

1 cup mayonnaise
1/2 cup sour cream
2 T. chopped cilantro leaves and stems
2 T. chopped basil leaves
2 T. chopped tarragon leaves
2 T. chopped dill
2 T. minced chives
minced zest of 1 lemon
1 T. fresh lemon juice
1/2 tsp. salt
1/4 tsp. freshly ground black pepper

Combine all the ingredients in a small bowl and whisk together. Cover and refrigerate for 1 hour before serving. The sauce will keep in the refrigerator for up to 3 days.

Serves 4

Salsa di Pomodoro

Basic Tomato Sauce

Chef//Proprietor Luca Sena, padre
Assistant to Chef, Luca Sena, figlio
Panorama at the Penn's View Hotel, Philadelphia, PA

4 cloves garlic
1 cup olive oil
4 vine ripened tomatoes, chopped into 1/4-inch squares
8 fresh basil leaves, chopped
salt and pepper

Peel garlic and crack open with the flat side of a knife. Sauté garlic in olive oil over low flame, about 5 minutes. Remove garlic from oil and discard. Add tomatoes, basil, and salt and pepper to oil. Sauté for 10 to 15 minutes.

Serves 4

NOTE: Serve over pasta with Parmesan cheese on the side. Garnish with fresh basil leaf. You may add baby clams, mussels, shrimp, chicken, or grilled beef for variation.

Fresh Tomato Sauce

Executive Chef David W. Brennan
DiLullo's, Philadelphia, PA

1/2 cup olive oil
3/4 cup minced red onion
1 tsp. minced garlic
2 lbs. plum tomatoes, diced into 1-inch pieces
1/2 cup fresh basil
salt and freshly ground pepper to taste

Place oil in a medium-sized saucepan over medium heat. Add onions and garlic and sauté for 3 to 5 minutes. Add tomatoes and basil. Season with salt and pepper. Simmer for 35 to 40 minutes. Remove from heat and pass through a food mill.

Tomato Olive Sauce

Chef/Proprietor Ben McNamara
Isabella's, Philadelphia, PA

1 large onion, diced
4 large cloves garlic, finely diced
4 T. extra virgin olive oil
1 cup white wine
16 oz. San Marzano tomatoes or your favorite canned stewed tomatoes
30 pitted Gaeta olives
6 large basil leaves, julienned and roughly chopped
salt and pepper to taste

In a heavy saucean, cook onions and garlic in olive oil until sweet and translucent. Add white wine and allow liquid to reduce by one third. Add diced tomatoes and their juice. Lower heat and allow liquid to reduce by two thirds. Add olives, basil, and salt and pepper.

Sweet Basil Pesto

Chef Jospeh E. Shilling C.E.C.
Serrano Restaurant, Philadelphia PA

"Great with pasta, spread on warm bread, or as an essence to liven up soup or stew."

2 cups sweet basil leaves, no stems
1/2 cup garlic cloves
1/2 cup pinenuts or walnuts, toasted
1/2 to 3/4 cup grated Parmesan cheese
1/3 cup olive oil
1 tsp. black pepper
1/2 tsp. salt

Combine all ingredients in a food processor and blend until smooth. Can be frozen or refrigerated.

About the Chef

Name: Jospeh E. Shillin, C.E.C., C.F.B.E

Education & Training: Graduate of Penn State (University Park) and Culinary Institute of America; trained at La Varenne and Cordon Bleu in Paris, France

Inspirations/Influences: world-wide traveling and tasting plus the history, culture, lifestyle, and individuality of the cuisine.

Hobbie: cookbooks, music, art, cooking shows, Food TV

Family: single; from a family of 12 brothers and sisters

Hometown: Emporium, PA

Favorite Food to Eat: fish, especially fresh Hawaiian fish!

Favorite Food to Prepare: fish: steamed, grilled, baked — mmm! (It's good for you too.)

Favorite Cookbook: *CIA Guide to Healthy Cooking* by Tim Ryan

Corn-Tomato Stock

Chef/Proprietor Kevin von Klause
White Dog Cafe, Philadelphia, PA

4 ears sweet corn
3 cloves garlic, peeled
1 small onion, peeled
6 basil stems
5 black peppercorns
1 bay leaf
1 tsp. salt
10 cups water
2 cups coarsely chopped tomatoes (fresh or canned)

With a sharp knife, remove the corn kernels from the ears of corn and reserve. Place the corn cobs, garlic, onion, basil stems, peppercorns, bay leaf, salt, and water in a large stockpot set over high heat. Bring to a boil. Reduce the heat and simmer for 1 hour. Strain the stock into a clean saucepan; discard the solids.

Combine 1 cup of the corn stock with the tomatoes in a blender or food processor and puree until smooth. Add the pureed tomatoes to the remaining corn stock and set over low heat.

Sun-dried Marmalade

Executive Chef Don Paone
Sonoma Restaurant, Manayunk, PA

1 large onion, diced
2 oz. butter
1 T. olive oil
1/2 cup balsamic vinegar
1/2 cup brown sugar
1/2 cup sun-dried tomatoes
salt and pepper to taste

Cook onions in butter and olive oil until tender. Add balsamic vinegar, brown sugar, and tomatoes. Simmer for 5 minutes. Season to taste with salt and pepper. Serve hot or cold.

Red Onion Marmalade

Executive Chef David Bennett
Kansas City Prime, Manayunk, PA

1 red onion, thinly julienned
1/2 tsp. minced garlic
2 T. honey
2 T. red wine vinegar
2 T. port wine

Sweat onion and garlic over low heat until onion begins to caramelize. Stirring frequently, add remaining ingredients and continue to cook until all liquids are reduced to a thick syrup.

Garlic Butter

Executive Chef Dany Chevalier
Nicholas Nickolas, The Rittenhouse Hotel, Philadelphia, PA

1 lb. butter (lightly salted), room temperature
1½ T. garlic powder
1/2 T. fresh garlic puree
1/8 cup chopped parsley
1/2 T. Worcestershire sauce
1/2 T. aromatic bitter
1/2 T. Tabasco sauce
1/8 cup white wine
1½ T. brandy

In a mixer, combine butter, garlic powder, garlic puree, and parsley. Mix until butter is soft. Add Worcestershire, bitter, Tabasco, wine, and brandy. Mix at least 30 minutes. Place into plastic tub and store.

Brandy, Basil and Tomato Butter

Executive Chef Don Paone
Sonoma Restaurant, Manayunk, PA

shells of 1½ lbs. shrimp
8 plum tomatoes, peeled, squeezed, and diced (all saved)
1 small onion, diced
1 small carrot, chopped
1 rib celery, chopped
1 clove garlic, smashed
1 bay leaf
1/2 cup basil, chiffonaded and stems reserved
1/4 cup brandy
1 lb. sweet butter
kosher salt and pepper to taste

Cover shrimp shells with cold water in a 1 quart pan. Add skin, juice, and seeds from tomatoes plus onion, carrot, celery, garlic, bay leaf, and basil stems. Bring stock to a boil; then reduce heat and simmer gently for 30 minutes. Strain stock and put liquid back into pot on medium high heat so that it will reduce. Add brandy and reduce liquid until about 1/4 cup remains. Add diced tomatoes and sliced basil.

With a whip, start to incorporate butter. Whip constantly over heat until butter is incorporated and mixture is nice and silky. Season with kosher salt and black pepper.

Desserts

Apricot-Ginger Biscotti 239

Classic Biscotti 240

Mexican Wedding Cookies 242

Black & White Cookies 243

Chocolate Macaroons with Raspberry Filling 244

Shortbread and Apple Chutney 245

Vanilla Pana Cotta with Oven-Roasted Strawberries 246

Harry's Crème Brûlée 247

Crème Brûlée with Fresh Raspberries 248

White Chocolate Mousse 249

Bittersweet Chocolate Sauce 249

Banana Bavarian Mousse 250

Chocolate Mousse 251

Irish Rice Pudding 252

Chocolate-Banana Bread Pudding 253

Summer Pudding 254

Black Forest Crepes with Cocoa Sorbet 256

Strawberry Napoleon 258

Star Anise Alfajor 259

Lemon Poached Pears with Berry Sauce 260

Summertime Rhubarb Mango Crumb 261

Harvest Fruit Crisp 262

Ricotta Cheesecake 264

Pumpkin Cheese Cake 265

Double Chocolate Banana Mousse Cake 266

Chocolate Buttermilk Cake 267

Kahlúa Flourless Fudge Cake.. 268

Blackberry Cream Streusel Cake 269

Carrot Cake with Orange Glaze Icing 270

Amazing Apple Spice Cake 272

Lemon Poppyseed Cake 274

French Apple Tart... 275

Lemon Tart 276

Fresh Fruit Tarts 278

Old Fashioned Apple Pie 279

Apricot-Ginger Biscotti

Pastry Chef Michael Vandergeest
Tony Clark's, Philadelphia, PA

2 bulbs fresh ginger, peeled and chopped
8 oz. plus 1 T. unsalted butter
2½ cups granulated sugar
6 eggs
1 lb. dried apricots (fresh plump ones)
5 cups flour
2 tsp. baking powder
1/2 tsp. salt
pinch ground ginger
2 cups whole toasted almonds

Preheat oven to 325°. Sweat ginger with 1 tablespoon butter. Reserve. Cream sugar with 8 ounces butter. Add eggs slowly. Incorporate the apricots, dry ingredients, and almonds until it forms a nice, clean dough. Portion into 4 slightly irregularly-shaped logs. Bake for 18 to 20 minutes. Slice on a bias cut into 1/2-inch thick pieces and return to oven for an additional 4 to 6 minutes. Store in airtight container.

About the Chef

Name: Michael Vandergeest

Education/Training: The Restaurant School; 8 years at the Four Seasons Hotel

Hobbies: fishing, carpentry work, gardening

Hometown: King of Prussia, PA

Favorite Food to Eat: any grilled fish, salads

Favorite Food to Prepare: cooking on the grill, seafood

Favorite Cookbook: *Art Culinaire* and *Bread Alone*

Classic Biscotti

Pastry Chef/Owner Gilda Ann Doganiero
Gilda's Biscotti, Inc., Philadelphia, PA

"Biscotti is proven to be magnificent with red wine, coffee, espresso, tea, milk, and — as was discovered most recently at a pairing at McNally's Tavern — Guiness Stout. Mangia!"

2 cups whole toasted almonds with skins
2 cups sifted unbleached all-purpose flour
1 cup less 2 T. granulated sugar
1/2 tsp. baking powder
1/2 tsp. baking soda
1/8 tsp. salt
2 large eggs
zest of 1 lemon
4½ tsp. fresh lemon juice
1/2 tsp. pure almond extract

Preheat oven to 375°. Line 2 flat baking sheets with parchment paper. Place almonds, flour, sugar, baking powder, baking soda, and salt in a KitchenAid mixer with a paddle attachment or a regular mixing bowl. Combine to evenly distribute the contents and crush some of the almonds. In a separate bowl, combine the eggs, zest, lemon juice, and extract. Add the egg mixture to the dry ingredients and combine until well moistened.

Turn mixture out onto work surface and separate into 4 equal sections. Roll each section into a long sausage-like shape, dusting work surface with flour if necessary. Place 2 rolls on each baking sheet. Leave about 2 inches between them and do not flatten the rolls.

Bake the rolls for abut 15 minutes. Check baking sheets as they may need to be rotated to bake the loaves evenly. Bake another 10 to 15 minutes until rolls are evenly browned and spring back quickly when touched.

Have a cutting surface and a sharp knife ready. When able to handle, remove one loaf at a time from parchment paper. Slice on a bias (diagonally) into 1/2-inch thick pieces. Return slices to parchment paper for the second baking. Bake about 5 to 10 minutes until biscotti are crisp, rotating pans again as needed. Allow biscotti to cool completely and store in airtight jars when not munching.

About the Chef

Name: Gilda Ann Doganiero

Education/Training: Culinary Institute of America, Class of 1990

Inspirations/Influences: the perfection of simplicity, my family

Hobbies: snowshoeing, outdoor winter activities, coffee with friends, running with my Rottweiler

Family: father Antonio Francesco from Abrozzi and mother Rita of Irish descent

Hometown: Haddonfield, NJ

Favorite Food to Eat: bucatini with garlic and oil

Favorite Food to Prepare: bucatini with garlic and oil

Favorite Cookbook: *The Book of Alain Ducasse*

Mexican Wedding Cookies

Executive Pastry Chef/Owner Diane Nussbaum
La Patisserie Francaise, Haddonfield, NJ

C

4½ sticks butter
1 cup 6x sugar
2 tsp. vanilla
3¼ cups flour
2/3 cup walnuts, broken into small pieces
10x sugar

Preheat oven to 350°. Cream butter and 6x sugar together. Add vanilla and flour. Mix until blended. Add walnuts. Roll into balls, using approximately 1 tablespoon dough per ball. Bake on aluminum foil-lined cookie sheet until lightly browned, approximately 10 minutes. Coat cookies with a dusting of 10x sugar while cooling.

Yields 96 cookies

Black & White Cookies

Pastry Chef/Owner Deborah Kaplan
Sud Fine Pastry, Philadelphia, PA

As seen on Seinfeld!

2½ cups granulated sugar
5 cups cake flour
2 cups bread flour
8½ tsp. baking powder
1/4 tsp. salt
1¾ cups vegetable shortening or oil
6 eggs
1½ cups water
1/4 tsp. vanilla
1/8 tsp. lemon extract
Fondant (see recipe)

Preheat oven to 370°. Place all dry ingredients in a mixing bowl. Add liquids slowly and mix until smooth. Place in a pastry bag with plain round tip and pipe into 2½-inch round pieces. Bake for 10 to 15 minutes until done. Cool completely. When cool, coat half of each cookie with plain fondant and let dry. When dry, coat the other half with chocolate fondant.

Fondant

3 cups confectioners' sugar
water
1/8 cup unsweetened cocoa

Mix confectioners' sugar with water until it is a creamy consistency. Divide mixture into 2 portions and add cocoa to one of them.

About the Chef

Name: Deborah Kaplan   **Education/Training:** self-taught

Hometown: Smithtown, NY   **Hobbies:** music, Latin dancing

Favorite Food to Eat and Prepare: avocado, broccoli di rape

Favorite Cookbook: anything edited by Craig Claiborne

Chocolate Macaroons with Raspberry Filling

Executive Chef Ed Doherty
La Campagne, Cherry Hill, NJ

4 egg whites
pinch of salt
12 oz. sugar
3 cups ground almonds
1 T. cocoa powder
raspberry preserves, jarred or your own recipe

Preheat oven to 400°. Whisk the egg whites lightly with a pinch of salt. In a separate bowl, mix the sugar and almonds thoroughly. Add the whites and cocoa powder. Pipe small heaps onto a greased baking tray and bake for 12 minutes. Let macaroons cool on a baker's wire rack.

To assemble, pipe raspberry jam into the centers of half the yield and then top with the remaining macaroons. Macaroons can be stored in an airtight container for 1 week.

Shortbread and Apple Chutney

Pastry Chef Kelly McGrath
City Tavern, Philadelphia, PA

8 oz. butter
1 cup brown sugar, firmly packed
1/2 cup molasses
1/2 tsp. salt
1 cinnamon stick
1 T. grated fresh ginger
zest and juice of 2 limes
6 tart apples (Granny Smith), peeled and cubed
1 cup raisins
1 cup chopped walnuts
Shortbread Cookies (see recipe)
caramel ice cream (optional)

Melt butter and add sugar, molasses, salt, cinnamon stick, ginger, and lime zest and juice. Bring mixture to a boil and add apples, raisins, and walnuts. Cook until apples are slightly soft but do not overcook. Place a shortbread triangle on plate and top with chutney. Add another triangle and more chutney; finish with a triangle. Drizzle syrup from chutney around plate and on top of dessert. Serve with caramel ice cream if desired.

Serves 8

Shortbread Cookies

12 oz. butter, softened
1 cup 10x sugar
3 cups all-purpose flour, sifted
1 tsp. salt
1 tsp. vanilla

Cream butter and sugar. Add flour and salt and combine well. Refrigerate dough 1 hour.

Preheat oven to 350°. Roll out dough and cut into triangle shapes. Bake for 15 to 20 minutes until golden. (Watch carefully as oven performance may vary.) Let sit until cool.

Yields 24 cookies

Vanilla Pana Cotta
with Oven-Roasted Strawberries

Pastry Chef Michael Vandergeest
Tony Clark's, Philadelphia, PA

4 gelatin sheets
3 cups heavy cream
1 cup whole milk
3 oz. sugar
2 Tahitian vanilla beans
2 pints strawberries, cleaned and cut in half
pinch of white pepper
finely julienned fresh mint to taste
lemon snap cookies (optional)

Soak gelatin sheets in cold water. Combine cream, milk, sugar, and vanilla beans in a saucepan and bring to a boil. Remove from heat, cover with plastic wrap, and steep for 45 minutes.

Add gelatin sheets. Strain mixture through a fine mesh strainer. Pour into 6 lightly oiled 4-oz. molds. Chill 4 to 6 hours.

Preheat oven to 325°. Combine strawberries, white pepper, and mint on a baking tray. Heat for 8 to 10 minutes. Serve on top of pana cotta. Garnish with additional fresh mint. Serve with lemon snap cookies if desired.

Serves 6

Harry's Crème Brûlée

Executive Chef David Leo Banks
Harry's Savoy Grill, Wilmington, DE

2 cups heavy whipping cream
1/4 cup granulated sugar
4 egg yolks
1 T. vanilla extract
3/4 cup granulated sugar (approximate)
3/4 cup brown sugar (approximate)

Preheat oven to 325°. Prepare a hot water bath for 4 (6-ounce) ramekins. Combine the cream and sugar in the top of a double boiler or in a saucepan over low heat. Heat to approximately 170°. Stir with a whip initially to combine cream and sugar; do not whip to froth.

In a small bowl, whisk the egg yolks. When cream/sugar mixture has reached desired temperature, whisk some of the hot mixture into the yolks to "temper" the yolks. Add a little at a time; stir with a whisk but do not froth. Return to hot cream/sugar mixture. Stir in the vanilla extract. Strain this mixture through a fine sieve. Skim air bubbles from top of custard mixture. Divide mixture evenly among the 4 ramekins; use a pitcher for this step.

Place ramekins in the hot water bath. Bake for approximately 30 minutes. DO NOT ALLOW WATER IN WATER BATH TO BOIL! Turn pan and allow to bake for approximately 15 minutes more. Remove ramekins from water bath and allow to cool. Refrigerate. Custard will firm up nicely under refrigeration.

Combine the topping sugars. Spread an even layer over the top of each ramekin. Heat under a hot broiler until sugar caramelizes.

Serves 4

VARIATIONS: Add 10 to 15 pieces of fresh blueberries or raspberries or blackberries to each ramekin before adding custard. You can make a chocolate Crème Brûlée by adding melted chocolate to the custard mixture.

Crème Brûlée
with Fresh Raspberries

Chef Steve Timlin
Garden State Park Clubhouse Restaurant, Cherry Hill, NJ

2 cups heavy whipping cream
4 large eggs, well-beaten
2 T. sugar
1/2 cup light brown sugar
1 pint fresh raspberries

Heat whipping cream in double boiler until hot. Pour cream slowly over the well-beaten eggs. Beat constantly while pouring. Return the mixture to the double boiler and stir in the sugar. Heat until the eggs thicken and the custard heavily coats a spoon. Divide mixture into 6 custard cups and chill overnight.

When well-chilled, cover custard with a 1/4-inch layer of light brown sugar. Place cups in a shallow baking dish and put dish under a hot broiler just long enough for the sugar to caramelize and form a crust. Rotate dish regularly to ensure even browning and eliminate scorching. Garnish with raspberries and serve at once.

Serves 6

White Chocolate Mousse

Pastry Chef Drew Smith
Rococo, Philadelphia, PA

6 oz. white chocolate, chopped
1½ cups heavy cream

Place the white chocolate into a bowl set over warm water (110° to 115°) until melted. Stir the melted chocolate until smooth. Keep the chocolate over the water. Meanwhile, whip cream in a separate bowl until soft peaks form.

Remove the melted white chocolate from over the water. Slowly fold in 1/3 of the whipped cream into the chocolate. (You will get the smoothest white chocolate mousse if you slowly incorporate the cold whipped cream into the warm white chocolate. Gradually lowering the temperature of the white chocolate will prevent it from "seizing" into an unusable mess.) Fold in the remaining cream in 2 more 1/3 additions. Serve chilled in a large bowl or individual serving dishes.

Serves 2 to 4

Bittersweet Chocolate Sauce

Pastry Chef Michael Vandergeest
Tony Clark's, Philadelphia, PA

14 oz. bittersweet chocolate, finely chopped
2 cups heavy cream
1 to 2 oz. Myers Dark Rum

Place chocolate in a bowl. In a saucepan, bring heavy cream to a boil; then pour over chocolate. Add rum and mix well.

Banana Bavarian Mousse

Pastry Chef Drew Smith
Rococo, Philadelphia, PA

"The Bavarian is flavored with banana extract. The flavor strength of banana extracts vary, so use this as a guideline and taste as you go."

2 gelatin sheets or 1 envelope powdered gelatin
3/4 cup milk
2 egg yolks
1/4 cup sugar
1 tsp. vanilla extract
1/2 to 1 tsp. banana extract to taste
1 cup heavy cream

Soften the gelatin sheets in cold water. If using the powdered gelatin, soak the gelatin in 1/4 cup cold water. Place the milk into a saucepan and bring to a boil. Remove from heat. Place the egg yolks into a bowl. Slowly pour the hot milk into the yolks, whisking as you pour. Add the sugar and the softened gelatin and whisk until dissolved. Add the vanilla and banana extracts.

Set the mixture over ice to cool, stirring occasionally. In a separate bowl, whip the cream until stiff peaks form. Stir the whipped cream into the cooled Bavarian mixture. Serve chilled in a large bowl or individual serving dishes.

Serves 2 to 4

Chocolate Mousse

Pastry Chef Drew Smith
Rococo, Philadelphia, PA

8 oz. semisweet chocolate, chopped
4 oz. unsalted butter
4 eggs, separated
1/8 tsp. cream of tartar or 1/8 tsp. lemon juice
1 tsp. sugar

Place the chocolate and butter into a bowl over warm water until melted. Whisk together until smooth. Remove bowl from over water and whisk in the eggs yolks. Set aside.

Place the eggs whites into a medium-sized bowl. Add the cream of tartar and beat with an electric mixer at low speed until frothy. Raise the speed to medium-high until the egg whites are stiff and shiny. Add the sugar and beat for another minute. Fold the beaten egg whites into the chocolate mixture until completely blended. Serve chilled in a large bowl or individual serving dishes.

Serves 2 to 4

NOTE: Eggs whites are easy to whip and overwhip. Many mixers are very powerful and when used at high speed, egg whites can overwhip. When beating egg whites, make sure your bowl and beaters are clean. Make certain that there are no bits of egg yolk in the whites or they won't whip correctly. Correctly beaten egg whites should be smooth, satiny, glossy, and creamy in appearance.

Irish Rice Pudding

Executive Chef/Owner Kathleen Sonsini
La Familia Sonsini, Medford, NJ

2 cups rice
10 cups half-and-half
1 cup sugar
2 tsp. pure vanilla extract
2 cups Bailey's Irish Cream

Rinse rice. Put half-and-half, sugar, and vanilla in a pot and bring to a boil. Add rice, stirring often over medium heat. When rice starts to absorb the liquid, add Bailey's Irish Cream. Continue cooking until rice has absorbed almost all the liquid (approximately 30 minutes). Serve warm or chilled.

About the Chef

Name: Kathleen Sonsini

Education/Training: self-taught

Inspirations/Influences: being able to create something

Hobbies: gardening, art

Family: husband and co-owner Frank, four kids, one grandchild, and one dog

Hometown: New Orleans, LA

Favorite Food to Eat: everything

Favorite Food to Prepare: breakfast

Favorite Cookbook: my collection of recipes culled from 25 years of reading cookbooks and magazines

Chocolate-Banana Bread Pudding

Pastry Chef Michael Vandergeest
Tony Clark's, Philadelphia, PA

☉

1 loaf moist banana bread (a recipe of your choice or from your favorite bakery)
Chocolate Custard (see recipe)
6 round lace cookies, 3 inches in diameter (available at your favorite bakery)
Bittersweet Chocolate Sauce (Recipe appears on page 249.)
6 ripe bananas, mashed
mint

Preheat oven to 350°. Place a sheet of parchment on a baking pan. Place six 2-inch round metal rings on sheet. Cube banana bread into 1/8-inch squares. Pack each round with bread.

Pour warm custard into rings. Allow bread to soak up custard and top with additional custard if needed. Bake for 12 to 15 minutes. Remove from oven and allow to rest for 10 to 15 minutes.

Place cookies on a baking sheet. Top with mashed bananas and sprinkle with sugar. Heat either under the broiler or with a torch, allowing sugar to caramelize.

Place pudding on dessert plate. Top with cookie and spoon warm sauce around pudding. Garnish with mint. Serve with malt ice cream if desired.

Serves 6

Chocolate Custard

1/4 cup unsalted butter, cubed
1½ lbs. semi-sweet chocolate, finely chopped
1½ cups heavy cream
1½ cups milk
5 whole eggs
3 egg yolks
2 oz. brown sugar, firmly packed

Place butter and chocolate in a bowl. Bring cream and milk to a boil in a saucepan. Pour over butter and chocolate. Mix eggs and yolks with brown sugar; then combine with warm milk mixture. Strain through a fine mesh strainer.

Summer Pudding

Pastry Chef Mary Ellen Hatch
Rose Tattoo Cafe, Philadelphia, PA

Angel Food Cake (see recipe)
2 pints strawberries, stemmed and quartered
1/2 cup sugar
2 pints blackberries
1 pint raspberries
1 pint necterberries, tayberries, or red currants
3 T. chambord or crème de cassis
1 tsp. lemon juice
pinch salt
whipped cream (optional)

Use either eight 6 ounce ramekins or a trifle bowl. If using ramekins, use a round, sharp cutter the same size as the inside of the ramekins to cut 24 pieces of angel food cake. If using a trifle bowl, cut a cardboard template (pattern) the same size as the inside of bowl. Use pattern to cut out 4 pieces of angel food cake.

Put strawberries and sugar in a saucepan and cook over low heat for about 10 minutes. Add other berries and continue cooking about 10 minutes more. Cool and add the chambord or crème de cassis, lemon juice, and salt to taste. Pour some berry sauce into ramekins or bowl just to cover bottom (do all 8 ramekins at once). Dip a piece of the base (cake) into the sauce in pan, saturating it. Place that over bottom of container. Spoon more sauce over that layer of base. Continue layering in this manner until the ramekins or bowl are overflowing slightly.

For ramekins: Line a cookie sheet with plastic wrap and place ramekins on top of the wrap. Cut another sheet of plastic wrap and place over the ramekins. Place another cookie sheet on top of the ramekins along with a 5-pound weight to compress the pudding. Refrigerate overnight. Unfold the individual puddings by running a paring knife along the inside edge of each ramekin and inverting them. Serve with or without whipped cream.

For trifle bowl: Cut a second cardboard circle. Wrap the cardboard circles in plastic wrap and place one on top of last layer of fruit in bowl. Be sure the cardboard fits inside the bowl. Wrap the trifle bowl in plastic wrap. Place second wrapped cardboard on top and put a 5-pound weight on top of cardboard. Refrigerate overnight. Leave pudding in bowl and scoop out with a rounded serving spoon. Serve with or without whipped cream.

Serves 8 as individual or trifle presentation

Angel Food Cake*

1 cup cake flour
1½ cup sugar
2 cups egg whites
1/2 tsp. salt
1½ tsp. cream of tartar
2 tsp. vanilla

Preheat oven to 375º. Sift flour and 3/4 cup sugar together 3 times. Whip egg whites on medium speed. Add salt and cream of tartar. Increase speed and add 3/4 cup sugar a little at a time. Whip until soft peaks form. (They should be stiff but not dry.) Transfer whites to a large bowl. Sift 1/3 of the flour/sugar mixture over egg whites. Fold in with balloon whip and repeat process 2 more times. Fold in vanilla. Pour into two 18 x 9-inch sheet pans and bake 30 minutes.

Serves 8

* This recipe is fat free.

About the Chef

Name: Mary Ellen Hatch

Education/Training: Bucks County Community College and La Vareen in Paris; also competed on the 1994 Bread Baking Team of the Coupe du Monde. This was the first time an American team was invited to join the competition.

Inspirations/Influences: French and New England styles

Hobbies: swimming, cooking, baking

Family: one brother, three sisters

Hometown: Levittown, PA

Favorite Food to Eat: risotto

Favorite Food to Prepare: New England-style desserts

Favorite Cookbook: *Star's Desserts*

Black Forest Crepes
with Cocoa Sorbet

Executive Chef Jim Coleman
Treetops Restaurant, Rittenhouse Hotel, Philadelphia, PA

⊚

"This dessert adapts the classic Black Forest cake, properly known as Schwarzwülder Kirschtorte. That rich and heavy dessert contains chocolate cake soaked in kirsch , sour cherries, and kirsch-flavored whipped cream. I have tried to mitigate the high calorie impact of the original by dropping the cream altogether and adapting the flavors of the cake into crepe form. It ready works!"

1½ cups pitted cherries
1/2 T. all-purpose flour
1/2 cup Merlot or other dry red wine
zest of 1/2 orange
3/4 cup all-purpose flour
2 T. cocoa powder
1 T. sugar
1 T. corn oil
1/3 cup lowfat (1%) milk
2 egg whites
Cocoa Sorbet (see recipe)

Combine first 4 ingredients in a saucepan, cover, and cook over low heat for about 15 minutes, stirring constantly, until the cherries are tender and the sauce has thickened. Remove from heat and set aside.

To prepare the crepes, sift the 3/4 cup flour, cocoa, and sugar into a mixing bowl and set aside. In a separate mixing bowl, combine corn oil and milk. Slowly add milk mixture to flour mixture, stirring constantly to prevent lumping. Whisk the egg whites until foamy and fold into the crepe batter.

Heat a nonstick sauté pan until very hot. Pour enough batter to just cover the bottom of the hot pan and let brown for 20 to 30 seconds on each side. Remove the crepe, place on a warm plate, and keep warm. Repeat for the remaining batter. Stack the crepes, using pieces of waxed paper to separate each crepe.

Place a large scoop of the sorbet in the center of each serving plate. With a spoon, make a small indentation in the middle of each sorbet. Fold each crepe like a handkerchief, creating a point with the center of the crepe, and press into the indentation in the sorbet. Spoon the cherries over the crepes and the plate and serve immediately.   *Serves 4*

Cocoa Sorbet

2 cups water
2/3 cup sugar
2 T. cocoa powder
1/4 cup freshly squeezed orange juice
1 T. kirsch or other cherry liqueur

Combine the water, sugar, and cocoa in a saucepan and stirring often, bring to a boil. Remove from the heat and let cool. Stir in the orange juice and cherry liqueur and pour into the tub of an ice cream maker. Freeze according to the manufacturer's directions.

About the Chef

Name: Jim Coleman

Education/Training: Culinary Institute of America; El Centro College

Inspirations/Influences: the excitement of mixing the flavors of the world

Hobbies: fishing, football fanatic

Family: married to Candace Hagan, two children — Katie (12) and Jimmy (7)

Hometown: Dallas, TX

Favorite Food to Eat: the fried chicken I grew up on; all kinds of ethnic and Asian foods

Favorite Food to Prepare: everything — enjoy experimenting and the challenge of cooking

Favorite Cookbook: I own over 1000 cookbooks; love the older ones especially.

Strawberry Napoleon

Executive Chef Ed Doherty
La Campagne, Cherry Hill, NJ

1 square (12 x 12-inch) puff pastry
1 quart milk
1 vanilla bean
4½ oz. sugar
4 egg yolks
1½ oz. flour, sifted
2 pints strawberries, sliced
1 cup whipped cream
10 tsp. confectioners' sugar

Preheat oven to 450°. Bake the whole sheet of puff pastry for 20 minutes. (Place a weight on top to keep it flat.)

Boil milk with vanilla bean. Reserve. In a bowl, whisk the sugar and yolks together until the mixture becomes white; then add the flour. Pour in milk and stir well until smooth. Return mixture to the milk pot. Stir over low heat until it gets thick.

After baking, cut the puff pastry into 12 squares, each measuring 4x3-inches. Put pastry cream into a pastry bag and pipe cream onto 4 of the squares. Place some sliced strawberries on top of the cream and pipe some whipped cream into the center. Using 4 more squares, make a second level and repeat the process. Powder the last 4 rectangles with the confectioners' sugar and place them on top to complete the assembly. Serve with a chocolate or fruit (any type) sauce.

Serves 4

Star Anise Alfajor

Executive Chef Guillermo Pernot
Vega Grill, Manayunk, PA

✖

4 T. sugar
2 cups cake flour
2 cups all-purpose flour
4 tsp. cream of tartar
2 tsp. baking soda
1 tsp. salt
pinch of nutmeg
1 tsp. ground star anise
8 oz. unsalted butter, cold and diced into 1-inch pieces
1/2 cup milk
1 cup heavy cream
1 pint heavy cream, whipped
1½ cups Dulce de Leche (see recipe)
2 T. confectioners' sugar
1 pint fresh berries

Preheat oven to 400°. Sift all dry ingredients together in a large bowl. Toss butter into bowl and cut with a dough cutter until it resembles a coarse cornmeal texture. Add milk and heavy cream and work until soft. Do not overwork.

Roll out to 3/4-inch thickness and cut into 3½-inch circles. Place in oven for 12 to 15 minutes until lightly browned. Remove from oven and cool for 20 minutes.

Cut pieces in half horizontally and fill with dulce de leche and whipped cream. Dust with confectioners' sugar and place onto plates garnished with fresh berries.

Serves 12

Dulce de Leche

3 cans sweetened condensed milk

Place cans in a pot with enough water to cover. Bring to a boil and reduce heat to slow simmer. Simmer for 3 hours, replenishing water as needed. Let can cool; then open and serve.

Yields 1½ cups

Lemon Poached Pears
with Berry Sauce

Chef/Owner Donna Leahy
Inn at Twin Linden, Churchtown, PA

⑤

"This elegant fruit dish is inherently low in calories and fat and may be made ahead and refrigerated until serving."

8 cups water
1 cup sugar
1/4 cup lemon juice
6 medium-sized firm pears
Berry Sauce (see recipe)
2 tsp. lemon zest
1/4 cup fresh raspberries

In a large stock pot, combine the water, sugar, and lemon juice. Bring the liquid to a boil. In the meantime, peel and core the pears, leaving the stem attached. Add the pears to the boiling liquid and reduce the heat to a simmer. Poach the pears for 12 to 15 minutes or until tender when pierced with a fork or sharp knife point. Remove from heat and cool completely. Refrigerate the pears in the liquid until ready to serve.

To serve, spoon a pool of sauce onto each plate and set a pear on top of the sauce. Drizzle the remaining sauce on top. Sprinkle lemon zest onto each pear and divide fresh raspberries evenly among plates.

Serves 6

Berry Sauce

1 cup raspberries
1/2 cup blackberries
1 cup strawberries, hulled and quartered
4 T. fresh orange juice
1/4 cup sugar (optional)

Combine the ingredients in a food processor or blender and process until smooth. Strain to remove seeds and refrigerate until ready to serve.

Adapted from *Morning Glories: Recipes for Breakfast, Brunch & Beyond from an American Country Inn* by Donna Leahy (Rizzoli International, 1996).

Summertime Rhubarb Mango Crumb

Executive Chef/Owner Bill Beck
Pompano Grille, Philadelphia, PA

1/4 cup butter
2 1 x 1-inch chunks ginger
3 cups chopped rhubarb
1 cup diced mango
1 cup sugar
1/4 cup flour
1/2 tsp. cinnamon
1 cup flour
1/2 cup crushed fried plantains
1 cup brown sugar, firmly packed
1/2 cup butter, melted

Preheat oven to 375°. Melt 1/4 cup butter in a large sauté pan. Add the ginger and rhubarb and sauté until it begins to be translucent. Add the mango. Cook for about 1 minute more. Remove the ginger. Combine sugar, cinnamon, and 1/4 cup flour. Add it to the rhubarb mixture and pour into a buttered 8x8x2-inch pan.

Combine 1 cup flour, plantain chips, and brown sugar. Add melted butter and mix with a fork. Sprinkle over the rhubarb mixture and bake 25 minutes.

Yields 16 2-inch squares

Harvest Fruit Crisp

Chef/Proprietor Kevin von Klause
White Dog Cafe, Philadelphia, PA

"Harvest fruits are all of the gorgeous fruits the farmers bring us: apples, pears, apricots, grapes, cranberries, cherries, blueberries—any combination of them can be baked into a bubbling crisp that will set your mouth to watering. This dessert is terrific for crowds; we make it when we have 80 people coming for a Table Talk dinner, and they all must be served dessert at the same time. It can be made in the morning and warmed just before serving. Top it with some vanilla ice cream or a dollop of whipped cream and a sprinkle of cinnamon."

4 large firm tart apples such as Granny Smith, Macintosh, or Ida Red,
   cored and sliced
3 ripe pears such as Bartlett or Bosc, cored and sliced
1½ cups seedless red grapes, stems removed
1½ cups fresh cranberries or thawed frozen cranberries
1½ cups granulated sugar
3 T. cornstarch
2 tsp. ground cinnamon
1 tsp. ground ginger
1/2 tsp. ground cloves
Crumb Topping (see recipe)

Preheat the oven to 350°. Butter an 11 x 9-inch baking dish.

Combine the apples, pears, grapes, and cranberries in a large mixing bowl. In a separate bowl, combine the sugar, cornstarch, cinnamon, ginger, and cloves and mix well. Add the sugar mixture to the fruit and toss to coat evenly.

Spread the fruit into the prepared baking dish. Cover with the crumb topping. Bake on the middle rack of the oven until the juice is thick and the topping is browned, about 50 minutes. If the topping browns before the fruit is cooked, cover with foil and bake until the fruit is tender. Serve warm or let cool to room temperature, cover, and refrigerate for up to 2 days. Rewarm before serving.

Serves 6

Crumb Topping

1 cup firmly packed light brown sugar
1 cup all-purpose flour
1½ cups rolled oats
pinch of salt
1 tsp. ground cinnamon
1/2 tsp. ground ginger
1 cup coarsely chopped pecans
8 T. (1 stick) unsalted butter, cold and cubed

Combine the brown sugar, flour, oats, salt, cinnamon, ginger, pecans, and butter in the bowl of an electric mixer fitted with a paddle attachment. Blend on low speed until the butter is incorporated and the topping is the consistency of coarse meal, about 2 minutes. Reserve for topping.

Ricotta Cheesecake

Pastry Chef Kelly McGrath
City Tavern, Philadelphia, PA

standard pie dough for 10-inch pan
3 lb. ricotta cheese
1/3 cup all-purpose flour
1 cup granulated sugar
1/2 cup amaretto
1¼ tsp. vanilla extract
9 eggs
1¼ cup heavy cream
3 tsp. orange zest

Preheat oven to 300°. Roll out pie dough to fit a 10-inch removable bottom (springform) pan. Spray bottom and sides of pan so dough doesn't stick. Refrigerate dough while making cheesecake.

In a large bowl, mix ricotta cheese, flour, sugar, amaretto, and vanilla. Add eggs and cream slowly; then add zest. Pour mixture into pan and bake approximately 1 hour until cake is set and light brown on top. Let cake cool completely before removing sides.

Serves 8

About the Chef

Name: Kelly McGrath

Education/Training: The Restaurant School

Inspirations/Influences: exotic ingredients with basic technique

Hobbies: cooking, reading

Family: large Italian and Irish family

Hometown: "South Philly"

Favorite Food to Eat: Thai and Chinese

Favorite Food to Prepare: chambord and chocolate frozen souffle

Favorite Cookbook: *Grande Finale*

Pumpkin Cheese Cake

Owner Joe Lovallo
New World Cafe, Cinnaminson, NJ

2 lb. cream cheese
4 eggs
1 cup pumpkin
2 cups sugar
1 T. cinnamon
1 T. nutmeg
pinch of salt
Gingersnap Crust (see recipe)

Preheat oven to 350°. In a mixing bowl, whip cream cheese until smooth. Add eggs and pumpkin. In a separate bowl, combine sugar, cinnamon, nutmeg, and salt. Add to wet ingredients. Pour mixture into prepared (greased, lined, and crust ready) springform pan. Place in a water bath and bake for 50 minutes.

Serves 10 to 12

Gingersnap Crust

1/2 lb. butter
7 oz. sugar
1 tsp. vanilla
1 egg
4 oz. gingersnap cookies, finely ground
12 oz. flour
1 tsp. baking powder

Combine butter, sugar, vanilla, and egg in a mixing bowl. Whip with paddle attachment until smooth. Add cookies. Mix flour and baking powder in a separate bowl; add to mixer. Lightly grease a 10-inch springform pan. Remove mixture from bowl and place in pan. Cover with another sheet of wrap and press with fingers to mold crust to line the pan. Remove plastic wrap.

Double Chocolate Banana Mousse Cake

Pastry Chef Drew Smith
Rococo, Philadelphia, PA

"Each layer of this cake — chocolate mousse studded with bananas, white chocolate mousse, and banana Bavarian mousse — is pretty good on its own. Combined, they fuse into a delicious play of flavor and texture. Since the cake is comprised of three layers, it can be assembled in stages over the course of two to three days. The cake is more mousse than "cake." Actually only one layer of chocolate buttermilk cake sits on the bottom. You will need to have the cake ready to use before you begin assembly."

Chocolate Buttermilk Cake (Recipe appears on page 267.)
2 T. dark rum (optional)
Chocolate Mousse (Recipe appears on page 251.)
3 to 4 bananas
White Chocolate Mousse (Recipe appears on page 249.)
Banana Bavarian Mousse (Recipe appears on page 250.)

Cut a 1/4-inch thick slice from the chocolate buttermilk cake and fit it into the bottom of a 10-inch springform pan. Brush the cake with dark rum if desired. Spread 2/3 of completed chocolate mousse onto the cake. Slice bananas into thirds crosswise; then halve each piece lengthwise. Press banana pieces into the mousse. Spread the remaining mousse over the bananas, cover, and refrigerate.

Spread the completed white chocolate mousse into the pan to cover the chocolate mousse. Cover and refrigerate.

Pour the completed banana Bavarian mousse into the pan over the white chocolate mousse layer. Do not cover. Refrigerate.

When ready to serve, remove cake from refrigerator. Warm a pairing knife under hot water; then wipe dry. Carefully run the warm knife around the outside edge of the pan before loosening the lock of the springform pan. Slice the cake with a warm knife, wiping the knife between cuts.

Serves 12 to 14

Chocolate Buttermilk Cake

Pastry Chef Drew Smith
Rococo, Philadelphia, PA

1 1/3 cups cocoa powder
2 1/3 cups all-purpose flour
2 2/3 cups sugar
1 tsp. baking soda
1 tsp. baking powder
1 tsp. salt
1 1/3 cups strong coffee, room temperature
1 cup buttermilk
2 eggs
2/3 cup vegetable oil

Preheat oven to 350°. Line a 10-inch round cake pan with a circle of wax or parchment paper. Grease and lightly flour the paper and the cake pan. Set aside.

Sift all the dry ingredients into a large mixing bowl. Mix together by hand until a uniform brown color is attained. In a separate mixing bowl, combine the coffee, buttermilk, eggs, and oil. Whisk until blended. Pour the liquid ingredients into the dry ingredients. Mix; then whisk the batter to remove any lumps. Pour the batter into the prepared pan. Place the pan onto the middle rack in the oven. Bake for 1 hour or until done. The cake will be firm to the touch; a cake tester or knife point inserted into the cake should come out clean. Remove cake from the oven and let cool.

The cake can be wrapped and refrigerated until needed. The cake will keep 2 to 3 days in the refrigerator or up to 2 to 3 weeks in the freezer.

Kahlúa Flourless Fudge Cake

Chef/Proprietor Ben McNamara
Isabella's, Philadelphia, PA

7 extra large egg whites
1 cup sugar
1/2 lb. unsalted butter, cut into small pieces
1/2 lb. European bittersweet chocolate, broken into small pieces
1 T. pure vanilla extract
1 T. espresso
3 T. Kahlúa

Preheat oven to 300°. Grease and flour a 10-inch springform pan.

Place egg whites and sugar into a mixer and whip into firm peaks. Meanwhile, melt butter over medium heat. When melted, add chocololate, stirring occasionally until smooth. Quickly add vanilla, espresso, Kahlúa, and chocolate butter mixture to the egg white mixture, gently folding until smooth. Pour into prepared cake pan and bake on center rack for 40 minutes.

Remove from oven. Wait 5 minutes and press sides down so the top of the cake is even. Cool and refrigerate for 4 hours or until set. Remove cake from pan and cut with a hot knife into 8 pieces. Serve with fresh berries and vanilla ice cream if desired.

Serves 8

About the Chef

Name: Ben McNamara

Education/Training: Westminster Culinary Institute, London, England

Inspirations/Influences: fresh ingredients

Hobbies: cooking, checkers, rollerblading

Family: married, two children — Nicholas and Isabelle

Hometown: Philadelphia, PA

Favorite Food to Eat: Indian, Greek

Favorite Food to Prepare: French, Italian

Favorite Cookbook: Becoming a Chef

Blackberry Cream Streusel Cake

Chef/Owner Donna Leahy
Inn at Twin Linden, Churchtown, PA

"This deliciously moist coffee cake may be made with other flavors of preserves."

2¼ cups all-purpose flour
3/4 cup sugar
3/4 cup butter, softened
1/2 cup sliced almonds
1 tsp. baking powder
1 tsp. baking soda
1 tsp. salt
1 cup sour cream
2 eggs
2 tsp. almond extract
8 oz. cream cheese
1 cup seedless blackberry preserves

Preheat the oven to 350°. Grease and flour a 9- or 10-inch springform pan. In a large bowl, combine the flour and 1/2 cup of sugar. With a pastry blender, cut in the butter until crumbly.

Remove 1 cup of the crumb mixture; stir the almonds into the reserved crumb mixture and set aside. To the remaining crumble mixture, add the baking powder, soda, and salt and combine well. In a separate bowl, whisk together 3/4 cup of sour cream, 1 egg, and 1 teaspoon almond extract. Stir the sour cream mixture into the dry mixture and combine well. Spread the batter into the pan evenly.

With an electric mixer, beat together the cream cheese, remaining sour cream, 1 egg, and remaining sugar. Mix in remaining almond extract. Pour the mixture over the batter. Spoon the preserves evenly over the cheese mixture. Sprinkle the reserved crumb mixture over top. Bake for 45 minutes or until firm and lightly browned.

Serves 8

Adapted from *Morning Glories: Recipes for Breakfast, Brunch & Beyond from an American Country Inn* by Donna Leahy (Rizzoli International, 1996).

Carrot Cake with Orange Glaze Icing

Chef De Cuisine Fritz Blank
Deux Cheminées, Philadelphia, PA

⊚

"There are many recipes for carrot cake. Some call for cooked carrots and some for raw; some have nuts; some have raisins; some have both nuts and raisins. Many recipes for carrot cake are mediocre; a few are good. This recipe is excellent!"

2 cups flour
1 tsp. salt
1½ tsp. baking powder
1 tsp. baking soda
3 tsp. ground cinnamon
1½ tsp. ground nutmeg
5 cups grated raw carrots
2 cups sugar
4 egg yolks
1½ cups vegetable oil (or peanut oil)
1/2 cup chopped pecans (or substitute English walnuts, black walnuts, or others)
4 egg whites

Preheat oven 350°. Butter and bread crumb a 3-quart turban mold. In a large bowl, thoroughly mix the flour, salt, baking powder, baking soda, and spices. Pass through a sieve to insure an even distribution, especially the baking soda. Grate the carrots either by hand using a box grater or a Robot Coupe.® In a separate large bowl (5-quart Kitchen Aid® mixer bowl), beat the sugar and egg yolks until light and fluffy. Add the oil, carrots, and pecans; combine well by hand and fold into the mixture of dry ingredients. Using a dry, clean, grease-free bowl, whip the egg whites until stiff peaks form. Fold the beaten egg whites, 1/3 at a time, into the base mixture. Pour batter into the prepared turbian mold. Bake for about 1 hour "until knife comes out clean." Allow to cool before unmolding!!

Orange Glaze Icing

2 cups sugar
1/2 cup cornstarch
2 cups orange juice
2 tsp. lemon juice
1/2 tsp. salt
4 T. grated orange zest
4 T. butter

In a saucepan, off heat, combine and blend together the sugar and cornstarch. Whisk the orange and lemon juice into the sugar and mix until smooth. Incorporate the salt, zest, and butter. Place over low heat and, whisking constantly, cook until thick, smooth, and glossy. Allow to cool completely; then pour evenly over carrot cake.

Amazing Apple Spice Cake

Jennifer Bingham Ballou
Private Resident Chef, Whitemarsh Township, PA

3 cups all-purpose flour
1 tsp. baking soda
1 tsp. salt
1 tsp. cinnamon
1/2 tsp. nutmeg
1½ cups vegetable or corn oil
2 cups sugar
3 large eggs, room temperature
2 tsp. vanilla extract
1¼ cups chopped pecans
2 cups peeled and finely chopped apples (Golden Delicious)
Brown Sugar Topping (see recipe)

Preheat oven to 325º. Grease and dust a 10-inch Bundt pan. Sift flour, baking soda, salt, cinnamon, and nutmeg into a small bowl. In a large bowl, beat oil, sugar, eggs, and vanilla on medium speed for 3 to 4 minutes or until well blended. Gradually add flour mixture, beating until smooth. Gently fold in apples and pecans. Pour batter into prepared pan and bake for 1 hour and 20 minutes or until tests done. Cool on rack for 20 minutes. While cake is still warm, drizzle brown sugar topping over top.

Serves 20 to 24

Brown Sugar Topping

1/2 cup butter or margarine
1/2 cup light brown sugar, firmly packed
2 tsp. milk

Combine all ingredients in a small pot and bring to boil over medium heat. Cook 2 minutes, stirring continuously. Immediately spoon mixture over warm cake.

About the Chef

Name: Jennifer Ballou

Education/Training: Le Cordon Bleu, London, England

Inspirations/Influences: fresh local ingredients, freshly ground spices

Hobbies: entertaining, friends, travel, tennis

Family: As a child I was always encouraged by my parents to try everything on my plate so as to broaden my palate.

Hometown: Chester, VT

Favorite Food to Eat: seafood of any form

Favorite Food to Prepare: soups with fresh breads

Favorite Cookbook: I rarely refer to one; but if I had to choose one in particular, it would be *Patricia Wells at Home in Provence.*

Lemon Poppyseed Cake

Pastry Chef Trish Brennan
Friday Saturday Sunday Restaurant, Philadelphia, PA

1½ cups sugar
9 T. unsalted butter
4 eggs
2 cups all-purpose flour
2½ tsp. baking powder
1/2 tsp. salt
3/4 cup milk
3/4 cup poppyseeds
1½ tsp. vanilla extract
grated lemon zest of 3 lemons
Lemon Glaze (see recipe)
confectioners' sugar

Preheat oven to 325°. Butter and flour a Bundt pan. Cream together the butter and sugar until light and fluffy. Add eggs, one at a time, to butter and sugar; mix after each addition. Sift together flour, baking powder, and salt in a bowl. Add the dry ingredients alternately with milk. Fold in poppyseeds, vanilla extract, and lemon zest. Pour batter into pan. Bake 50 to 60 minutes. Cool cake for 15 minutes and unmold. Poke holes on top and pour lemon glaze over the cake. Cool and dust with confectioners' sugar.

Lemon Glaze

1/2 cup fresh lemon juice
1/2 cup sugar

Combine ingredients in a saucepan and bring to a boil. Cool before serving.

French Apple Tart

Executive Chef Ed Doherty
La Campagne, Cherry Hill, NJ

6 Granny Smith apples, peeled
2 oz. butter
1 vanilla bean
Shortcrust (see recipe)
sugar

Cut 3 apples into quarters and put them in a small pot with 1.5 ounces of butter and the vanilla bean. Add a touch of water and cover with a lid. Cook for 25 minutes or until soft. Mash into a sauce. Spread the apple sauce on the bottom of the crust. Slice the remaining 3 apples into thin slices and cover the filling. Sprinkle some sugar on top and dot with the remaining butter. Bake in a preheated 450° oven for 20 minutes. Serve warm or at room temperature.

Shortcrust

9 oz. flour
1 pinch salt
3 oz. sugar
4.5 oz. cold butter
1 egg
cold water

Combine flour, salt, and sugar in a bowl. Cut in butter. Mix in egg and enough water to form a ball. Let sit for 2 hours. Preheat oven to 400°. Line a 10-inch tart pan with the dough and bake for 10 minutes.

Lemon Tart

Executive Chef Joel Gaughan
Braddock's Tavern, Medford, NJ

1 prebaked Sweet Pastry Shell (see recipe)
9 eggs
14 oz. sugar
zest of 2 lemons
juice of 5 lemons
9 oz. heavy cream

Preheat oven to 250°. Whisk eggs with the sugar and the lemon zest. Stir in lemon juice and then fold in the cream. Remove any froth from the top of the mixture. Pour the filling into the pastry shell and bake for 30 to 35 minutes.

Serves 8

About the Chef

Name: Joel Gaughan

Education/Training: Atlantic County College

Inspirations/Influences: eating great food

Hobbies: stunt kites, kayaking, camping

Family: married, two children — daughter Lianna and son Jonathon

Hometown: Medford Lakes, NJ

Favorite Food to Eat: French food

Favorite Food to Prepare: French cuisine

Favorite Cookbook: *Simply French*
by Joel Robuchon

Sweet Pastry Shell

1 plump moist vanilla bean
4 T. unsalted butter, softened
1/2 cup confectioners' sugar, sifted
2 large egg yolks, room temperature
1 cup plus 2 T. all-purpose flour, sifted
pinch of salt

Flatten the vanilla bean and cut it in half, lengthwise. With a small spoon, scrape out the seeds and place them in the bowl of a food processor.

Add the butter to the food processor and mix until very light, smooth, and well aerated. Add the sugar and process until thoroughly blended. The mixture should have the consistency of a thick frosting. Add the egg yolks and process to blend. Add 1 cup of flour and salt and process just until the flour is incorporated. (If the dough is exceptionally sticky, add remaining flour and quickly process again.) The dough should not form a ball. Do not overprocess.

Transfer the dough to a sheet of waxed paper. With your hands, gently form the dough into a ball and flatten it into a circle. Wrap and refrigerate for at least 1 hour or up to 24 hours.

Preheat oven to 425°. Butter a 9 x 1½-inch round tart pan. Remove dough from refrigerator. Place on plastic wrap that is large enough to accomodate a 14-inch circle of dough.

Flatten dough ball into circle and cover with another piece of plastic wrap. Roll out dough to a 14-inch circle. Remove top layer of plastic wrap.

Roll dough around rolling pin (Do not worry if dough breaks and falls apart.) Place dough in pan and unroll starting at one edge. If dough falls apart, press together with fingertips. Line shell with dough and crimp edges.

Place foil inside pie shell on top of dough and fill with dried beans. Bake for 10 minutes. Remove beans and foil and bake for another 8 minutes or until golden brown.

Fresh Fruit Tarts

Head Pastry Chef Diane Nussbaum
La Patisserie Francaise, Haddonfield, NJ

1 package frozen puff pastry dough
1 cup heavy cream
1/4 cup sugar
Pastry Cream (see recipe)
apricot jam, warmed and strained
fresh fruit (pineapple, strawberries, kiwi, mango, grapes, bananas)

Roll out defrosted puff pastry dough to an 1/8-inch thickness. Dough should measure about 2 inches larger than tart pan to be used. Ease dough into pan, making edges slightly thicker than the base. Prick entire bottom of tart with a fork. Put shell in freezer for about 1/2 hour to relax dough. Bake in preheated 375° oven until dough is golden brown, about 20 to 25 minutes.

Beat heavy cream with sugar until light peaks form. Add 2 cups pastry cream(custard) to whipped cream and mix thoroughly. Place mixture in baked pastry shell. Clean and cut desired fruits. Arrange nicely on the custard. Brush apricot jam, thinned with water if needed, onto fruits. Refrigerate until serving time.

Serves 12 to 14

Pastry Cream

4 cups milk
1 cup sugar
7 whole eggs
2 egg yolks
3/4 cup cornstarch

Heat milk and 1/2 cup of sugar to just boiling. In a separate bowl, beat eggs, egg yolks, and remaining sugar for 3 to 5 minutes. Add cornstarch and beat until combined. When milk has come to a boil, take 1 cup of it and add to egg mixture, beating constantly. Now add egg mixture to hot milk, stirring constantly. Turn heat to medium and stir egg-milk mixture until custard is thick. Be careful not to let the bottom burn.

Remove from heat and put in a bowl. Coat top of custard with butter to prevent "skin" from forming. Cover surface of custard directly with plastic wrap. Cool completely. Will keep 1 week in refrigerator.

Old Fashioned Apple Pie

Owner Julie Van DeGraaf
Pink Rose Pastry Shop, Philadelphia, PA

2 cups flour
1/4 cup cake flour
1/4 tsp. baking powder
8 oz. cold butter, cut into small pieces
5 to 6 T. water
4 T. butter
1/4 cup brandy
1 T. cinnamon
1/4 tsp. nutmeg
1/4 tsp. cloves
1/4 tsp. ginger
10 Granny Smith apples, peeled and sliced 1/2 inch thick

Combine flours and baking powder in a mixing bowl. Add butter. Beat with a flat paddle for about 10 minutes or until dough looks crumbly. Leave mixer on and add water just until dough comes together, about 3 minutes. Chill dough for 30 minutes. Cut dough in half and set one portion aside. Roll out bottom crust to 1/4 inch thick and fit into a 10-inch pie shell.

Melt butter in a heavy saucepan. Add brandy, spices, and apples and sauté for 15 minutes. Cool.

Preheat oven to 450°. Pour apple mixture into bottom crust. Roll out top crust using remaining dough. Cover apples and crimp the edge. Bake for approximately 45 minutes.

Brunch

Tarragon and Fresh Corn Cakes
  with Smoked Salmon and Caviar 283
Asian Spiced Gravlax with Curry Oil and
  Sesame Seed-Ginger Blinis 284
Open-faced Salmon B.L.T 286
Salmon Loaf 287
Southwestern Smoked Salmon Roll Ups 288
Salmon and Whitefish Terrine 289
Crabmeat Cheesecake with Pecan Crust 290
Crab and Tomato Napolean with Goat Cheese Vinaigrette 292
Cedarbrook Imperial 293
Crisp Cornmeal-crusted Oysters, Baby Greens
  and Apple Vinaigrette 294
Escargots in Pastry with Pernod, Garlic and Cream 296
Southwestern Crepes 297
Stuffed Orange Zest Crepes with Strawberry Orange Glaze 298
Rolled Basil Souffle with Roasted Red Pepper Coulis 300
Poached Figs with French Toast in Port Wine 302
Tamale Dulce 303
Biscuits with Fresh Cream and Berries 304
Metropolitan Millet Muffins 305
Banana-Walnut Bread 306
Nutty Chocolate Tea Loaf 307

Tarragon and Fresh Corn Cakes with Smoked Salmon and Caviar

Executive Chef Allyson Thurber
Striped Bass, Philadelphia, PA

5½ cups fresh corn kernels
10 egg yolks
1/2 cup all-purpose flour
1½ T. kosher salt
1½ T. fresh ground black pepper
2 T. minced garlic
2 T. chopped fresh tarragon
2 oz. olive oil
1 lb. smoked salmon, sliced
1 cup crème fraîche
4 oz. salmon caviar
4 oz. American sturgeon caviar
2 T. chopped chives

Combine corn, eggs, flour, salt, pepper, garlic, and tarragon and let rest for 10 minutes. In a preheated sauté pan, add oil and bring to a medium heat. Drop corn mixture by tablespoon into oil and flatten each to 2-inch circles. Lightly brown and then turn. Remove and drain on paper towels.

Corn cakes may be made ahead of time, then lightly heated in a preheated 350º oven for 5 minutes. Top each with smoked salmon, then crème fraîche and small amounts of both caviars. Garnish with chopped chives. Yummmmmmm!

Serves 6 to 8

About the Chef

Name: Allyson Thurber

Education/Training: Culinary Institute of America

Hobbies: gardening, cats, white water rafting **Hometown:** Sacramento, CA

Favorite Food to Eat: baguette with sun-dried tomato olive pesto, chicken tacos

Favorite Food to Prepare: BBQ

Favorite Cookbook: *Fish and Shellfish* by James Peterson and *An American Place* by Larry Forgione

Asian Spiced Gravlax with Curry Oil and Sesame Seed-Ginger Blinis

Chef/Owner Philippe Chin
Chanterelles, Philadelphia, PA

1/2 lb. kosher salt
1/4 lb. sugar
1 T. cracked black pepper
3 T. Chinese five-spice powder
1 lb. center-cut salmon side, deboned, skin on
1 lb. mashed potatoes
5 eggs
1 oz. milk
1 oz. heavy cream
1 pinch baking powder
3/4 oz. grated ginger, skin on
1 tsp. toasted black sesame seed
1 tsp. toasted white sesame seed
1 T. extra virgin olive oil
Curry Oil (see recipe)

Combine salt, sugar, pepper and 2 tablespoons Chinese five-spice powder. Pour half of the mixture on a sheet pan. Place salmon on top and cover with the remaining mixture. Cover with plastic wrap and refrigerate for 36 hours. After marinated, remove salmon from pan and soak in cold water for 15 minutes. Dry the fish and sprinkle with remaining five-spice powder. Put aside until ready to serve.

In a large mixing bowl, whisk next 8 ingredients together until smooth. Pre-heat large skillet pan with olive oil over medium heat. Spoon approximately 1 tablespoon of batter for each blini into the skillet (blini should be silver dollar size). Cook blinis for approximately 2 minutes per side. Blinis can be made in advance and kept warm in the oven before serving.

Slice thin slivers of salmon on an angle. Roll salmon to form a rosette, place on top of warm blini, and drizzle with curry oil.

Serves 8

Curry Oil

1/2 cup vegetable oil
1 T. curry powder
2 bay leaves, cracked
salt and pepper

In a small saucepan over medium heat, whisk the curry into the oil. Add cracked bay leaves and salt and pepper; simmer slowly for 15 minutes. Strain.

About the Chef

Name: Philippe Chin

Education/Training: Restaurant School, Paris, France

Inspirations/Influences: great ingredients

Hobbies: Harley Davidson motorcycle, snowboarding, windsurfing

Family: single

Hometown: Paris, France

Favorite Food to Eat: ethnic

Favorite Food to Prepare: fish

Favorite Cookbook: *Escoffier*

Open-faced Salmon B.L.T

Executive Chef David Leo Banks
Harry's Savoy Grill, Wilmington, DE

☾

4 small fresh plum tomatoes
1 tsp. salt
1 tsp. freshly ground black pepper
2 tsp. balsamic vinegar
fresh basil and oregano, chopped (optional)
2 T. capers, drained
1½ cups mayonnaise
juice of 2 lemons
8 slices good quality smoked bacon
4 5-oz. boneless salmon fillets
butter, oil, or nonstick spray for grilling
4 slices sunflower honey wheat bread or Branola
4 pieces green leaf lettuce, washed and dried
flat-leaf Italian parsley, washed and dried

Slice the tomatoes into 4 slices per tomato. Sprinkle each slice with salt, pepper, and vinegar. Toss gently in a bowl with the herbs. Allow to stand at room temperature.

Crush the capers slightly and combine with the mayonnaise. Stir in lemon juice to taste; set aside. Cook the bacon in a single layer in a 350° oven. Do not allow the bacon to get too crisp. Drain on paper towels and set aside. Leave the oven on.

Skin the fillets. Use a charcoal grill or a raised-grill skillet on high heat. Coat the salmon fillets with the butter, oil, or nonstick spray. Grill, skin side up, until deep brown grill marks appear on the meat side of the fish. Turn the fish over and briefly grill the other side. (Fish should not be cooked through or this will hinder the slicing. Remove fish from the heat or out of the pan.)

Toast the bread in the oven: the inside of each slice should be "spongy." Spread an even layer of the lemon-caper mayonnaise on the toast and place 1 piece of lettuce on top. Cut the salmon fillets 1 time diagonally and put into the hot oven to finish cooking. (The fish is best left slightly rare.)

Place a piece of salmon on top of the leaf lettuce. Place 2 slices of bacon on salmon; top with another piece of salmon to hold bacon in place.

Layer 4 slices of marinated tomatoes in the center of the sandwich and spread a generous amount of the lemon-caper mayonnaise on the tomatoes. Garnish with parsley and serve.

Serves 4

Salmon Loaf

Chef William Love
Country Club Restaurant, Philadelphia, PA

3/4 cups soft breadcrumbs
1 tsp. salt
1 tsp. paprika
1/2 green pepper, diced
1 stalk celery, diced
1/2 bunch scallions, sliced
1/4 bunch parsley, chopped
1 egg
1/4 cup heavy cream
2 T. melted butter
1 T. lemon juice
1 T. Worcestershire sauce
1 lb. cooked, flaked salmon trimmings
Dijon-Dill Sauce (Recipe appears on page 223.)

Preheat oven to 350°. Generously butter an 8- to 10-oz. loaf pan or cupcake pan.

Whisk together all ingredients except the salmon; then stir in salmon. Pour mixture into pan. Bake 30 minutes or until set in the middle. Serve with Dijon-dill sauce.

Serves 12

About the Chef

Name: William Love

Education/Training: Chef David Brown

Inspirations/Influences: the customer's satisfaction

Hobbies: sports

Family: married, two children

Hometown: Memphis, TN

Favorite Food to Eat: chicken

Favorite Food to Prepare: matzo balls

Favorite Cookbook: *Magic Chef*

Southwestern Smoked Salmon Roll Ups

Executive Chef Chris Todd
Arroyo Grille, Manayunk, PA

12 12-inch flour tortillas
1 lb. smoked salmon, sliced thin
2 cups mildly spicy tomato salsa
3 ripe avocados, sliced
3 medium bunches arugula, cleaned and destemmed

Lay all ingredients out on tortillas. Roll up like egg rolls. Serve immediately.

Serves 12

Salmon and Whitefish Terrine

Executive Chef Tom Hannum
Hotel Dupont, Wilmington, DE

2 lbs. salmon, ground
12 eggs
salt and pepper to taste
2 quarts heavy cream
2 lbs. whitefish, ground
caviar
baby lettuces
citrus zests

Place ground salmon in food processor. Process for 30 seconds; then add 6 eggs. Process again until well blended, scraping down sides occasionally. Season with salt and pepper. Add 1 quart heavy cream and process until well incorporated. Set aside.

Process whitefish for 30 seconds; then add remaining eggs. Process again until well blended, scraping down sides occasionally. Season with salt and pepper. Add remaining heavy cream and process until well incorporated.

Preheat oven to 350°. Using 2 pastry bags, pipe mousses into a terrine mold in a checkerboard pattern, alternating layers and colors. Poach terrine in a water bath for approximately 45 minutes. When firm, remove and cool. Slice and arrange on serving plates with caviar, baby lettuces, and citrus zests.

Serves 8

About the Chef

Name: Thomas A. Hannum

Education/Training: Culinary Institute of America, also trained at Le Bec-Fin and Die Ente Vom Lehel in the Hotel Nassauer in Weisbbaden,Germany

Inspirations/Influences: fresh ingredients

Hobbies: bowling   **Family:** recently married to Michelle

Hometown: Wilmington, DE

Favorite Food to Eat: roasted veal loin

Favorite Food to Prepare: anything that is fresh, quick, easy and delicious

Favorite Cookbook: No "one" favorite - I always try to keep up with latest cooking trends and "hot" new talents in the industry

Crabmeat Cheesecake with Pecan Crust

Chef/Owner Joe Brown
Melange Cafe, Cherry Hill, NJ

☺

1/2 small onion, finely diced
butter
4 oz. crabmeat, shell removed
8 oz. cream cheese, room temperature
1/3 cup Creole cream cheese (or substitute equal parts plain yogurt and sour cream)
2 eggs
salt and white pepper to taste
hot sauce to taste
Pecan Crust, baked (see recipe)
2 T. chopped shallots
4 oz. sliced mixed wild mushrooms
1 T. lemon juice
3 oz. Worcestershire sauce
1 oz. hot sauce
3 oz. heavy whipping cream
3 T. soft unsalted butter
24 crab claw fingers
salt and pepper to taste

Cook the onion in a bit of butter over medium heat until translucent. Add the crabmeat and cook until just heated through. Set this aside. In a mixer fitted with a paddle or by hand, using a wooden spoon, cream the cream cheese until smooth. Add the Creole cream cheese and then the eggs, one at a time. Fold in the crabmeat mixture. Season to your liking with salt and white pepper and hot sauce. Pour the mixture into the prepared crust. Bake for about 30 minutes until set and firm to the touch.

Sauté shallots until translucent. Add mushrooms and cook until sweated. Add lemon juice, Worcestershire, and hot sauce and reduce by 3/4. Add heavy cream and reduce by 1/2. Whisk in unsalted butter.

In a separate sauté pan, add crab claw fingers. Salt and pepper to taste and pour reduction over crab fingers. Place 3 crab claws and 2 tablespoons sauce on each slice of cheesecake.

Serves 8

Pecan Crust

3/4 cup pecans
1 cup flour
1/2 tsp. salt
5 T. cold butter
3 T. ice water

Preheat oven to 350°. Grind the pecans, flour, and salt in the food processor until fine. Transfer to a bowl. Add butter. Work the butter into the flour mixture until you have crumbs about the size of a pea. Toss in the water, lifting the dough up with your fingers to evenly incorporate. The dough will remain fairly crumbly. Starting with the sides and then the bottom, press the dough into a 9- or 10-inch tart pan. Bake for about 20 minutes.

About the Chef

Name: Joseph J. Brown

Education/Training: The Restaurant School

Inspirations/Influences: family and other chefs

Hobbies: basketball, music

Family: youngest of 10

Hometown: Willingboro, NJ

Favorite Food to Eat: just about anything

Favorite Food to Prepare: whatever is different

Favorite Cookbook: too many to name

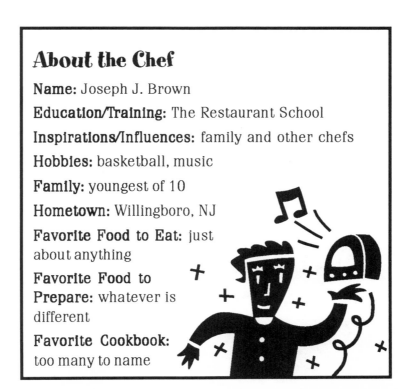

Crab and Tomato Napoleon with Goat Cheese Vinaigrette

Executive Chef Trish Morrissey
Philadelphia Fish & Co., Philadelphia, PA

4 oz. goat cheese, crumbled into small pieces
3 T. champagne vinegar
1/4 cup chicken stock
1 small shallot, minced
1/2 cup vegetable oil
1/4 cup olive oil
1 tsp. sugar
salt and pepper to taste
1 lb. jumbo lump crab (pick through for shells)
I T. chopped fresh basil
2 large ripe tomatoes
1/4 lb. young arugula or fresh watercress
1 T. extra virgin olive oil
1 tsp. lemon juice

Place 2 ounces of goat cheese, vinegar, chicken stock, and shallot in a blender and blend until smooth. Add the vegetable oil, olive oil, and sugar. Pulse the blender twice, season with salt and pepper, and set aside. In a bowl, toss together the crab meat with 3/4 of the vinaigrette, the remaining goat cheese, and the basil. Check for seasoning.

Slice the tomatoes into 12 slices and season each slice with salt and pepper. On 4 plates, place a slice of tomato in the center. Divide the crab meat mixture in half; set one half aside. Spoon crab meat onto each of the 4 tomato slices. Place another slice of tomato on top. Divide the remaining crab meat and repeat the process.

Toss the arugula with the extra virgin olive oil, lemon juice, and salt and pepper to taste. Top each tomato stack with a handful of greens. Drizzle remaining vinaigrette around each plate and serve immediately.

Serves 4

Cedarbrook Imperial

Executive Chef Jerry S. Truxell
Cedarbrook Hill Country Club, Wyncote, PA

1/4 cup diced red onion
1/4 cup diced green pepper
1 tsp. butter
2 lb. jumbo lump crabmeat
1 lb. salmon, cubed
1/2 cup mayonnaise
1 tsp. Old Bay seasoning
1 T. chopped fresh tarragon
1 tsp. dry mustard
1 T. capers
6 slices white bread, diced
1/4 cup Locatelli cheese
1 tsp. Hungarian paprika

Sauté onion and pepper in butter until soft. Cool to room temperature; then combine with all remaining ingredients except cheese and paprika. Place in even portions into 6 gratin dishes or large scallop sea shells and dust with cheese and paprika. Cook in a 350° preheated oven for 20 to 25 minutes or until light brown.

Serves 6

Crisp Cornmeal-crusted Oysters, Baby Greens and Apple Vinaigrette

Executive Chef David Leo Banks
Harry's Savoy Grill, Wilmington, DE

16 oysters
variety of baby greens and herbs: red oak leaf, frisée, Lolla Rosa, arugula,
 radicchio, watercress, dill, tarragon, Italian flat-leaf parsley
2 cups fine yellow cornmeal
1 T. curry powder
1 T. freshly ground white pepper
1 T. salt
16 oz. olive oil or peanut oil for frying
2 bunches flat-leaf Italian parsley, washed and dried
Apple Vinaigrette (see recipe)

Shuck the oysters ahead of service; set aside in some of their juice. Reserve the best-looking shells. Gently wash the greens and dry well; set aside. Combine the cornmeal, curry, pepper, and salt; mix well and set aside.

Just before service, heat the oil in a sauté pan over medium heat until it is hot. Fry the parsley quickly until it is very crisp. Drain and set it in the center of a plate or serving platter.

Toss the greens with half of the prepared vinaigrette; arrange them around the parsley. "Nest" the reserved oyster shells on the greens.

Reheat oil if necessary. Drain the oysters and dredge them in the cornmeal mixture. Fry in the hot oil until they are crisp and golden. Place quickly on paper towels. Place an oyster in each shell. Spoon the remaining vinaigrette onto the oysters and around the outside of the plate. Serve immediately.

Serves 4

Apple Vinaigrette

1 unpeeled Granny Smith apple, diced
1 shallot, minced
1/4 cup sherry wine vinegar
2 T. apple cider vinegar
1 tsp. salt
1 tsp. freshly ground black pepper
1/4 cup finely chopped chives
9 oz. extra virgin olive oil

Combine the first 6 ingredients in a small bowl. Allow to sit at room temperature for 15 minutes. Then whisk in the chives and oil; do not refrigerate.

About the Chef

Name: David Leo Banks, C.E.C.

Education/Training: Culinary Institute of America

Inspirations/Influences: pureness, natural flavors, spontaneity

Hobbies: organic gardening, home canning, wood cutting

Family: married 14 years to Kathryn, three children — Wesley (5), Gail (2), and Mason (6 mos.)

Hometown: Parkersburg, WV

Favorite Food to Eat: osso bucco

Favorite Food to Prepare: cassoulet

Favorite Cookbook: *Charlie Trotter's*

Escargots in Pastry with Pernod, Garlic and Cream

Chef/Owner Peter Lamlein
Overtures, Philadelphia, PA

6 cups heavy cream
4 T. finely chopped garlic
1/2 cup Pernod or to taste
chopped parsley
fresh ground pepper
1 pkg. (12) prebaked pastry shells
1 can extra small French snails

Over low heat, cook heavy cream with garlic, whisking at regular intervals to prevent the formation of a skin. Cook cream until thick and reduced by half. Add Pernod, parsley, and pepper.

Bake pastry shells according to their instructions. Rinse off snails. Put 8 to 12 per person into the sauce. Once heated, place sauce into shells.

Serves 12

About the Chef

Name: Peter Lamlein

Education/Training: self-taught (25 years experience)

Inspirations/Influences: tasting — learned alot as a traveling hippie in Europe!

Hobbies: opera, theatre, talking to people

Hometown: Torresdale, PA

Favorite Food to Eat: pizza

Favorite Food to Prepare: things that freak people out, desserts

Favorite Cookbook: *In Madeleine's Kitchen* by Madeleine Kamman

Southwestern Crepes

Executive Chef Jerry S. Truxell
Cedarbrook Hill Country Club, Wyncote, PA

2 eggs
2 cups sifted flour
pinch salt
1 T. butter, melted
1 tsp. butter
1 lb. vanilla ice cream
1/2 cup graham cracker crumbs
1/2 cup apricot jelly
2 T. horseradish
1/4 cup butter
1/4 cup brown sugar
2 T. Melba sauce
1/4 cup chopped pecans
1 cup whipped cream

To make crepes combine eggs, flour, salt, and melted butter. Heat a 6-inch non-stick sauté pan and add 1 teaspoon butter. Add crepe mixutre in 2 ounce intervals and spread evenly around pan. Cook until firm and lightly browned; then turn over and cook for 1 minute more. Place on a greased pan and set aside.

Form ice cream into 12 even-portioned logs and roll in graham cracker crumbs to coat. Wrap each log with a crepe and chill in the freezer.

Combine apricot jelly with horseradish. Mix together butter and brown sugar and spread evenly on top of each crepe. Put crepes on a sheet pan and heat under broiler until brown.

Place 2 crepes each on chilled plates and top with apricot sauce, melba sauce, chopped pecans, and whipped cream.

Serves 6

Stuffed Orange Zest Crepes with Strawberry Orange Glaze

Chef/Owner Donna Leahy
Inn at Twin Linden, Churchtown, PA

⑥

"These crepes make an elegant breakfast main course or a wonderful addition to a brunch buffet. The crepes, filling, and orange syrup may be made up to 24 hours in advance."

1¼ cups ricotta cheese
4 oz. cream cheese
5 T. sugar
1 T. orange extract
3 tsp. grated orange zest
3/4 cup all-purpose flour
1 egg
1 egg yolk
3/4 cup half-and-half
1/4 cup water

With an electric mixer, beat the ricotta cheese, cream cheese, and 3 tablespoons sugar until smooth. Add the orange extract and 1 teaspoon orange zest and mix until just combined. Set aside.

In a large mixing bowl, combine the flour with the remaining 2 tablespoons of sugar and 2 teaspoons orange zest. In a smaller bowl, whisk together the egg, egg yolk, half-and-half, and water. Pour the wet ingredients into the dry ingredients and stir until just combined. Spray a 10-inch nonstick frying pan with no-stick spray and heat on medium until hot but not smoking. Ladle in 2 to 3 tablespoons of crepe batter, just enough to coat the bottom of the pan, and swirl rapidly side to side to coat the pan evenly. Cook the crepe until the edges just begin to curl and brown (1 to 2 minutes), loosen, and flip to cook the other side 1 to 2 minutes. Continue until 6 crepes are completed. Layer with waxed paper and store covered until ready to use.

When ready to serve, preheat the oven to 375°. Fill each crepe with 2 to 3 tablespoons cheese filling and fold the bottom 1/3 up. Fold the both sides in; then finish rolling the bottom until a neat rectangular package is formed. Place the crepes on a lightly greased baking sheet. Bake for 8 to 10 minutes until just heated through. Spoon strawberry glaze over warm crepes to serve.

Serves 6

Strawberry Orange Glaze

1½ cups orange juice
1/2 cup corn syrup
1/2 cup plus 3 T. sugar
2 naval oranges, peeled and cut into 1/4-inch wedges
3 T. butter
2 cups fresh strawberries, hulled and quartered
3 T. Grand Marnier or similar orange liqueur

In a medium saucepan, combine the orange juice, corn syrup, and ½ cup sugar over medium heat. Stir in the orange wedges. Bring just to a boil; then reduce heat to low and simmer for about 15 minutes until mixture is syrupy and slightly thickened. Set aside.

Melt the butter in a medium saucepan. Add the strawberries and cook for 1 minute on high heat. Sprinkle in the remaining 3 tablespoons sugar and continue cooking and stirring until strawberries begin to release juice, about 2 to 3 minutes. Ladle in the orange syrup mixture and cook for 1 minute. Add the liqueur and flame if desired.

Adapted from *Morning Glories: Recipes for Breakfast, Brunch & Beyond from an American Country Inn* by Donna Leahy (Rizzoli International, 1996).

Rolled Basil Souffle
with Roasted Red Pepper Coulis

Chef/Owner Donna Leahy
Inn at Twin Linden, Churchtown, PA

1/4 cup butter
1/2 cup all-purpose flour
1/2 tsp. salt
1/2 tsp. pepper
2½ cups milk, scalded
5 eggs, separated
2 T. basil pesto
1 T. extra virgin olive oil
1 T. minced shallots
1/4 cup chopped prosciutto
1½ cups chopped shiitake mushrooms
5 oz. crumbled goat cheese
5 oz. cream cheese
1/2 cup chopped roasted red peppers
Roasted Red Pepper Coulis (see recipe)
2 T. chopped fresh basil

Preheat the oven to 350°. Grease a 15½ x 10½ x 1-inch jelly roll pan and line with parchment. Melt the butter over medium heat in a medium saucepan. Stir in the flour, salt, and pepper and cook for 2 minutes, stirring constantly. Add the warm milk and bring to a boil. Lower heat and simmer for 2 minutes. Add the egg yolks and cook 1 minute longer. Remove from heat and allow to cool.

Beat egg whites until stiff. Fold pesto into cooled mixture and then fold in egg whites. Spread the mixture into pan and bake for 15 to 20 minutes. Immediately invert the roll onto a dish towel topped with parchment and roll up jelly-roll style. Allow to cool.

Heat the olive oil in a large sauté pan. Add the shallots and sauté over medium heat for 30 seconds. Add the prosciutto and mushrooms and sauté for 2 to 3 minutes until mushrooms soften. Remove from heat and cool slightly. Stir in the goat cheese, cream cheese, and peppers. Cover and allow to soften to spreading consistency. Unroll the souffle, spread the filling on evenly, and roll up without the towel or parchment. Place on a lightly greased baking sheet and cover with foil. Bake in a preheated 350° oven for 10 minutes.

Heat the coulis in a medium saucepan. Slice the souffle into 12 pieces. Divide sauce among 6 individual plates. Place 2 souffle slices on top of each plate and sprinkle with fresh basil.

Serves 6

Roasted Red Pepper Coulis

1 cup chopped roasted red peppers
1/2 cup fresh tomato sauce

Process the roasted peppers and tomato sauce in food processor or blender until smooth.

Adapted from *Morning Glories: Recipes for Breakfast, Brunch & Beyond from an American Country Inn* by Donna Leahy (Rizzoli International, 1996).

Poached Figs with French Toast in Port Wine

Executive Chef Ed Doherty
La Campagne, Cherry Hill, NJ

1/2 quart port wine
1 lemon peel
1 orange peel
1 cinnamon stick
1 vanilla bean
3 black pepper seeds or 1 chunk ginger
16 figs
1/2 cup milk
1 egg, beaten
2 T. sugar
1 oz. butter
4 thick slices stale bread

In a pot, simmer the port wine with orange and lemon peels, cinnamon stick, vanilla bean, and pepper seeds or ginger. Poach the figs for 10 minutes and then place a lid on top and let them sit in the liquid for 30 minutes.

Mix together the milk, egg, sugar, and 2 tablespoons of the port reduction from the pot. Soak bread in milk mixture. Heat butter in a pan. Fry the bread in the butter until golden brown. Meanwhile, reduce the remaining port mixture over medium heat until syrupy. Serve bread topped with figs and the reduction.

Serves 2

Tamale Dulce

Kithen Staff
Zocalo, Philadelphia, PA

1 package dried corn husks (available at Hispanic grocery)
1/2 lb. rice flour (not sweet rice flour)
2 tsp. baking powder
1½ sticks unsalted butter
1 cup powdered sugar
2 eggs
3 egg yolks
1/4 cup milk
3/4 tsp. vanilla

Soak corn husks in water overnight or for at least 2 hours. Sift together the rice flour and baking powder and put aside. Cream the butter and sugar with an electric mixer. In a separate bowl, beat the eggs, egg yolks, milk, and vanilla. Alternately add the dry ingredients and the egg/milk mixture to the creamed butter and sugar. Scrape the sides of the bowl to ensure an even blend. Spoon batter into softened corn husks, folding ends to contain it. Place the filled husks upright in a steamer. Steam 30 to 45 minutes. Present each tamale slightly unwrapped to show cake inside. Serve with vanilla ice cream and/or a warm fruit sauce of your choice.

Serves 8

About the Chef

Name: Our kitchen is run with the team of Mexican and American trained staff members.

Education/Training: We combine classical training with hands-on experience in Mexico.

Inspirations/Influences: the traditional and contemporary cuisine from many regions of Mexico

Favorite Food to Eat: We love the complex combinations in Oayaran mol sauces.

Favorite Food to Prepare: It's wonderful to bring dishes from ports of Mexico usually not represented in America.

Favorite Cookbook: Anything by Diana Kennedy is brilliant.

Biscuits with Fresh Cream and Berries

Pastry Chef Kelly McGrath
City Tavern, Philadelphia, PA

2¼ cup all-purpose flour
1/2 cup granulated sugar
1½ tsp. baking powder
3/4 tsp. baking soda
1/2 tsp. salt
6 T. butter
1/2 cup buttermilk
1 egg yolk
2 cups heavy cream, whipped
strawberries, blueberries, blackberries, raspberries

Preheat oven to 400°. Combine all dry ingredients and butter in food processor and process until crumbly. Add buttermilk and yolk. Process until dough holds together. (Do not overwork dough.) Roll out on floured surface and cut out biscuits using a biscuit cutter. Brush top of bisquits with milk and bake for 15 to 20 minutes or until golden brown. When cool, cut biscuits in half. Place whipped cream and berries on bottom half and then replace top half.

Serves 8

Metropolitan Millet Muffins

Owners James Barrett and Wendy Smith Born
Metropolitan Bakery, Philadelphia, PA

"Delicious for breakfast with freshly brewed coffee."

6 oz. unsalted butter
1 cup brown sugar, firmly packed
3 eggs
1/4 cup milk
1 T. pure vanilla
2 cups all-purpose flour
1¼ tsp. baking powder
1/2 tsp. baking soda
3/4 tsp. kosher salt
1 cup millet, lightly toasted and cooled

Preheat oven to 375°. Prepare muffin pan. Using the paddle attachment of your mixer, cream the butter and sugar well. In a small bowl, combine the eggs, milk, and vanilla. In another bowl, sift together the flour, baking powder, baking soda, and salt. Toss in the toasted millet. Alternating between the milk mixture and the flour mixture, fold them into the creamed butter. Do not overmix. Spoon into prepared muffin pan and bake for 20 to 25 minutes or until skewer comes out clean.

Yields 12 muffins

Banana-Walnut Bread

Owner Joe Lovallo
New World Cafe, Cinnaminson, NJ

1 lb. unsalted butter
4 cups sugar
8 eggs
1 T. vanilla
4 bananas
6 cups flour
1 T. baking soda
1 T. nutmeg
1 tsp. salt
2 cups half-and-half
1 cup toasted walnuts

Preheat oven to 350°. Grease three 9 x 5-inch loaf pans. Cream eggs and sugar in mixer on slow speed. Add eggs, vanilla, and bananas. Combine flour, baking soda, nutmeg, and salt. Add slowly to mixer. Add half-and-half slowly. Add walnuts and mix well. Pour batter into loaf pans. Bake for 1½ hours.

About the Chef

Name: Joe Lovallo

Education/Training: B.S. in Food Marketing from St. Joseph's University

Inspirations/Influences: necessity

Hobbies: sports

Family: wife Denise, two sons — Will and Joey

Hometown: Voorhees, NJ

Favorite Food to Eat: crabcakes, pizza

Favorite Food to Prepare: all types of breads and desserts

Favorite Cookbook: *Larousse Gastronomique*

Nutty Chocolate Tea Loaf

Chef/Owner Lisa Wilson
BoDine's Catering, Collingswood, NJ

2 cups sugar
3/4 cup cocoa
1 tsp. baking powder
2 tsp. baking soda
3 cups flour
2 eggs
1 cup milk
1/2 cup cooking oil
1 tsp. pure vanilla extract
1 cup cold coffee
1 cup finely chopped walnuts

Preheat oven to 350°. Grease and flour a 9 x 5-inch loaf pan. Combine dry ingredients. In a separate bowl, beat eggs, milk, cooking oil, and vanilla. Add coffee. Combine wet with dry ingredients. Add walnuts and mix well. Pour into pan and bake approximately 40 minutes. Test for doneness. Let cool. Slice to serve.

Index

A

Allen, Patrick 150
Alo Gohbi 204
Anderson, John 76, 88, 144
Ann, Gilda Doganiero 240
Apple
    amazing spice cake 272
    chutney 245
    French tart 275
    harvest fruit crisp 262
    old fashioned pie 279
    vinaigrette 295
Arroyo Grille 31, 59, 288
Asparagus
    and lobster risotto 81
    grilled jumbo with truffles and morels 195
    with rouget and fava beans 136
Avocado, puree 115
Azalea Restaurant 36, 195

B

Banana
    -cilantro salsa 217
    -walnut bread 306
    Bavarian mousse 250
    chocolate bread pudding 253
    double chocolate mousse cake 266
Banks, David Leo 40, 247, 286, 294
Barbeque
    salmon on grilled romaine 140
    salmon with crispy yams 139
    sauce 224
    South American chocolate shrimp 108
Baretto, Luigi 45, 117, 181, 208, 226
Barrett, James 305
Baskette, Michael 16, 49, 184
Beans
    black, cakes with clams 107
    green, garden salad 200
    Nicola Shirley's rice and 212
Beau Rivage Restaurant 133
Beck, Bill 22, 132, 138, 148, 217, 261
Beef

coffee mop steak 167
    filet ricardo 166
    filetto di manzo alla barolo 165
    london broil Jack Daniel's 170
    marinated steak wrap 32
    medallion and seafood combo 168
Beer
    sauce with mussels 104
    seafood fest 124
Beets, roasted with gorgonzola 196
Bennett, David 176, 234
Berks, Andrew 58
Big Fish Restaurant 56, 91, 166
Bingham, Jennifer Ballou 272
Biscotti
    apricot-ginger 239
    classic 240
Biscuits, with fresh cream and berries 304
Blackberry
    berry sauce 260
    biscuits with fresh cream and berries 304
    cream streusel cake 269
Blank, Fritz 105, 174, 198, 199, 270
Blinis, sesame seed-ginger 284
BLT's Cobblefish 131
Blueberry, sauce 181
BoDine's Catering 307
Braddock's Tavern 276
Brasserie Perrier 84
Bread
    banana-walnut 306
    Metropolitan millet muffins 305
    Navajo fry 19
    nutty chocolate tea loaf 307
    pudding, chocolate-banana 253
Brennan, David W. 83, 231
Brennan, Trish 274
Brown, Joe 290
Buckley's Tavern 201
Buker, Mark 48, 142
Buono, Lynn 38, 177, 218
Butter
    bacon-shallot 152
    brandy, basil and tomato 235
    garlic 234

C

Café Portobello 24
Caffé Aldo Lamberti 171, 225
Cajun Bouillabaisse 122
Cake
  amazing apple spice 272
  angel food 255
  blackberry cream streusel 269
  carrot with orange glaze icing 270
  chocolate buttermilk 267
  double chocolate banana mousse cake 266
  Kahlúa flourless fudge 268
  lemon poppyseed 274
Calamari
  calamari sarento 33
  grilled with cucumbers 69
Cancelliere, John 87
Cardillo, Antonio 172
Carrot, cake with orange glaze icing 270
Catelli Ristorante & Café 80
Caviar
  easy gravlox and smoked salmon mousse
    appetizers 17
  oyster gratin with caviar 34
  tarragon and fresh corn cakes with smoked
    salmon a 283
Cedarbrook Hill Country Club
    63, 159, 293, 297
Chanterelles 68, 70, 128
Charmoula 146
Cheesecake
  crabmeat with pecan crust 290
  pumpkin 265
  ricotta 264
Cherry, soup 60
Chevalier, Dany 33, 99, 234
Chicken
  and shrimp Sante Fe 190
  breast au poirve with roasted pepper 185
  curried with orange, grapes and star fruit
    189
  Dijon 186
  grilled lemon 187
  grilled tandoori breast with mint raita sa
    188
  ravioli polla verde 87
  smoked chicken and cheddar roll ups 31
  smothered with onions 184
  with Maine lobster and lump crab 191

Chin, Philippe 68, 70, 128, 284
Chocolate
  -banana bread pudding 253
  banana mousse cake 266
  black forest crepes with cocoa sorbet 256
  buttermilk cake 267
  cocoa sorbet 256
  custard 253
  Kahlúa flourless fudge cake 268
  macaroons with raspberry filling 244
  mousse 251
  nutty tea loaf 307
  sauce, bittersweet 249
  South American BBQ shrimp 108
  white mousse 249
Chowder
  New Jersey clam 45
  New Orleans clam 46
  roasted vegetable with curry 48
Chrysanthemum 109
Chutney, apple 245
Ciboulette 79
Circa 75, 101
City Tavern 245, 264, 304
Clam
  chowder, New Jersey 45
  chowder, New Orleans 46
  with black bean cakes 107
Clark, Tony 120
Clubhouse Restaurant 153
Coconut
  and macadamia encrusted scallops 117
  fried shrimp 110
Codfish, pan seared with caramelized
    onions 126
Coleman, Jim 55, 66, 81, 256
Compote
  cranberry 183
  olive and roasted pepper 151
Conch, Key West fritters 22
Cookies
  Biscotti
    apricot-ginger 239
    classic 240
  black & white 243
  chocolate macaroons with raspberry 244
  Mexican wedding cookies 242
  shortbread 245
Corn
  -tomato stock 233
  crusted crab and crab cakes 112

hash with roasted peppers 202
ragout 36
risotto with rock shrimp, and basil 80
roasted and scallion mashed potato 205
roasted polenta 211
roasted, salsa 219
tarragon and fresh corn cakes 283
tomato risotto, 78
Corned Beef Academy 61
Cornish Game Hens, sage-rubbed 182
Coulis
　red pepper 301
　tomato 40
Country Club Restaurant 223, 287
Couscous, sun-dried cranberry 209
Crab
　and shrimp cakes 112
　and tomato napoleon with goat cheese
　　vinaigre 292
　cakes, Phoenix 113
　cakes with roasted pepper and corn hash
　　114
　Cedarbrook imperial 293
　cheesecake with pecan crust 290
　dumplings 25
　grilled stuffed portobello 24
　little juicy steamed buns 28
　risotto with fava beans 79
　soup, creamless tomato with fennel and 54
　stone crab empanadas 30
Crabs, soft shells 116
Cranberry
　compote 183
　sun-dried couscous 209
Crea, George 167
Creative Catering Company 32, 77, 182
Crème Brûlée
　Harry's 247
　with raspberries 248
Crepes 298
　black forest with cocoa sorbet 256
　southwestern 297
　stuffed orange zest 298
Crisps/Crumbs
　harvest fruit 262
　summertime rhubarb mango 261
Crust
　gingersnap 265
　pecan 291
　shortcrust 275
Curry Oil 285

Custard, chocolate 253
Cuvee Notredame Restaurant 104

D

Daggett, Tony 170, 189
Daggett's Catering 170, 189
De Saint Martin, Olivier 124, 126
Deux Cheminées 105, 174, 198, 199, 270
Devine, Jeffrey 123
DiLullo's 83, 231
Dip, vodka 23
Dock Street Brewery & Restaurant 124, 126
Doherty, Ed 60, 244, 258, 275, 302
Dough, empanadas 24. *See also* Crust
Dover Sole 127. *See also* Fish
Dressing, pesto 68. *See also* Vinaigrette
Duck, roast with blueberry sauce 181
Duffy, Brian W. 56, 91, 166
Dumplings
　crab 25
　Har Gow, shrimp 26
　little juicy steamed buns 28
　shrimp 26
Dupont, Hotel 289

E

Eggplant, pate 16
Ellen, Mary Hatch 254
Empanada, stone crab 30
Escargot
　in pastry with pernod, garlic and cream 296
　napoleon with shiitake and cream 35

F

Fava beans
　with crab risotto 79
　with rouget and asparagus 136
Feast Your Eyes Catering 38, 218
Figs, with French toast in port wine 302
Fischer, William 171, 225
Fish. *See* Monk Fish; Codfish; Dover
　　Sole; Flounder; Pompano; Red
　　Snapper; Rouget; Salmon; Sea
　　Bass; Trout; Tuna
　Provencal 129
　steamed 125
Flounder, mushroom crusted 128

Foie Gras, stuffed tuna steak 156
Foo, Susanna 178, 222
Fortunato, Michael 90
Four Seasons Hotel Philadelphia 136, 227
Fowl. *See* Cornish Game Hens
Francis, Trzeciak 149, 228
Francois, Jean Taquet 141
Frederick's Regional Italian Cuisine 134, 165
French toast 302
Friday Saturday Sunday Restaurant 50, 107, 186, 220, 274
Friedman, Ian 76, 158

G

Garden of Eden Natural Foods and Country Kitchen 200
Garden State Park Clubhouse 248
Gaughan, Joel 276
Gazpacho
clear tomato 57
prickly pear and pineapple 59
tropical fruit 58
Gehin, Gerard P., 133
GG's Restaurant 46, 154
Gilbert, Clark 69
Gilda's Biscotti, Inc. 240
Glaze
ancho honey 138
apricot chipotle 176
lemon 274
orange icing 270
strawberry orange 299
Gnocchi
potato basil 89
three cheese with tomato cream 88
Gottlieb, David 54, 111, 207
Gravlax
and smoked salmon mousse appetizers 17
Asian spiced 284
Grear, David R. 156, 224

H

Halibut, pot au feu 56
Hall, Eric 75, 101
Hannan, Francis 113
Hannum, Tom 15, 179, 183, 213, 289

Har Gow Shrimp Dumplings 26
Harry's Savoy Grill 40, 247, 286, 294
Hepner, Edwin 185
Hilton at Cherry Hill 167
Hotel Dupont 15, 179, 183, 213, 289
Huffman, Liz 201
Husch Restaurant & Bar 76, 88, 144

I

Imbesi, Louis 80
Inn at Twin Linden 269, 298, 300
Isabella's 89, 191, 231, 268

J

Jake and Oliver's House of Brews 140
Jake's Restaurant 139
Jalapeño Pepper Puree 222
Jamaican Jerk Hut 212
Jambalaya 123
Jason Ruch 47
Joe's Peking Duck House 147
Joseph Poon Restaurant 26, 125
Just Between Friends Restaurant and Catering 157

K

Kansas City Prime 176, 234
Kaplan, Deborah 243

L

La Campagne 60, 244, 258, 275, 302
La Famiglia Ristornate 127
La Familia Sonsini 252
La Patisserie Francaise 242, 278
La Terrasse 69
Lacroix, Jean-Marie 136, 227
Lamb
fire-grilled rack 180
honey-grilled chops 178
pot au feu 55
racks au jus with pureed sweet potatoes 179
Lamlein, Peter 296
Landsman, Howard and Melissa Killeen 17, 18
Laurel Springs Smoke House 17, 18

Leahy, Donna 269, 298, 300
Lee, Patrick 147
Lemon Poached Pears 260
Lichtenstein, Alan 108, 224
Lim, Bruce 79
Lobster
  and asparagus risotto 81
  and mussel stir-fry 102
  beef medallion and seafood combo 168
  red and spicy 100
  roasted Maine 99
  sauteed with ginger basil beure blanc 100
  with chicken and lump crab stuffing 191
London Grill 152
Long, Alex 109
Loose Ends Restaurant 190, 217
Los Amigos's "New Mexico Grille" 106, 219
Lovallo, Joe 265, 306
Love, William 223, 287
Lucskos Káposziá 198

M

Marmalade
  red onion 234
  sun-dried 233
Martini Cafe 168
Martini's Lounge & Restaurant 19
Martorella, Francesco 84
McAndrews, Peter 35
McConnell, Bill 19
McConnell, Daniel 53, 188, 204
McGill, James 139
McGrath, Kelly 245, 264, 304
McNally, Michael 152
McNamara, Ben 89, 191, 231, 268
Meeker, Kevin 102, 129
Melange Cafe 290
Melchiorre, Diana 200
Metropolitan Bakery 305
Millan, Yudi 110
Monkfish
  Brazilian baked 130
  panchetta 131
Morrissey, Trish 51, 122, 203, 292
Mousse
  banana Bavarian 250
  chocolate 251
  double chocolate banana cake 266
  easy gravlox and smoked salmon 17

white chocolate 249
Muratore, Frank 24
Mushroom
  -crusted flounder 128
  charred tomato essence 118
  exotic, with grilled veal chop 171
  five ragout 201
  soup, Billy Weavers's cream of 50
  soup, roasted shallot and 51
  with salmon 144
Mushrooms
  Portobello, grilled stuffed portobellos 24
    pizza 40
  Shiitake, escargot napoleon with shiitake
    and cream 35
Mussels
  and lobster stir-fry 102
  mescalero 106
  moules a la mariniere 105
  with beer sauce 104

N

Napoleon
  crab and tomato with goat cheese 292
  escargot with shiitake and cream 38
  grilled vegetable with baby lettuces 38
  strawberry 258
Napoleon Restaurant-Bar 150
New World Cafe 25, 108, 224, 265, 306
Nicholas Nickolas 33, 99, 234
Nicola Shirley's Rice and Beans 212
Noodles, Asian sesame 93
Notredame, Michel 104
Nussbaum, Diane 242, 278
Nutinsky, Howard 61

O

Old Original Bookbinder's Restaurant
    100, 116, 118, 219
Olive
  and roasted pepper compote 151
  tomato sauce 231
Onion
  caramelized with codfish 126
  chicken smothered 184
  red, marmalade 234
Overtures 296
Oysters
  crisp cornmeal-crusted 294

gratin with caviar 34
stew with verbena 120

P

Pana Cotta 246. *See also* Pudding
Panorama 82, 230
Paone, Don 86, 173, 211, 235
Papaya
  -cilantro sauce 226
  salsa 218
Paradigm 156, 224
Pasta
  cavatelli alla Scarpinato's 85
  cavatelli with sun-dried tomato pesto 84
  penne with sweet roasted pepper sauce 83
  potato basil gnocchi 89
  ravioli polla verde 87
  scallop with pesto and cream 90
  shrimp Amelia 91
  Sonoma shrimp ravioli 86
  three cheese gnocchi with tomato cream 88
  with cold tomato salad 82
  with venison sausage and smoked mozza-
    rella 92
Pears, lemon poached 260
Pecan
  -pistachio butter 133
  crust 291
Peppers
  jalapeño pepper puree 222
  olive and roasted pepper compote 151
  patria chile vinaigrette 71
  roasted poblano vinaigrette 71
  roasted with corn hash 202
  Serrano's five pepper hot sauce 221
  sweet roasted sauce 83
Pernot, Guillermo
  30, 52, 71, 206, 226, 259
Pesto
  crusted salmon with roasted tomato oil 142
  dressing 68
  over scallops and penne 90
  sun-dried tomato 84
  sweet basil 232
Pfeffer, Michael 100, 116, 118
Pheasant, roasted with cranberry compote
  183
Phifer, Annemarie 190, 217
Philadelphia Fish & Co.
  51, 102, 122, 129, 203, 292

Philadelphia Tea Party 53, 188, 204
Phoenix Restaurant 113
Pie, old fashioned apple 279. *See also* Tart
Pineiro, Charles 168
Pink Rose Pastry Shop 279
Pizza, portobello 40
Polenta
  grilled 210
  roasted corn 211
Pompano, fire grilled with banana-
    cilantro salsa 132
Pompano Grille
  22, 132, 138, 148, 217, 261
Poon, Joseph 26, 125
Poppyseed, cake, lemon 274
Pork
  apricot chipotle glazed roast tenderloin 176
  escalopes, aux cœurs de celeris 174
  grilled tenderloin with papaya salsa 177
  loin with pistachios 175
  roasted tenderloin with roasted corn
    polenta 173
Pot Au Feu
  braised lamb shank 55
  halibut 56
Potato
  alo gohbi 204
  basil gnocchi 89
  Cajun roasted 203
  melted leek risotto 76
  roasted corn and scallion mashed 205
  sweet, pureed 179
  tarragon 140
Provencal
  fish 129
  sauce 228
  sauce with sea bass 149
Provence 149, 228
Pudding. *See* Custard; Mousse
  chocolate-banana bread 253
  Irish rice 252
  summer 254
Pumpkin
  cheesecake 265
  seed vinaigrette 66
  soup, cream of 49

Q

Quay, Kimberly 114, 202
Quinoa, salad with citrus vinaigrette 64

R

Ram's Head Inn 45, 117, 181, 208, 226
Raspberry
  berry sauce 260
  biscuits with fresh cream and berries 304
  chocolate macaroons with raspberry filling
    244
  crème brûlée with 248
Ravioli
  polla verde 87
  Sonoma shrimp 86
Red Snapper
  with four vinegars 134
  with pecan/pistachio butter 133
Rembrandt's Restaurant 35
Remi's Cafe 90
Restaurant Taquet 141
Rhubarb Mango Crumb 261
Rice
  and beans 212
  pudding, Irish 252
  wild 213
Risotto
  California 76
  crab with fava beans 79
  lobster and asparagus 81
  roasted corn, rock shrimp, and basil 80
  tomato 75
  tomato-sweet corn risotto 78
Ristorante Volare 87
River City Diner 185
Rococo
  67, 146, 180, 205, 227, 249, 250, 251, 266
Roscoe's Kodiak Cafe 114, 202
Rose Tattoo Cafe 254
Rouget, with fava beans and asparagus
  136
Rouissiya, Mustapha
  67, 146, 180, 205, 209, 227
Ruch, Jason 25

S

Sage Cafe 76, 158
Salad
  Asian vegetable 63
  Caren's shrimp 61
  cold tomato over hot pasta 82
  grilled calamari 69
  mixed tomato, proscuitto and mozzarella
    62
  quinoa with citrus vinaigrette 64
  Rococo with limestone and tat-soi 67
  watercress, bibb and jimaca 66
Salmon
  ancho honey glazed 138
  barbequed with crispy yams 139
  barbequed with grilled romaine 140
  grilled with tomato, olive oil and herbs 141
  Moroccan roasted 146
  pesto crusted with roasted tomato oil 142
  southwestern smoked roll ups 288
  steamed with ginger and scallion 147
  with exotic mushrooms 144
Salmon - smoked
  and whitefish terrine 289
  easy gravlox and 17
  loaf 287
  open-faced B.L.T. 286
  with tarragon and fresh corn cakes 283
Salsa
  banana-cilantro 217
  black bean 217
  cruda 218
  fresca 219
  papaya 218
  roasted corn 219
  tomatillo 220
Sandwich
  marinated steak wrap 32
  open-faced salmon B.L.T 286
  smoked chicken and cheddar roll ups 31
  southwestern smoked salmon roll ups 288
Sauce
  basic cream 223
  basic tomato 230
  BBQ 224
  berry 260
  beurre blanc 224
  bittersweet chocolate 249
  demi-glace 225
  Dijon 186
  Dijon-dill 223
  dulce de leche 259
  fresh tomato 231
  mint raita 188
  mojo criollo 226
  papaya cilantro 226
  port wine reduction 156
  Provencale 228

red wine 227
saffron honey 227
sorrel 126
summer herbs 229
Tomato
    olive 231
    sun-dried pesto 84
    sweet roasted pepper 83
Sausage
    with farfelle and smoked mozzarella 92
Scallops
    and penne with pesto and cream 90
    beef medallion and seafood combo 168
    grilled with wild mushroom charred
      essence 118
    jambalaya 123
    macadamia and coconut encrusted 117
Scanlon, Gerald 64
Scarpinato, Vincenzo 85
Scarpinato's Ristorante 85
Sea Bass
    Chilean, citrus and rum 148
    with sauce Provencale 149
Seafood Fest 124
Seafood Jambalaya 123
Sena, Luca 82, 127, 230
Sensational Cook Caterers 20
Serrano Restaurant 221, 232
Sesame
    Asian noodles 93
    crusted tuna loin 70
    seed-ginger blinis 284
Shilling, Joseph E. C.E.C. 221, 232
Shirley, Nicola 212
Shrimp
    Amelia 91
    and chicken Sante Fe 190
    and crab cakes 112
    beef medallion and seafood combo 168
    Caren's salad 61
    coconut fried 110
    dumplings 26
    grilled Oriental kabobs 20
    pan seared in pernod cream sauce 111
    risotto with corn and basil 80
    Sonoma ravioli 86
    South American chocolate BBQ sauce 108
    Szechuan style 109
Simon, Paul 140
Sirirathasuk, Chakapope 107, 186, 220

Smith, Drew 249, 250, 251, 266, 267
Smith, Mark 20
Sonoma Restaurant 86, 173, 211, 235
Sonsini, Kathleen 252
Sorbet, cocoa 256
Souffle, rolled basil 300
Soup
    Billy Weavers's cream of mushroom 50
    clear tomato gazpacho 57
    cream of pumpkin 49
    creamless tomato and fennel with crabmeat
      54
    halibut pot au feu 56
    lamb shank pot au feu 55
    New Jersey clam chowder 45
    New Orleans clam chowder 46
    prickly pear and pineapple gazpacho 59
    rasam 53
    roasted shallot and wild mushroom 51
    roasted vegetable with curry 48
    seafood bisque 47
    sour cherry 60
    South American squash 52
    tropical fruit gazpacho 58
Southwestern
    chicken and shrimp Sante Fe 190
    crepes 297
    smoked salmon roll ups 288
Squash
    risotto 77
    soup, South American 52
Star Anise Alfajor 259
Steak. See Beef
Stewart, Joe 46, 154
Strawberry
    berry sauce 260
    biscuits with fresh cream and berries 304
    napoleon 258
    orange glaze 298
    oven-roasted with vanilla pana cotta 246
Striped Bass 283
Strudel, vegetable 208
Sturm, Adam 36, 195
Sud Fine Pastry 243
Summertime Rhubarb Mango Crumb 261
Susanna Foo Chinese Cuisine 178, 222
Swordfish, grilled 150. See also Fish

T

Tamale Dulce 303

Tart
  French apple 275
  fresh fruit 278
  lemon 276
  sweet pastry shell 277
Tarzy, Michael 157
Taylor, Curt 106, 219
Terrine
  salmon and whitefish 289
  wild boar and Scottish hare 15
The Art Institute of Philadelphia 16, 49, 184
The Dilworthtown Inn 54, 111, 207
The Five Spot 130
The Inn at Sugar Hill 48, 142
The Inn Philadelphia 62, 187, 210
The Mansion 123
The Pacific Grille 110
The Restaurant School 64, 175
Thurber, Allyson 283
Timlin, Stephen 153, 248
Todd, Chris 31, 59, 288
Tomato
  -corn stock 233
  basic sauce 230
  clear gazpacho 57
  cold salad over hot pasta 82
  cream, with three cheese gnocchi 88
  oil, roasted 142
  olive sauce 231
  risotto 75
  risotto, sweet corn and 78
  salad with proscuitto and mozzarella 62
  sauce 231
  soup, creamless with fennel and crabmeat 54
  tomatillo salsa 220
  with grilled salmon, olive oil and herbs 141
Tony Clark's 120, 239, 246, 249, 253
Treetops Restaurant 55, 66, 81, 256
Trout
  rainbow 153
  sautéed with corn-peanut crust 152
  smoked, with horseradish honey mustard
    sauce 18
Truxell, Jerry S. 63, 159, 293, 297
Tulipano Nero 172
Tuna
  anise-seared, black currant balsamico 155
  Asian with wasabi vinaigrette 154
  foie gras stuffed 156
  grilled Caribbean salsa 157

  puttanesca 158
  sesame crusted loin 70
  wasabi crusted 159

V

Van, Julie DeGraaf 279
Vandergeest, Michael 239, 246, 249, 253
Vanilla Pana Cotta 246
Vannoy, John, C.E.C. 175
Veal
  grilled chop with exotic mushrooms 171
  vitello alla principessa 172
Vega Grill 30, 52, 71, 206, 226, 259
Vegetable.
See also Asparagus; Mushroom
  alo gohbi 204
  beets, roasted 196
  celery hearts, braised 199
  green bean garden salad 200
  julienne 207
  lucskos káposziá 198
  napoleon with grilled 38
  roasted peppers and corn hash 202
  yuca con mojo criollo 206
Vidi, Frederick 134, 165
Vinaigrette. *See* Dressing, Salad
  apple 295
  balsamic 39
  cabrales and patria chiles 71
  mint peppercorn 180
  orange-rosemary 197
  ponzu-wasabi 70
  roasted poblano 71
  tarragon 140
  tomato 151
  wasabi 154
Vinegar
  black currant balsamico 155
  fruit flavored 135
von Klause, Kevin
    78, 112, 155, 196, 229, 233, 262

W

Ward, Steven 131
Wasabi
  crusted tuna 159
  vinaigrette 154
Wei, Michael 28
Weitzman, Toby 32, 77, 182

Welcovitz, Wendy 62, 187, 210
White Dog Cafe
    78, 112, 155, 196, 229,
    233, 262
Wilson, Craig 130
Wilson, Lisa 307

Y

Yangming 28
Yuca con Mojo Criollo 206

Z

Zocalo 218, 303
Zucchini, crisps 115

Pictured on back cover

William Love
Country Club Restaurant

Kelly McGrath
City Tavern

David Banks
Harry's Savoy Grill

Joel Gaughan
Braddock's Tavern

Tom Hannum
Hotel DuPont

Ed Doherty
La Campagne

John L. Anderson
Husch

George Crea
Hilton at Cherry Hill

Jeffrey Devine
The Mansion

Gerald Scanlon
The Restaurant School

Mike Vandergeest
Tony Clark's

Howard Nutinsky
Corned Beef Academy

Philippe Chin
Chanterelles

Olivier De Saint Martin
Dock Street Restaurant

Louis Imbesi
Catelli Restaurant

Joseph K.K. Poon
Joseph Poon Restaurant

Diane Nussbaum
La Patisserie Francaise

Charles Pineiro
Martini Cafe

Annemarie Phifer
Loose Ends

Andrew Berks
Park Hyatt

Joseph Brown
Melange

Gilda Doganiero
Gilda's Biscotti

Jennifer Ballou
Private Residence Chef

Howard Landsman
Laurel Springs Smoke House

Tony Daggett
Daggett's Catering

Kevin Meeker
Philadelphia Fish & Co.

Trish Morrissey
Philadelphia Fish & Co.

Lynn Buono
Feast Your Eyes Catering

Peter McAndrews
Rembrandt's Restaurant

Brian W. Duffy
Big Fish Restaurant

Mark Buker
Inn at Sugar Hill

Michael Baskette
School of Culinary Arts

Guillermo Pernot
Vega Grill

Joe Lovallo
New World Cafe

Alan Lichtenstein
New World Cafe

Jason Ruch
New World Cafe

About the Editor

Name: Joanne Correia

Education/Training: Temple University

Inspirations/Influences: formerly my family's likes and dislikes; presently, this cookbook

Hobbies: stitchery, bike riding, church choir, spending time with family

Family: husband John, four children — Connie, Christopher, Joel, and Jennie

Hometown: Cherry Hill, NJ

Favorite Food to Eat: garden salads

Favorite Food to Prepare: quick breads, pasta

Favorite Cookbook: *Betty Crocker's New Picture Cook Book* and *Local Flavor*

About the Author

Name: Connie Correia Fisher

Education/Training: Johnson & Wales University

Inspirations/Influences: the seasons, cravings

Hobbies: movies, reading, trash picking, restoring furniture

Family: married to Bill, two cats — Neuman and Little Jerry Fisher

Hometown: Cherry Hill, NJ

Favorite Food to Eat: *panzanella* with Jersey tomatoes, pasta, Bill's chocolate chip cookies

Favorite Food to Prepare: soups, pies

Favorite Cookbook: *The New Professional Chef;* books by Mollie Katzen

Connie Correia Fisher (pictured center, no jacket)
is the editor and publisher of *Cuizine* Magazine,
a regional food magazine, which she founded in 1993.

Local Flavor Mail Order Form

Please send the following:

❑ _____ copies of *Local Flavor: Favorite Recipes of Philadelphia Area Chefs* $15.95

❑ _____ yearly subscriptions (5 issues) to *Cuizine* magazine $9.00

Sales Tax on *Local Flavor:* NJ addresses please add $.96 (6%)
Shipping: $3.00 for the first book; $1.00 for each additional book
Payment: Please make your check or money order payable to:

Small Potatoes Press
1106 Stokes Avenue
Collingswood, NJ 08108

SHIP TO: _____

_____

_____

SHIP TO: _____

_____

_____

❑ Is this a gift? If so, please include your name and full address.

_____

_____

 **Thank you!**